THE BLACK BELT THESIS:
A READER

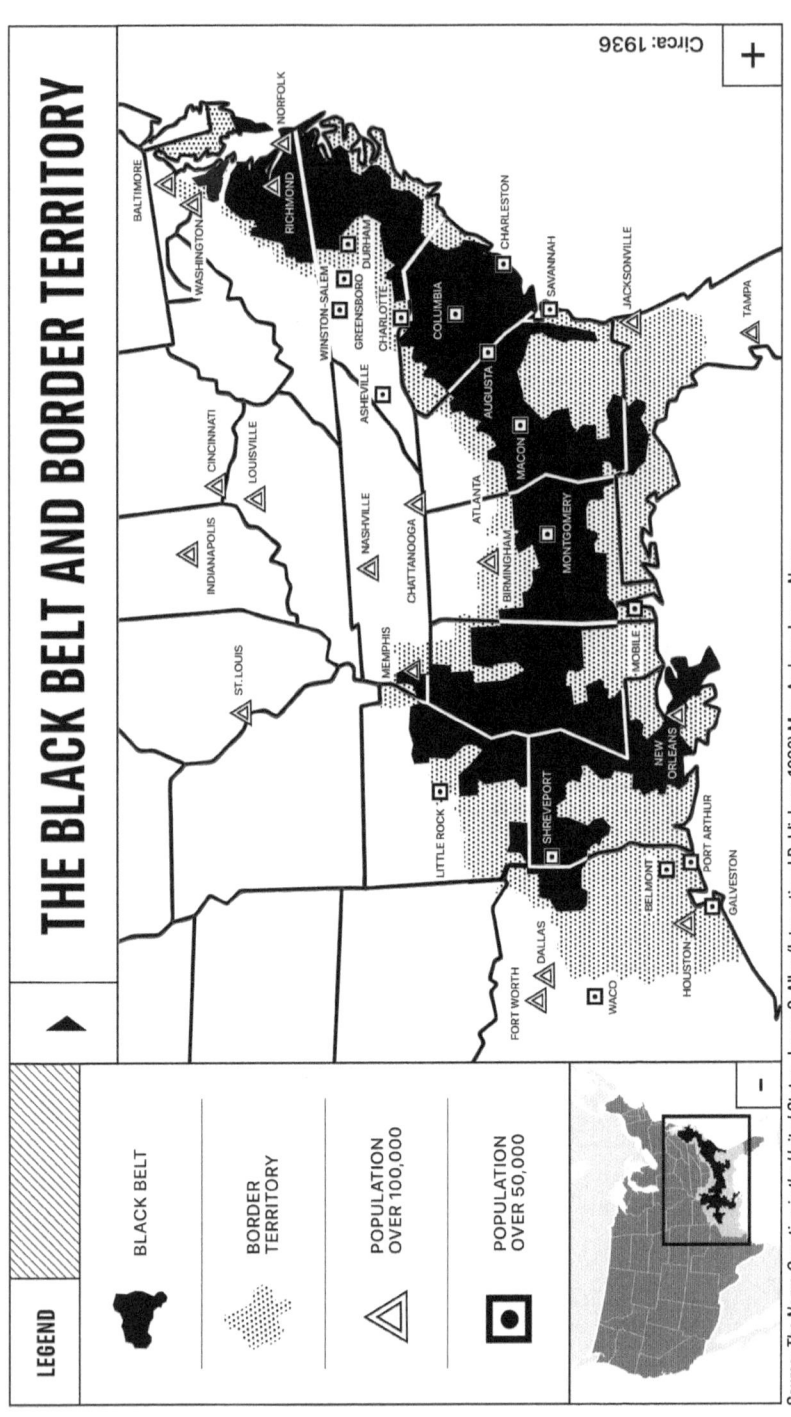

Source: *The Negro Question in the United States*, James S. Allen (International Publishers, 1936) Map: Andrew James Nance

THE BLACK BELT THESIS: A READER

First published in August 2023 by
1804 Books, New York, NY
1804Books.com
This selection © 1804 Books, New York, NY
"Sharecroppers with Guns: Organizing the Black Belt" originally published in *Black Bolshevik: Autobiography of an Afro-American Communist*. Copyright 1978 by Harry Haywood.
ISBN: 978-1-7368500-7-7
Library of Congress Control Number: 2023942391
Cover: Andrew James Nance

TABLE OF CONTENTS

IX   PREFACE

XIX   INTRODUCTION
         EUGENE PURYEAR

THE COMINTERN RESOLUTIONS

1   I. THE 1928 COMINTERN RESOLUTION ON THE NEGRO QUESTION IN THE UNITED STATES

11   II. THE 1930 COMINTERN RESOLUTION ON THE NEGRO QUESTION IN THE UNITED STATES

SECTION ONE: HISTORY

33   'CAPITALISM AND AGRICULTURE IN THE UNITED STATES OF AMERICA'
         V.I. LENIN

41   'LIFE AMONG NEGRO FARMERS IN AMERICA'
         GEORGE PADMORE

47   SELECTIONS FROM *THE LIFE AND STRUGGLES OF NEGRO TOILERS*
         GEORGE PADMORE

71   'LYNCH JUSTICE IN AMERICA'

75   'CHAPTER 1: THE PROBLEM'
         HARRY HAYWOOD

85   'NEGROES AND THE CRISIS OF CAPITALISM IN THE US'
         W. E. B. DU BOIS

TABLE OF CONTENTS

SECTION TWO: ORGANIZATION

99 'FURTHER NOTES ON NEGRO QUESTION IN SOUTHERN TEXTILE STRIKES'
CYRIL BRIGGS

105 'A NEGRO TUUL ORGANIZER IN THE SOUTH OF THE USA'
GILBERT LEWIS

109 'A SOUTHERN TEXTILE WORKER: LETTER TO FIFTH CONGRESS OF THE RED INTERNATIONAL OF LABOR UNIONS'

111 'ALABAMA MASSACRE'
EUGENE GORDON

115 EXCERPT FROM *LET ME LIVE*
ANGELO HERNDON

137 'SOUTHERN TERROR'
LOUISE THOMPSON

145 'SHARECROPPERS WITH GUNS: ORGANIZING THE BLACK BELT'
HARRY HAYWOOD

169 'REPLY TO MISLED WORKER'

175 'SAVE THE SCOTTSBORO BLACK YOUTHS'
CLARA ZETKIN

SECTION THREE: THEORY

183 'THE NATIONAL REVOLUTIONARY STRUGGLE OF THE NEGROES'
TOM JOHNSON

191 SELECTIONS FROM *THE REDS IN DIXIE: WHO ARE THE COMMUNISTS AND WHAT DO THEY FIGHT FOR IN THE SOUTH?*
TOM JOHNSON

213 SELECTIONS FROM *THE NEGRO QUESTION IN THE UNITED STATES*
JAMES ALLEN

TABLE OF CONTENTS

- **247** 'ON THE RIGHT TO SELF-DETERMINATION FOR THE NEGRO PEOPLE IN THE BLACK BELT (A DISCUSSION ARTICLE)'
  CLAUDIA JONES
- **261** 'CHAPTER 6: LAND AND FREEDOM'
  HARRY HAYWOOD
- **279** 'WHAT DO WE STAND FOR?'
- **283** GLOSSARY
- **289** ACKNOWLEDGMENTS
- **291** ENDNOTES

PREFACE

The Black Belt. A crescent of fertile soil, the heart of North American agriculture for generations before European settlers colonized it. Following the genocidal "removals" of the so-called Five Civilized Tribes, it became the homeland of slavery. After emancipation, agriculture was sustained here through sharecropping. Historically, it has had a Black majority population. Its very name, the Black Belt, signals an unbroken chain of struggles for land, and for freedom.

The Black Belt comprises about two hundred counties in the southern US, from Texas to Virginia, concentrated especially in central Alabama and Mississippi. It is the historic heartland of the Cotton Kingdom, where short-staple cotton was cultivated on massive plantations by the forced labor of enslaved Africans. This cotton was an essential raw material for the Industrial Revolution, fueling changes as far as India and Egypt. This bloodstained harvest, in turn, maintained the oligarchic control of slave owners over the US government.

Every site of great exploitation is also home to a long history of resistance. The communities of the Black Belt incubated the struggle against slavery, and the radical promise of Reconstruction. In the 1930s, communities in the Black Belt engaged in fierce class struggles, which would provide a seedbed for the emergence of the civil rights movement a few decades later. For centuries, liberation struggles in the Black Belt had drawn international connections, particularly with Haiti, and the broader Caribbean. The Black Belt Thesis was part of this trajectory.

In 1928, the Third International (Communist Interntional or Comintern) adopted the Black Belt Thesis, linking the struggles of workers and farmers in the US South with the international fight against imperialism, in the period between the First and Second World Wars. Doing so, the international communist movement recognized Black people in the US as an oppressed nation with the territorial right of self-determination, marking a strategic turn during a period of deep structural crisis in the capitalist system. At the onset of the 1930s, the Great Depression rapidly swelled the ranks of the poor in the US. In an era of militancy, mass working-class organizations blossomed. The Black Belt Thesis responded to these conditions, prioritizing the organization of Black and white workers and farmers against state and vigilante violence, against inhumane conditions in fields and factories, and more broadly, against all manifestations of racism. Taking life through centuries-old local traditions of struggle against slavery and racism, the Black Belt Thesis transformed the culture, philosophy, and practice of communism in North America.

The Black Belt Thesis also defined the work of the Communist Party USA (CPUSA) during this time of working-class radicalization. Attentive to local conditions and communities, the CPUSA established itself as a leading organization in the struggle against racism. It cultivated local leadership, spearheaded international campaigns against lynching, and organized multiracial unions of urban and rural workers. While the turn to the popular front later in the decade would dissipate some of the organizational momentum that had developed around the Black Belt Thesis, its impacts would reverberate in later decades in the youth wings of the party, and in Black struggles that moved away from the party itself. Studying the Black Belt Thesis today offers important lessons on the histories of working-class and anti-racist struggles in the US. It also offers important perspectives on the task of building a unified and independent working-class movement, to meet the current crisis.

Extreme exploitation, racist violence, and freedom struggle persist in our day, and the Black Belt itself remains home to militant struggles over land, labor, and democracy. The Black Belt has become a center of US manufacturing (particularly German, Japanese, and Korean auto assembly). It hosts a high concentration of military bases, suggesting the strategic importance of controlling the region, and the significance of war for the area's economy. This preface introduces the historical context of the Black Belt Thesis, and some of its key theoretical and practical interventions. Named for the beating heart of repression, anti-democratic reaction, acute racist terror, brutal exploitation, and environmental degradation in the US, named also for the spiritual and organizational reservoir of some of the most profound freedom struggles in the modern world, the Black Belt Thesis offers lessons in histories of struggle, methods of analysis, and proposals for liberation, lessons that we can carry into our work today.

Historical Context

The Communist Party USA was formed in 1919, but for the first several years of its existence it paid scant attention to the oppression of Black people, or to the political and economic role of the former slave states of the South. The initial push to reorient the party towards these questions came from Lenin, who had often compared the situation of Russian peasants to that of the Black sharecroppers and tenant farmers of the US South. Lenin's insistence on the importance of the "Negro Question," as well as his focus on the remnants of slavery in Southern agriculture, were in keeping with the revolutionary strategy he advanced in the years following World War I. Seeing vast revolutionary potential in the anti-colonial struggles of oppressed peoples—most of whom were peasants—Lenin urged the European and North American parties of the Communist International to support national liberation movements in the colonized countries, arguing for an alliance of urban industrial workers with rural peasants and landless workers. These insights were central to the Communist break with European social democracy.

As part of its anti-imperialist efforts, the Third International formed a Negro Commission in 1921 to study questions related to Black oppression in Africa and the Americas. CPUSA member William Patterson participated on the commission, later joined by Harry Haywood. For the next several years, they and their comrades from communist parties around the world developed a theory of the "Negro Question" and its relationship to imperialism, anti-colonial struggles, and world revolution. By 1928, the Comintern issued a new set of theses at the Sixth Congress of the Communist International, addressing the "Negro Question" in the United States. These theses would shape the future of the Communist Party USA, and its impact on US life and politics in the ensuing decades.

Coming out of the Sixth Congress, the CPUSA launched new fronts of struggle in the Deep South, establishing District 16 (Virginia and the Carolinas), and District 17, (including Alabama, Georgia and Tennessee). In 1929, the Party assigned its first two organizers to District 17. Tom Johnson and Harry Jackson arrived just in time for the onset of the mass unemployment crisis of the Great Depression, and Alabama would become the epicenter of the Party's Southern work throughout the 1930s.

The early years of the Great Depression were some of the most dynamic in the Communist Party's history, especially in the South. From 1929 to 1931, the CPUSA and its affiliated organizations rapidly gathered a mass base in the Black Belt and in nearby Appalachia, sinking roots among sharecroppers and tenant farmers, textile workers, miners, and the unemployed. The Party's strength was among Black sharecroppers and proletarians, but a significant number of poor whites, and a handful of white intellectuals, joined as well.

Nevertheless, the Party had to function as a clandestine organization. In the Black Belt, the planter class maintained a total lock on state power. Democratic rights simply did not exist. Communists encountered brutal repression, with known party members facing assassination and imprisonment. Despite this, party members organized key struggles: the 1929 Loray Mill strike of mostly white textile workers in Gastonia, North Carolina; the Alabama Sharecroppers Union in rural counties surrounding Birmingham; and multiracial unemployed councils in Atlanta, Birmingham, and other cities.

A cadre of new leaders was forged in the crucible of these struggles, from among the ranks of the Southern masses. Political education was key to this growth. The party held schools for new members, and the most promising recruits were sent to the national training school in New York for more intensive training in Marxism-Leninism and organizational methods. The party launched a biweekly tabloid, *Southern Worker*, on August 16, 1930, and meetings often included reading articles aloud, followed by political discussion.

This work laid a firm foundation for what would become one of the most significant popular struggles of the decade. In 1931, nine young unemployed Black men were falsely accused of raping a white woman in Scottsboro, Alabama. Their story became a rallying cry for antifascists and trade unionists worldwide, and a symbol of the deeply unjust Jim

Preface

Crow system. The case of the Scottsboro Boys was taken up by the International Labor Defense (ILD), a legal defense organization led by William Patterson. The ILD employed a mass organizing strategy to defend the accused, including a rally organized in July 1931 by the German Communist Party, at which 150,000 German workers gathered in solidarity.

By the mid-1930s, communist revolutions in Western Europe had failed, and the prospect of war loomed over the world. Fascism posed a challenge to communists everywhere, threatening the very survival of the Soviet Union. Mussolini and Hitler had captured state power in Italy and Germany. In the United States, the planter class of the Black Belt was widely viewed as the potential cornerstone of a North American version of fascist rule. At the same time, communist parties and broad-based Left movements in many countries—including in the United States—had attained new levels of power over the course of the depression, and were preparing to respond. In August 1935, the Seventh World Congress of the Communist International assembled to assess the situation and point a way forward. Their answer was the people's front, a policy of broad alliances against fascism and imperialism that signaled a shift in the work of the Party, moving towards greater cooperation with all of those elements in the United States hostile to fascism, including parts of the Roosevelt administration.

In the South, this involved reconfigurations at every level. The CPUSA's trade union work in the South fully absorbed itself into Congress of Industrial Organizations (CIO) organizing drives, and began working more closely with Myles Horton's Highlander Folk School. The Sharecroppers Union, which by this time had thousands of members in Alabama, Georgia, and Louisiana, was dissolved as an independent union, merging first into the National Farmers Union, and then into the CIO's United Cannery, Agricultural, Packing and Allied Workers of America (UCAPAWA). The party-led League of Struggle for Negro Rights was replaced with the National Negro Congress (NNC), which included a wide spectrum of Black-led organizations. This in turn led to the formation of the NNC's youth wing, the Southern Negro Youth Congress. Finally, in 1937, the *Southern Worker* ceased publication, and party units were reorganized along the lines of traditional American political party structures.

The capstone of the Communist Party's attempt to build a people's front in the Black Belt was the formation of the Southern Congress for Human Welfare (SCHW) in 1938. That November, SCHW held its first public gathering in Birmingham, convening a crowd of 1,200 people. High-level government officials like Supreme Court Justice Hugo Black mingled with Black sharecroppers and the unemployed, including party members such as Hosea Hudson. It was at this meeting that Birmingham's public safety commissioner, Bull Connor, first became notorious, entering a confrontation with Eleanor Roosevelt over whether the meeting would be segregated. In more extended collaborations, SCHW and the Southern Negro Youth Congress organized literacy classes and voter registration drives in Birmingham in the late 1930s.

The Black Belt Thesis emerged during a period when the international working-class movement prioritized African American struggles in the South, making these priorities concrete through base building work, the organization of the Southern working class, and the recognition of the South as the key region for class struggle in North America. These efforts paved the way for the strategic shift in the next period, which sought to forge broad alliances in order to defeat fascism at home and abroad. Studying the historical context for the Black Belt Thesis paves the way to understand its theoretical breakthroughs for the communist movement in North America.

Theoretical Context

As part of his contribution to the Marxist theory of emancipation, Lenin drew parallels between the conditions of landless workers and peasants in imperial Russia, and the conditions of Black sharecroppers and farmers in the US. In his 1915 analysis of US agriculture, Lenin noted the stark divides between Black and white agricultural workers in the US. Black farmers tended to be tenants and sharecroppers working under semi-feudal and semi-slave conditions, while white farmers typically owned their land. Lenin concluded that "there is a startling similarity in the economic status of the Negroes in America and the peasants in the heart of agricultural Russia who 'were formerly landowners' serfs.'" These insights informed the development of the worker-peasant alliance, which marked the communist break from European social democracy's lack of attention to fighting class exploitation in rural areas.

"Self-determination," in the politics of the Third International, involved the right of oppressed nations to claim political autonomy.

In the context of their revolution against the multinational Russian Empire, the Bolsheviks defined self-determination as the right of oppressed nations to establish separate states. By applying this concept to the North American context, the Third International insisted on the collective right of Black people to define their political future. The theory of self-determination in the Black Belt opened up whole new fields of creative and revolutionary work. The CPUSA began to devote real resources to organizing Black and white industrial workers and tenant farmers in the South, transforming itself into a front-line fighter for the needs and demands of Black people, especially Black workers, throughout the United States.

The Black Belt Thesis aimed squarely at the separation of race and class as separate issues. It argued that US imperialism overall relied on the violent, naked dictatorship of wealth in the South, especially in the plantation system of the Black Belt. Ending this dictatorship, which resembled the situation of the colonized world, meant putting political power in the hands of the region's people. This was impossible without a determined multiracial struggle against the Jim Crow system in its entirety. In these core respects—the centrality of the US South to US imperialism worldwide; the need to establish genuine democracy in the region; the necessity of a multiracial struggle against white supremacy—the theory of the Black Belt Thesis offers guiding principles for our own day.

The Black Belt Thesis and Organizing Today

"The Party must consider the beginning of the systematic work in the south as one of its main tasks." This was part of the 1928 Comintern Resolution on the Negro Question, and almost a century later, organizing the US South today remains fundamental for building the working-class movement broadly. While it has often been dismissed as "backwards" or a lost cause, the South's identity, both as a distinctive region, and as a representation of American society as a whole, means that it holds strategic significance for the popular and democratic transformation of the US overall.

Rooted in the historic strategy of violent, racist oppression, the South continues to be ground zero for attacks on the working class. From its foundations in colonization and slavery, through the Jim Crow era, and to the present, ruling class strategies and policies have kept workers divided, using racism to maintain the class hierarchy. Anti-union right-to-work laws, first created in an attempt to prevent interracial organizing, shape organizing conditions in the majority of Southern states, resulting in the lowest levels of unionization in the US, with less than half of the national average. Consequently, the South is still the poorest region in the US, with nine of the twelve poorest states in the country. The South also trails behind the rest of the US, with the lowest levels of public education and health care. Migration patterns notwithstanding, nearly all majority-Black counties are located in the South. Additionally, the white poverty rate in the region is the highest in the country. All of these factors point to both the crisis and opportunity of organizing the US South today.

The US South must be understood as a strategic source of leadership for the movement overall. It is ripe for working-class organization, the true reason behind ruling class attempts to disorganize the region. The South has been the cradle of the most powerful anti-racist and anti-poverty struggles in US history, an unbroken legacy of resistance, from centuries of Black abolitionist struggle, to the radical promise of Reconstruction, to the Southern civil rights movement of the 1960s, on to the Black Lives Matter movement's origins and various labor struggles today. When united and consolidated by their common cause, the leadership of the working class in the South is indispensable to forming a strong revolutionary movement.

Organizing the US South, however, hinges on a concerted battle against centuries-long strategic divisions of the poor. The region is the most polarized expression of the fight between the white supremacist ruling class and the multiracial working class. This division is illustrated by reactionary, xenophobic rhetoric in political discourse, the hardening of racial hierarchies and divisions in the workplace, and the physical division of the working class across segregated geographies. Additionally, the rapidly changing population of the South demonstrates a need to go beyond the focus on Black-white organizing that characterized the movements of the 1930s and 1960s. The Latinx population represents the fastest-growing population in the region, accounting for over half of its population growth between 2010 and 2019. The vast majority of Latinx workers in the US South occupy construction, manufacturing, service, and agricultural jobs, and the ruling class imposes a particularly heinous form of labor control on

Preface

migrants through documentation status. The specific experiences of Latinx workers, and their connections to the experiences of workers across the South, are of critical importance for organizing the region's working class. When the working class is able to establish unity across all forms of division imposed by the ruling class, a transformative movement for the South, the US, and the world can emerge.

Speaking to the Southern Negro Youth Congress, W. E. B. Du Bois insisted that "the future of the Negro is in the South." Because Black workers suffered the harshest forms of exploitation and violence in the South, he argued, the region was the most fertile battleground for the working-class movement. However, Du Bois looked beyond the region, declaring that the South "is the firing line not simply for the emancipation of the American Negro but for the emancipation of the African Negro and the Negroes of the West Indies; for the emancipation of the colored races; and for the emancipation of the white slaves of modern capitalistic monopoly." Du Bois linked the US South, North America and the Caribbean, and the world at large. Understanding the South's economic significance as a center of global capitalist production and manufacturing holds the central lever for connecting the US South to the Global South. The strategic significance of organizing the US South today comes into focus, as the key for working-class emancipation.

This book is the outcome of a months-long collective study in 2022 by a group of organizers and educators, working on the fronts of abolition, health care, housing, and labor. It is intended as a resource for collective political education. The book is organized into sections on the history, organization, and theory of the Black Belt Thesis. We have chosen selections which provide insight into the Black Belt Thesis, as it was informed by experiments in working-class struggles against racism, for the construction of socialism. This book is intended as a resource to study the distinct tradition of communism in North America, particularly its methods of analysis and struggle. We hope it can be a tool to facilitate the renewal and the unity of our movements, in order meet the demands that history places before us.

INTRODUCTION
EUGENE PURYEAR

"What time is it?! Nation Time!"
—African American Proverb

The "Black Belt Thesis," is foundational to "Black national consciousness." The first universalized theory that Black people in the United States make up a "nation within a nation." Even though its origins are in the communist movement, its insights are behind fundamental intellectual, cultural and political pillars of the Black liberation movement.

The Black Belt Thesis solidified a particular communist contribution to the Black liberation movement, producing a unified understanding of the economic status, geographic distribution, and second-class citizenship of Black Americans. It named particular enemies (capitalists) and strategic "allies" (the working class) of the Black liberation movement. It prescribed the process (socialist revolution) by which Blacks could gain the practical ability to alter their subaltern circumstances (preferential access to the means of production).

Communists identified an example of similar handling of the "National Question" in the Soviet Union, offering the Union of Soviet Socialist Republics (USSR) as a proof of concept in their strategies, even more so since the Soviets enthusiastically supported the Black fight in the US. The communists wrapped all this in a cloak of militant protest against the oppression of Blacks. "Reds" were unafraid to risk the lynch mob or the electric chair when in battle with Jim Crow.

Even today, the thesis's observations that Black people are indeed a nation with our historical and contemporary cultural anchor in the South resonates: soul food, soul music, jazz, hip-hop, "Ebonics," the Mississippi Delta and the Southside of Chicago. The Black Belt Thesis is less of an imposition of some "new idea," as opposed to a generalized understanding of an already clear reality, as a cursory examination of a few (mainly) contemporary facts reveals.

First, there is the question of geography and how the Black Belt Thesis came to be focused on the South. In the entire history of the country, never have fewer than 53 percent of Black people lived outside the South. A number that never dropped below 60 percent until 1960.[1] Not to mention that number has been steadily rising since 2000, with roughly 56 percent of Blacks living in the South currently.[2] Texas, Florida, and Georgia are the three states with the most Black people numerically.[3] Thirty-six percent of Blacks live in just ten cities.[4]

No matter where they live, Black people tend to live mainly among other Black people, and overwhelmingly around other people of color. The average Black person lives in a neighborhood that is 45 percent Black, 62 percent Black and Latino, and 69 percent Black, Latino, and Asian.[5] Among Blacks who are deemed "low-income," making less than 80 percent of the median income in their metro area, 80 percent live in "low-income" neighborhoods.

And then there is the question of Black workers' economic status, a question the thesis sought to raise. Black people in the US tend to experience the economy on the underside of $100,000. Eighty-one percent of Blacks fall below that threshold, 71 percent below $75,000 and 54 percent below $50,000.[6] Black families only hold 1 percent of unrealized capital gains (wealth in the stock market) and 3 percent of the overall wealth in society.[7] Additionally, Black people at every level of the job market get paid less than their white counterparts. Even Black lawyers, doctors, pharmacists and dentists make, on average, $39,330 a year less than whites in the same professions.[8] Less than 25 percent of Black people have a bachelor's degree (23 percent) and of Black churchgoers, 66 percent are Protestants.[9]

And so taken as a whole, one might say the Black community meets, quite well, the definition of a "nation" set forth in Joseph Stalin's 1913 text, *Marxism and the National Question,* a definition considered to be foundational to not only the Bolshevik's approach to national identity, but also that of the international communist movement, particularly in the US:

> A nation is a historically constituted, stable community of people, formed on the basis of a common language, territory, economic life, and psychological make-up manifested in a common culture.[10]

The texts in this volume comprise a range of foundational documents of the Black Belt Thesis, laying out the overall communist analysis that there was a direct relationship between Black freedom and socialist revolution, one could not exist without the other. This literature however raises some key questions: How did such a thesis come about? What made the communists take the issue up and how did it impact their work? How did it grow beyond and within the Black community? And, why study it today?

(Pre)History

It's impossible to understand the Black Belt Thesis unless you understand the Bolsheviks. National oppression was a critical weapon used by the czars to divide the working class and the peasantry. Upon taking power, the Bolsheviks threw open the cell doors of the "prison house of nations," stopping the pogroms in their tracks and plunging into a complex series of interpretations of "self determination" unique in their clear empowerment of formerly oppressed peoples. Making the Bolsheviks' approach to what was to become known as the "national and colonial question," a topic of intense interest worldwide after World War, I brought into question the colonial world order. In China, Vietnam, India, Mexico, and all across Africa, anti-colonialists moved toward the Comintern as their only reliable ally, and, by extension, communism as the most reliable means by which to achieve true liberation.

This broader phenomenon was also true in the US, where Black Americans were also seeing a model for liberation and peace through the USSR. A. Phillip Randolph and Chandler Owen were two such people for whom the Bolshevik Revolution was a revelation. They jointly edited a monthly magazine called *The Messenger* that emerged at about the same time the Bolsheviks took the Winter Palace in St.

Petersburg. In its second issue, January 1918, Owens and Randolph editorialized about the Bolshevik Revolution:

> The Bolsheviki are in control of Russia at present. They represent the extreme radicals—not in the sense of being unreasonably extreme in their demands, but in the sense of being unwilling to take half a loaf, but in the sense of being unwilling to take half a loaf when they are entitled to a whole loaf. They have sounded the tocsin of farewell, the death knell of half pay to the workers of Russia. They demand that the land which the workers till and mine with their toil shall be owned and operated by the workers for the welfare of the workers. They are uncompromising proponents of peace, too.[11]

In the next issue, *The Messenger* editors mentioned further that Bolshevism was the "foreword to true world democracy. The Soviets represent the needs and aims of the masses." And that the USSR had led "the world in making a concrete application of the principles of self-determination."[12] Notably, early communist leader C. E. Ruthenberg was arrested during the postwar crackdown on radicals for selling *The Messenger*, which had been banned by authorities for its revolutionary messages.[13]

The Crusader was another radical Black newspaper of the time, and was linked to the African Blood Brotherhood, an organization that arose to defend Black communities around the country from the American pogroms of 1919. Its editor was Cyril Briggs, an immigrant to Harlem from the Caribbean. In later years, Briggs noted that he and some in his circle gained a keen interest in communism explicitly because of: "The national policy of the Russian Bolsheviks and the anti-imperialist orientation of the Soviet state."[14] In an issue, the newspaper explained to its readers fighting on the "home front" that the Black liberation movement was a natural ally of the Bolsheviks, noting: "the Negro seeks relief in the class war of the proletariat against the conscienceless capitalists and makes common cause with the Bolsheviki of the world."[15]

Even Marcus Garvey, who at this point had become deeply hostile to the Communist Party, noted at a meeting just after Lenin's death that he was: "One of Russia's greatest men, one of the world's greatest characters, and probably the greatest man in the world between 1917 and 1924, when he breathed his last and took his flight from this world . . . We as Negroes mourn for Lenin because Russia promised great hope not only for Negroes but to the weaker people of the world."[16] From the perspective of the Black liberation movement at the time, it was already apparent that the Bolshevik Revolution had much to offer to the oppressed masses; and so the Black Belt Thesis fits into place as an effort to strengthen and concretize this international relationship.

'Absolutely Necessary'

As much as Black Americans identified with the October Revolution, the USSR also saw important links between their own struggle and the plight of Black people in the US. Lenin felt strongly that Black people in the United States were an oppressed nation. In one early writing Lenin noted: "The Negroes were the last to be freed from slavery, and they still bear, more than anyone else, the cruel marks of slavery."[17] Noting in another piece that:

> They should be classed as an oppressed nation, for the equality won in the Civil War of 1861–65 and guaranteed by the Constitution of the republic was in many respects increasingly curtailed in the chief Negro areas (the South) in connection with the transition from the progressive, premonopoly capitalism of 1860–70 to the reactionary, monopoly capitalism (imperialism) of the new era.

Adding:

> For the "emancipated" Negroes . . . "the American South is a kind of prison where they are hemmed in, isolated and deprived of fresh air."[18]

Much of Lenin's early knowledge of the condition of Blacks in the United States came from the 1910 census, where much of the work on Blacks in the South was compiled and prepared by none other than W. E. B. Du Bois, and already demonstrating how both movements referred to each other.

At the Second Congress of the Communist International in 1920, the issue of the "national and colonial question" was high on the agenda. In the midst of the discussion, US communist John Reed passed a note to Lenin: "Should I say something about the Negroes in America?" Lenin wrote back: "Yes, absolutely necessary." Reed, in his speech on the Black struggle, put an emphasis on the post-WWI upsurge in radicalism detailing in particular the role of *The Messenger*.[19] When presenting his "Draft Theses on the National Colonial Question," Lenin asked for comrades to make comments or additions concerning a number of places around the world. The only struggle not in Asia or Europe was the "Negroes in America."[20]

Despite the above, the early communists struggled to make much headway in Black America. Top party leaders went out of their way to recruit Black radicals, which led to the recruitment of Briggs, as well as fellow Harlem radicals Richard Moore and Grace Campbell, and a few other leaders in their broader national network, adding in a handful year-by-year. Many of them would go on to play major roles in the communist movement.

And so, the stage was already set for the declaration of the Black Belt Thesis. Both movements saw the potential of the other, and the common enemy of imperialism that oppressed them. The seed of international solidarity had already been planted, and now it was a matter of cultivating it, and turning that spirit into reality.

The Thesis: Foundations

The Comintern saw this issue as having theoretical roots: a lack of understanding the revolutionary potential of national liberation struggles. That there could be no revolution in the US without an explicit alliance between the working class and what they viewed as a Black nation, just like in the Soviet Union. Eager to see revolution in the US the Soviets were active in promoting their view, which came together with the general unhappiness of Black communists about the stagnant progress the party was making becoming a voice for Black liberation.

In 1924, Zinoviev instructed the representative of the Young Communist International to raise the issue.[21] Sen Katayama, a major Comintern figure on questions of national liberation, had also tried to press the idea a bit on Black students in the USSR and, according to some accounts, Stalin had also advanced Lenin's views on Black people

Introduction

being a nation when he met with some Black students who had come to the Soviet Union.[22]

But it was in 1927 when the issue came to a head. A Russian Young Communist International representative, Nasanov, toured the United States and became very convinced that Lenin's conception was correct. When he returned to the Soviet Union he sought out the main theoretical mind among communist Blacks in the USSR: Harry Haywood. Haywood had already been studying the question, and was further influenced that changes had to be made from the steady stream of complaints about the party's activity coming from new arrivals from the US.

Haywood, in his autobiography, notes that he was skeptical of Nasanov's position, but nonetheless, he began to discuss the issue with Nasanov and some other young Soviets. The crux of the discussion hinged on whether or not the Black experience needed to conform to every element of Stalin's 1913 description of what makes up a nation, for the Black liberation movement to be seen as a national liberation struggle. Nasanov and friends argued with Haywood that there did not need to be an exact identity and that it was ahistorical to even approach it that way.[23]

The Bolshevik view of the national question linked the formation of "nations" to the rise of capitalism, emerging from absolutist Europe. In some cases, like Russia and the United States, the oppressor nation incorporated "colonialism" into its state across a contiguous territory, forming "multinational" states. In this context, the various aspects of "nationhood" in a Marxist, or materialist approach, was as much about the whole as opposed to the aliquot parts.

Communists uphold the right of nations to "self-determination," including independence if desired. Haywood was worried that advocating for the legitimacy of an independent Black state was contradictory to demanding equal rights for Blacks within the American system. His Russian friends argued that the only guarantee of equality was some form of power or "self-determination" for Blacks.[24] Or, as comedian Dick Gregory would later say: *"A Negro with a gun is always mister."* [25]

The Thesis Proper

Haywood embarked on a study of the Garvey movement as a foundation for new theoretical excursions that would lead to the first explication of the Black Belt Thesis.[26] For Haywood the Garvey movement revealed the tremendous power that "group" or "national" uplift could inspire in the Black masses. It defined the question in terms of "nationality," and addressed its appeal to the most direct manifestation of national oppression: total economic destitution and marginalization.

Even more, the Garvey movement activated "dockworkers, manual laborers, miners, industrial workers, and seamen," plus, it's "greatest concentrations" were "the cotton belt areas of southwest Georgia, the Arkansas Delta, and the Yazoo-Mississippi Delta . . . and a few other sections of the South."[27] Flourishes and eccentricities aside, Garveyism "was an indigenous product, arising from the soil of Black super-exploitation and oppression . . . it expressed the yearnings of millions of Blacks for a nation of their own."[28]

Armed with these observations, Haywood started, as Lenin did, with slavery, where an explicit "Blackness" emerged from the brutal process whereby many African peoples were molded into one. The betrayal of Reconstruction and the military defeat of populism in the South "Froze . . . Blacks in their post-Reconstruction position: landless, semi-slaves in the South. It blocked the road to fusion of Blacks and whites into one nation on the basis of equality and put the final seal on the special oppression of Blacks."[29]

The defeat of democracy in the South, embraced by the ruling class as a whole meant that: "the path toward equality and freedom via assimilation was foreclosed and the struggle for Black equality thenceforth was ultimately bound to take a national revolutionary direction."[30]

The upshot of the analysis was that it "destroys forever the white racist theory . . . which relegated the struggle of Blacks to a subsidiary position in the revolutionary movement." And that the "new line established that the Black freedom struggle is a revolutionary movement in its own right, directed against the very foundations of US imperialism, with its own dynamic pace and moment . . . it places the Black liberation movement and the class struggle of US workers in their proper relationship as two aspects of the fight against the common enemy—US capitalism."[31]

Self-Determination and the Comintern

The timing of the new theory was a propitious one as it concerned the international communist movement. The Sixth Congress of the

Comintern came at a time of significant changes in the relationship of forces worldwide. Inside the Soviet Union, the contradictions of trying to manage a socialist system had created a number of challenges. Internationally, the Comintern's non-communist allies had betrayed them in the two biggest incidents of class struggle in the 1920s, the British General Strike of 1926 and the Chinese Revolution of 1927.

International communism was anxious to change course. Emerging as the leading figure of the Soviet Union was Stalin, whose new course, which would later become known as the "Third Period," foregrounded the possibility of revolution. He and his co-thinkers argued that the capitalist system was on the verge of a major crisis due to sharpening contradictions on all fronts. So much so, that in addition to the economic crisis, a new imperialist war offensive could also be expected.

Thus, while the moment was ripe for a new revolutionary offensive, key to that would be "exposing" and struggling against the social democrats (who they would soon start referring to as "social fascists") and conservative trade union leaders for leadership of all working-class struggles, to ultimately prevent them from moving in a counter-revolutionary direction.

Without a doubt, if there was one unified principal across the US political spectrum it was that Blacks should remain second-class citizens. So any policy of intensifying the struggle for Black dignity and equality was guaranteed to put one in conflict with all sections of the capitalist class, and most of the social democratic leaders. Advocates of a new course, as it concerned Black liberation, headed into the Sixth Congress of the Comintern, in a strong position. Despite spirited attempts to refute the thesis, as the debate proceeded, the position that Blacks in the US were a nation, and that the party should adopt the position of support for self-determination in the Black Belt was able to win the day.

Praxis

The new course arguing for an approach grounded in the need for "self-determination" reoriented the entire party around the relationship between Black freedom and socialism, underlining that one couldn't exist without the other, and, as such, suffused all of the party's work with this new appreciation.

In the early Depression era, the party engaged in a remarkable series of attacks on the racist edifice. All across the nation the members of the Communist Party USA (CPUSA) led an upsurge of millions of newly unemployed people seeking relief after the market crash. In Atlanta this led to six party members facing the electric chair for daring to hold an interracial rally "against unemployment and racism" in 1930.[32] In 1932 Black communist Angelo Herndon, whose voice is featured in this reader, was hit with the same charge, and the same death sentence, in a case that would become a worldwide cause célèbre. Communists dared to run for office and challenge the poll tax and lynch law, as well as organized thousands of Black sharecroppers.

The communists became household names with every Black American when they took up the infamous case of the nine Scottsboro Boys in 1931, who were viciously railroaded for a false charge of rape. While this was a normal occurrence in the South, almost never did it meet with real resistance. The communists organized a massive worldwide effort to free the Scottsboro Boys in a brash challenge to Jim Crow, the likes of which hadn't been seen in Alabama, or anywhere in the South, since the 1890s.

Back up north in Harlem, the communists "tried" one of their own members for racism in front of thousands. From rent strikes to fighting police brutality, communists became the go-to community activists in most of America's large urban ghettos for anyone who needed to stand up to authority.

The March 1931 issue of the internal *Party Organizer* tackled the ongoing shift in understanding in a piece titled "Mass Work Among Negroes (how not to work)." The piece emphasized that Black comrades should not be pigeonholed into "Negro work," It insisted that it was the responsibility of every member, especially white members, to become conspicuously involved in the fight for Black self-determination and equality, in particular, organizing other white workers into the fight. As the authors noted, while critiquing the New York district around their tactics in an anti-lynching struggle:

> While debating this question all comrades were, however, agreed that two leading Negro comrades should be sent to New Jersey to organize this struggle. The question of selecting a white comrade for this work never even entered their mind. So accustomed are we to relegating work among

Negro masses to Negro comrades that even the defense of
a Negro in danger of lynching is left to Negro comrades.³³

The difference in emphasis is clear from the content of the communist newspaper the *Daily Worker* as well. In the May 2, 1927 issue there is not one mention of the Black struggle. The May 2, 1932 issue urged its readers to "Carry on the struggle" after the massive May 1 demonstrations, by making May 7 "a day of struggle for the Scottsboro Boys."³⁴ It further contained, in four pages, five articles explicitly about the Black liberation movement, including Black CPUSA leader James Ford's article "Communism and the Negro."³⁵ By the mid-1930s, the communists were second to none in attacking racism.

This coincided with a coming together of broad forces in the labor movement who wanted to make a large push for industrial unions. Together this created a basis for a broad-based labor-Black-liberal coalition to extend and deepen the social reforms kicked off by President Roosevelt. This further corresponded with a shift in the broader international situation. First, the economic crisis began to stabilize. Second, and more importantly, the rise of Hitler in Germany had created deep unease among many capitalists, socialists, and communists.

Ultimately this would lead communists around the world, at the behest of the USSR, to pursue a new course, one that sought to formalize these broad cross-class alliances against fascism and for various types of social reform. On the one hand, this led the communists into a leading position in the Black liberation movement, by setting up the National Negro Congress that became the premier civil rights organization. On the other hand, it meant downplaying the issue of self-determination and nationhood. However correct it might be, it also foregrounded differences between Black organizations as opposed to their broad unity. So, in the name of unity, the communists decided to let the issue of self-determination fade to the background, while continuing to emphasize the struggle for equal rights.

Cold War Blues

After WWII, wartime exigency had given advocates of Black liberation a modicum of leverage in the national political scene. This led to the most significant gains in the arena of "civil rights" since the century had begun. Black America added its second congressman, and Black representatives began to populate municipal councils across the Northern and Midwestern industrial areas. Labor shortages during the war had seen limited but noticeable improvement in breaking down the de facto prohibition on access to skilled labor and associated higher incomes as well as greater access to "white-collar" professional occupations.

However, Blacks were still living in an apartheid status in the South, and it wasn't terribly better in the North. Further, Blacks remained at the bottom of all the various socioeconomic categories that mattered. As the war came to a close, these realities coincided with a few others to create a confused, combustible context around the contours of a postwar world. This took place alongside an upsurge of worker militancy, anti-colonial movements, and a sharpening of the international class struggle as the US launched the Cold War.

At this moment, the communists decided to respond: they re-emphasized their dormant thesis on self-determination. Similar to the original unveiling of the thesis, the reemphasis served primarily to reorient the party toward making Black liberation the "red thread" that ran through their work. Once again, then, the communist's ideological turn on the Black Belt Thesis put them at the center of Black militancy. They proved that the enduring value of the thesis was linking Black liberation to socialist revolution, focusing the mind of the party on fighting racism and white supremacy allowed them to punch above their weight.

Black workers either in or influenced by the party had serious strongholds across the nation: from Detroit and Cleveland's industrial plants; public sector workers in Washington, DC; in the Merchant Marine; to teachers' unions up and down the East Coast; tobacco workers in North Carolina; steel workers in Birmingham; General Electric workers in Louisville—even in the United Electrical Workers, America's largest and most progressive union, whose hundreds of thousands of members toiled in all sorts of industrial activities.

The examples of the Communist Party's presence and activity continued far and wide across the nation. In Harlem, the South Side of Chicago, the Black community in Los Angeles, Washington, DC, Detroit, and Cleveland (to name a few) the party's presence was ubiquitous. New York City saw communist Ben Davis become elected to the city council twice, with essentially total support of even "estab-

Introduction

lishment" Black leaders. The party was at the center of the postwar maelstrom, especially as it concerned the desire of Black people to shed second-class citizenship.

In Birmingham, Bessemer communists led struggles for the right to vote, at one point taking one hundred uniformed Black veterans to the Jefferson County Courthouse to register. In New Orleans, the party helped organize a group of hundreds of Black and white youth who picketed segregated stores, and integrated streetcars and buses by refusing to obey Jim Crow laws. In North Carolina, the party led militant strikes of the majority-Black tobacco workers, organizing nearly twenty thousand into unions across the state. Communists organized the pioneering Black women's group the Sojourners for Truth and Justice who, among other things, launched a militant campaign to defend Rosa Lee Ingram, a Black woman in Georgia who defended herself against a white rapist and was charged with murder. The outcry from the Sojourners commuted her death sentence and set the stage for her future freedom.

Even on the cultural front, the communist-published *Masses & Mainstream* featured "more articles by and about Black writers than any other journal except for Black ones."[36] Names one might recognize today, including Lorraine Hansberry, Paul Robeson, Alice Childress, Harry Belafonte, Sidney Poitier, Max Roach, Lena Horne, and Charlie Parker, among others were either in the party, or in its broader cultural orbit. Intellectually, the Dean of American Letters W. E. B. Du Bois had grown close to the party as well.

Ultimately, however, the realities of the Cold War offensive blunted many communist efforts, driving them semi-underground, causing their militant anti-racist work to flounder, then mainly disappear under the heat of the witch hunt. And, along with it, the Black Belt Thesis.

Legacies

As much as these histories of the communist movement and Black liberation have been erased, their impact can still be felt as it transformed through the decades following. The radical upsurge of the 1960s and 1970s saw the idea of "nationhood" reemerge and go mainstream. Afro hairstyles, dashikis, African and Muslim names, "buying Black," Black caucuses, and more all exploded into the US cultural landscape with a brash defiance best summed up by the political slogan "Black Power!" and the famous James Brown song: "Say It Loud! I'm Black and I'm Proud!" that spent six weeks at the top of the R&B charts in 1968. The Black Arts Movement launched names like Amiri Baraka and Nikki Giovanni into major cultural figures while consciously cultivating a national culture, as one manifesto noted: "The Black Arts and the Black Power concept both relate broadly to the Afro-American's desire for self-determination and nationhood."[37]

This "national consciousness" would also find expression in the National Black Political Assembly in Gary, Indiana in 1972; the Wattstaxx cultural festival in 1972; the Newark Black Power Conference in 1967; The Black Expos organized by Operation PUSH in the early 70s; the Atlanta conference of the Congress of Afrikan People in 1970 and others. One biography of Elijah Muhammad notes that "throughout the early 1960s, the idea of a separate Black state was Muhammad's biggest calling card. In fact, the national notoriety of the Nation of Islam was largely due to its avowed willingness to territorially withdraw from the United States."[38]

At the same time, a series of mass uprisings exploded in Black communities across the United States. Thousands rose up in Harlem in 1964 after a cop gunned down 15-year-old James Powell. A week later Governor Rockefeller had to send a thousand National Guardsmen to Rochester after the Black community retaliated to an attempted mass arrest of racist cops.

The next year, Watts, California gave the new mood a slogan: "Burn, Baby, Burn!" In 1967 and 1968, hundreds of cities burned, including at least 150 in the summer of 1967 and 110 in the four weeks after the Rev. Dr. Martin Luther King Jr. was assassinated in 1968.

This cauldron was what produced organizations and leaders that would become famous around the world; in particular, the Black Panther Party, the Republic of New Afrika, the League of Revolutionary Black Workers, and, before his assassination, Malcolm X. In these networks there were a number of older mentors who had history in the Communist Party and directly seeded ideas related to the Black Belt Thesis, including Queen Mother Audley Moore, Nelson Peery, Harry Haywood himself, and Abner Berry, among others. In that context, the Black Belt Thesis, in various modified forms, crept into the political lexicon.

Introduction

This is evident when you look to 1967, when Kwame Ture (then Stokely Carmichael) and Charles Hamilton released *Black Power: The Politics of Liberation in America*. The book was the first ideological treatment of the broader cultural-political phenomenon that was embodied by the rallying cry "Black Power!" which had emerged from the depths of the civil rights movement in Mississippi.[39]

The first chapter is subtitled "the colonial situation" and develops the nation-like formulation that "Black people . . . stand as colonial subjects in relation to white society," and further that institutional racism "has another name: colonialism."[40] Similar to Haywood, the authors addressed the fact that perhaps the situation of Blacks in the United States, was not exactly analogous to what people thought of as colonies, they similarly noted "but is the differentiation more than a technicality?"[41] They further noted that the Black population was located "geographically' in "majority blocs."[42] Also that the Black community was, in an overall sense, in a situation of uniform state of "economic deprivation."[43]

The echoes of the Black Belt Thesis in the "internal colonialism" concept make even more sense when one adds that Ture and Hamilton were building on a 1962 essay by Harold Cruse, a former Communist Party member, arguing the same, and, explicitly, contrasting his views to Haywood's.[44] Haywood, was making his own interventions as a contributor to the radical Black journal *Soulbook*.[45] In a series of essays Haywood defended, updated and explicated the Black Belt Thesis and also commented on current events. Notably, *Soulbook* was published by a group of Northern California radicals affiliated with Revolutionary Action Movement whose close circle included Huey Newton and Bobby Seale. Unsurprisingly then, the "internal colonialism" thesis was also adopted by the Black Panthers for a time.[46]

The Republic of New Afrika, centered on a program of creating a Black Nation in the six states of the Deep South, consciously drawing on the thesis. Its founding convention drew everyone from Amiri Baraka to H. Rap Brown, Queen Mother Moore, Robert F. Williams and Betty Shabazz. Making it clear how much currency "nationhood" had by the second half of the 1960s. Notably, the thesis would be taken up in its entirety by dozens of communist groups in the 1970s as well. It would become the subject of many a polemic, and make the thesis a topic of great discussion among the broader left-wing milieu in the US.

Why Now?

Taken as a whole the Black Belt Thesis has had one major enduring impact: theorizing the absolute centrality of racism to the construction of the broader American polity and culture. Foundational not simply to communist thinking, but to many attempts at similar theorizing moving forward, especially in the high-tide of Black resistance in the middle of the twentieth century.

By linking the defeat of racism to the defeat of capitalism, and vice versa, the thesis opened up critical intellectual and practical space in the struggle for Black liberation. For Black communists it created the space for a range of innovations and interventions that have gone on to be widely considered landmarks in the broader struggle for freedom. Perhaps more importantly, for non-Black communists, and other progressives, it created, and solidified, an understanding of the indispensable role that the struggle for Black liberation must play in any truly transformative future.

Revisiting the foundational documents of the Black Belt Thesis, then, takes on a critical importance in our current moment. The uprisings that have followed since Ferguson, the right-wing assaults on anti-racist education, the election of the first Black president, and the persistence of racial inequalities are all crying out for creative interventions and new theoretical innovations that can provide solutions. The essays and articles in this volume offer an opportunity to reflect on how, even ninety-five years later, the core observations about how racism is a feature, not a bug, of capitalism remains obviously true. At the same time, the reality of a shared history, culture and relationship to the US economy among Black Americans is as clear now as it was in 1928.

For the many millions who hope to banish white supremacy and the constant oppression of Black people to the dustbin of history, the Black Belt Thesis is a firm foundation on which to build new insights.

THE COMINTERN RESOLUTIONS

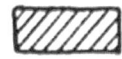

I. THE 1928 COMINTERN RESOLUTION ON THE NEGRO QUESTION UNITED STATES*

1. The industrialization of the South, the concentration of a new Negro working-class population in the big cities of the East and North, and the entrance of the Negroes into the basic industries on a mass scale, create the possibility for the Negro workers, under the leadership of the Communist Party, to assume the hegemony of all Negro liberation movements, and to increase their importance and role in the revolutionary struggle of the American proletariat.

The Negro working class has reached a stage of development which enables it, if properly organized and well led, to fulfill successfully its double historical mission:

(a) To play a considerable role in the class struggle against American imperialism as an important part of the American working class; and

(b) To lead the movement of the oppressed masses of the Negro population.

---

* Communist International, "1928 and 1930 Comintern Resolutions on the Black National Question in the United States" (Revolutionary Review Press, 1975), From Marx to Mao, http://www.marx2mao.com/Other/CR75.html.

2. The bulk of the Negro population (86 percent) live in the southern states; of this number 74 percent live in the rural districts and are dependent almost exclusively upon agriculture for a livelihood. Approximately one-half of these rural dwellers live in the so-called "Black Belt," in which area they constitute more than 50 percent of the entire population. The great mass of the Negro agrarian population are subject to the most ruthless exploitation and persecution of a semi-slave character. In addition to the ordinary forms of capitalist exploitation, American imperialism utilizes every possible form of slave exploitation (peonage, sharecropping, landlord supervision of crops and marketing, etc.) for the purpose of extracting superprofits. On the basis of these slave remnants, there has grown up a superstructure of social and political inequality that expresses itself in lynching, segregation, Jim Crowism, etc.

Necessary Conditions for National Revolutionary Movement

3. The various forms of oppression of the Negro masses, who are concentrated mainly in the so-called "Black Belt," provide the necessary conditions for a national revolutionary movement among the Negroes. The Negro agricultural laborers and the tenant farmers feel most the pressure of white persecution and exploitation. Thus, the agrarian problem lies at the root of the Negro national movement. The great majority of Negroes in the rural districts of the south are not "reserves of capitalist reaction," but potential allies of the revolutionary proletariat. Their objective position facilitates their transformation into a revolutionary force, which, under the leadership of the proletariat, will be able to participate in the joint struggle with all other workers against capitalist exploitation.

4. It is the duty of the Negro workers to organize through the mobilization of the broad masses of the Negro population the struggle of the agricultural laborers and tenant farmers against all forms of semifeudal oppression. On the other hand, it is the duty of the Communist Party of the USA to mobilize and rally the broad masses of the white workers for active participation in this struggle. For that reason the Party must consider the beginning of systematic work in the south as one of its main tasks, having regard for the fact that the bringing together of the workers and toiling masses of all nationalities for a

joint struggle against the landowners and the bourgeoisie is one of the most important aims of the Communist International, as laid down in the resolutions on the national and colonial question of the Second and Sixth Congresses of the Comintern.

For Complete Emancipation of Oppressed Negro Race

5. To accomplish this task, the Communist Party must come out as the champion of the right of the oppressed Negro race for full emancipation. While continuing and intensifying the struggle under the slogan of full social and political equality for the Negroes, which must remain the central slogan of our Party for work among the masses, the Party must come out openly and unreservedly for the right of the Negroes to national self-determination in the southern states, where the Negroes form a majority of the population. The struggle for equal rights and the propaganda for the slogan of self-determination must be linked up with the economic demands of the Negro masses, especially those directed against the slave remnants and all forms of national and racial oppression. Special stress must be laid upon organizing active resistance against lynching, Jim Crowism, segregation, and all other forms of oppression of the Negro population.

6. All work among the Negroes, as well as the struggle for the Negro cause among the whites, must be used, based upon the changes which have taken place in the relationship of classes among the Negro population. The existence of a Negro industrial proletariat of almost two million workers makes it imperative that the main emphasis should be placed on these new proletarian forces. The Negro workers must be organized under the leadership of the Communist Party, and thrown into joint struggle together with the white workers. The Party must learn to combine all demands of the Negroes with the economic and political struggle of the workers and the poor farmers.

American Negro Question Part of World Problem

7. The Negro question in the United States must be treated in its relation to the Negro questions and struggles in other parts of the world. The Negro race everywhere is an oppressed race. Whether it is a minority (USA, etc.), majority (South Africa), or inhabits a so-called independent state (Liberia, etc.), the Negroes are oppressed

by imperialism. Thus, a common tie of interest is established for the revolutionary struggle of race and national liberation from imperialist domination of the Negroes in various parts of the world. A strong Negro revolutionary movement in the USA will be able to influence and direct the revolutionary movement in all those parts of the world where the Negroes are oppressed by imperialism.

8. The proletarianization of the Negro masses makes the trade unions the principal form of mass organization. It is the primary task of the Party to play an active part and lead in the work of organizing the Negro workers and agricultural laborers in trade unions. Owing to the refusal of the majority of the white unions in the USA, led by the reactionary leaders, to admit Negroes to membership, steps must be immediately taken to set up special unions for those Negro workers who are not allowed to join the white unions. At the same time, however, the struggles for the inclusion of Negro workers in the existing unions must be intensified and concentrated upon, special attention must be given to those unions in which the statutes and rules set up special limitations against the admission of Negro workers. Primary duty of Communist Party in this connection is to wage a merciless struggle against the American Federation of Labor (AFL) bureaucracy, which prevents the Negro workers from joining the white workers' unions. The organization of special trade unions for the Negro masses must be carried out as part and parcel of the struggle against the restrictions imposed upon the Negro workers and for their admission to the white workers' unions. The creation of separate Negro unions should in no way weaken the struggle in the old unions for the admission of Negroes on equal terms. Every effort must be made to see that all the new unions organized by the left wing and by the Communist Party should embrace the workers of all nationalities and of all races. The principle of one union for all workers in each industry, white and black, should cease to be a mere slogan of propaganda, and must become a slogan of action.

Party Trade Union Work among Negroes

9. While organizing the Negroes into unions and conducting an aggressive struggle against the anti-Negro trade union policy of the AFL, the Party must pay more attention than it has hitherto done to the work in the Negro workers' organizations, such as the Brother-

hood of Sleeping Car Porters, Chicago Asphalt Workers' Union, and so on. The existence of two million Negro workers and the further industrialization of the Negroes demand a radical change in the work of the Party among the Negroes. The creation of working-class organizations and the extension of our influence in the existing working-class Negro organizations, are of much greater importance than the work in bourgeois and petty-bourgeois organizations, such as the National Association for the Advancement of Colored People, the Pan-African Congress, etc.

10. The American Negro Labor Congress[47] continues to exist only nominally. Every effort should be made to strengthen this organization as a medium through which we can extend the work of the Party among the Negro masses and mobilize the Negro workers under our leadership. After careful preparatory work, which must be started at once, another convention of the American Negro Labor Congress should be held. A concrete plan must also be presented to the Congress for an intensified struggle for the economic, social, political and national demands of the Negro masses. The program of the American Negro Labor Congress must deal specially with the agrarian demands of the Negro farmers and tenants in the south.

11. The importance of trade union work imposes special tasks upon the Trade Union Educational League (TUEL).[48] The TUEL has completely neglected the work among the Negro workers, notwithstanding the fact that these workers are objectively in a position to play a very great part in carrying through the program of organizing the unorganized. The closest contact must be established between the TUEL and the Negro masses. The TUEL must become the champion in the struggle for the rights of the Negroes in the old unions, and in the organizing of new unions for both Negroes and whites, as well as separate Negro unions.

White Chauvinism Evidenced in the American Party

12. The Central Executive Committee of the American Communist Party itself stated in its resolution of April 30, 1928, that "the Party as a whole has not sufficiently realized the significance of work among the Negroes." Such an attitude toward the Party work among the Negroes

is, however, not satisfactory. The time is ripe to begin within the Party a courageous campaign of self-criticism concerning the work among the Negroes. Penetrating self-criticism is the necessary preliminary condition for directing the Negro work along new lines.

13. The Party must bear in mind that white chauvinism, which is the expression of the ideological influence of American imperialism among the workers, not only prevails among different strata of the white workers in the USA, but is even reflected in various forms in the Party itself. White chauvinism has manifested itself even in open antagonism of some comrades to the Negro comrades. In some instances where Communists were called upon to champion and to lead in the most vigorous manner the fight against white chauvinism, they instead yielded to it. In Gary, white members of the Workers Party protested against Negroes eating in the restaurant controlled by the Party. In Detroit, Party members, yielding to pressure, drove out Negro comrades from a social given in aid of the miners on strike.
Whilst the Party has taken certain measures against these manifestations of white chauvinism, nevertheless those manifestations must be regarded as indications of race prejudice even in the ranks of the Party, which must be fought with the utmost energy.

14. An aggressive fight against all forms of white chauvinism must be accompanied by a widespread and thorough educational campaign in the spirit of internationalism within the Party, utilizing for this purpose to the fullest possible extent the Party schools, the Party press and the public platform, to stamp out all forms of antagonism, or even indifference among our white comrades toward the Negro work. This educational work should be conducted simultaneously with a campaign to draw the white workers and the poor farmers into the struggle for the support of the demands of the Negro workers.

Tasks of Party in Relation to Negro Work

15. The Communist Party of the USA in its treatment of the Negro question must all the time bear in mind this twofold task:

(a) To fight for the full rights of the oppressed Negroes and for their right to self-determination and against all forms of chauvinism, especially among the workers of the oppressing nationality.

(b) The propaganda and the day-to-day practice of international class solidarity must be considered as one of the basic tasks of the American Communist Party. The fight—by propaganda and by deeds—should be directed first and foremost against the chauvinism of the workers of the oppressing nationality as well as against bourgeois segregation tendencies of the oppressed nationality. The propaganda of international class solidarity is the necessary prerequisite for the unity of the working class in the struggle.

"The center of gravity in educating the workers of the oppressing countries in the principles of internationalism must inevitably consist in the propaganda and defense by these workers of the right of segregation by the oppressed countries. We have the right and duty to treat every socialist of an oppressing nation, who does not conduct such propaganda, as an imperialist and as a scoundrel." (Lenin, selected articles on the national question.)

16. The Party must seriously take up the task of training a cadre of Negro comrades as leaders, bring them into the Party schools in the USA and abroad, and make every effort to draw Negro proletarians into active and leading work in the Party, not confining the activities of the Negro comrades exclusively to the work among Negroes. Simultaneously, white workers must specially be trained for work among the Negroes.

17. Efforts must be made to transform the *Negro Champion*[49] into a weekly mass organ of the Negro proletariat and tenant farmers. Every encouragement and inducement must be given to the Negro comrades to utilize the Party press generally.

Negro Work Part of General Work of Party

18. The Party must link up the struggle on behalf of the Negroes with the general campaigns of the Party. The Negro problem must be part and parcel of all and every campaign conducted by the Party. In the

election campaigns, trade union work, the campaigns for the organization of the unorganized, anti-imperialist work, labor party campaign, International Labor Defense, etc.,[50] the Central Executive Committee must work out plans designed to draw the Negroes into active participation in all these campaigns, and at the same time to bring the white workers into the struggle on behalf of the Negroes' demands. It must be borne in mind that the Negro masses will not be won for the revolutionary struggles until such time as the most conscious section of the white workers show, by action, that they are fighting with the Negroes against all racial discrimination and persecution. Every member of the Party must bear in mind that "the age-long oppression of the colonial and weak nationalities by the imperialist powers, has given rise to a feeling of bitterness among the masses of the enslaved countries as well as a feeling of distrust toward the oppressing nations in general and toward the proletariat of those nations." (See resolution on Colonial and National Question of Second Congress.)

19. The Negro women in industry and on the farms constitute a powerful potential force in the struggle for Negro emancipation. By reason of being unorganized to an even greater extent than male Negro workers, they are the most exploited section. The AFL bureaucracy naturally exercises toward them a double hostility, by reason of both their color and sex. It therefore becomes an important task of the Party to bring the Negro women into the economic and political struggle.

20. Only by an active and strenuous fight on the part of the white workers against all forms of oppression directed against the Negroes, will the Party be able to draw into its ranks the most active and conscious Negro workers—men and women—and to increase its influence in those intermediary organizations which are necessary for the mobilization of the Negro masses in the struggle against segregation, lynching, Jim Crowism, etc.

21. In the present struggle in the mining industry, the Negro workers participate actively and in large numbers. The leading role the Party played in this struggle has helped greatly to increase its prestige. Nevertheless, the special efforts being made by the Party in the work among

the Negro strikers cannot be considered as adequate. The Party did not send enough Negro organizers into the coalfields, and it did not sufficiently attempt, in the first stages of the fight, to develop the most able Negro strikers and to place them in leading positions. The Party must be especially criticized for its failure to put Negro workers on the Presidium of the Pittsburgh Miners' Conference, doing so only after such representation was demanded by the Negroes themselves.

22. In the work among the Negroes, special attention should be paid to the role played by the churches and preachers who are acting on behalf of American imperialism. The Party must conduct a continuous and carefully worked out campaign among the Negro masses, sharpened primarily against the preachers and the churchmen, who are the agents of the oppressors of the Negro race.

Party Work among Negro Proletariat and Peasantry

23. The Party must apply united front tactics for specific demands to the existing Negro petty bourgeois organizations. The purpose of these united front tactics should be the mobilizing of the Negro masses under the leadership of the Party, and to expose the treacherous petty bourgeois leadership of those organizations.

24. The Negro Miners Relief Committee and the Harlem Tenants League are examples of joint organizations of action which may serve as a means of drawing the Negro masses into struggle. In every case the utmost effort must be made to combine the struggle of the Negro workers with the struggle of the white workers, and to draw the white workers' organizations into such joint campaigns.

25. In order to reach the bulk of the Negro masses, special attention should be paid to the work among the Negroes in the South. For that purpose, the Party should establish a district organization in the most suitable locality in the South. Whilst continuing trade union work among the Negro workers and the agricultural laborers, special organizations of tenant farmers must be set up. Special efforts must also be made to secure the support of the sharecroppers in the creation of such organizations. The Party must undertake the task of working out

a definite program of immediate demands, directed against all slave remnants, which will serve as the rallying slogans for the formation of such peasant organizations.

Henceforth the Workers (Communist) Party must consider the struggle on behalf of the Negro masses, the task of organizing the Negro workers and peasants, and the drawing of these oppressed masses into the proletarian revolutionary struggle, as one of its major tasks, remembering, in the words of the Second Congress resolution, that "the victory over capitalism cannot be fully achieved and carried to its ultimate goal unless the proletariat and the toiling masses of all nations of the world rally of their own accord in a concordant and close union. (Political Secretariat, Communist International, Moscow, USSR, Oct. 26, 1928.)

II. THE 1930 COMINTERN RESOLUTION ON THE NEGRO QUESTION UNITED STATES

(Final text, confirmed by the Political Secretariat of the ECCI, October 26, 1930.)

The Communist Party (CP) of the United States has always acted openly and energetically against Negro oppression, and has thereby won increasing sympathy among the Negro population. In its own ranks, too, the Party has relentlessly fought the slightest evidences of white chauvinism, and has purged itself of the gross opportunism of the Lovestoneites. According to the assertions of these people, the "industrial revolution" will sweep away the remnants of slavery in the agricultural South, and will proletarianize the Negro peasantry, so that the Negro question, as a special national question, would thereby be presumably solved, or could be put off until the time of the socialist revolution in America. But the Party has not yet succeeded in overcoming in its own ranks all underestimation of the struggle for the slogan of the right of self-determination, and still less succeeded in doing away with all *lack of clarity* on the Negro question. In the Party discussion the question was often wrongly put and much erroneous counterposing of phases of the question occurred, thus, for instance, should the slogan of social equality or the slogan of the right of self-determination of the Negroes be emphasized. Should only propaganda for the Negroes' right to self-determination be carried on, or should this slogan be considered as a slogan of action; should separatist tendencies among the Negroes be supported or opposed; is the Southern region, thickly populated by Negroes, to be looked upon as a colony, or as an "integral part of the national economy of the United States," where presumably a revolutionary situation cannot arise independent of the general revolutionary development in the United States?

In the interest of the utmost clarity of ideas on this question the Negro question in the United States must be viewed from the standpoint of its peculiarity, namely as the question of an *oppressed nation*, which is in a peculiar and extraordinarily distressing situation of national oppression not only in view of the prominent *racial distinctions* (marked difference in the color of skin, etc.), but above all because of considerable *social antagonism* (remnants of slavery). This introduces into the American Negro question an important, *peculiar* trait which is absent from the national question of other oppressed peoples. Furthermore, it is necessary to face clearly the inevitable distinction between the position of the Negro in the *South* and in the *North*, owing to the fact that at least three-fourths of the entire Negro population of the United States (12 million) live in compact masses in the South, most of them being peasants and agricultural laborers in a state of semi-serfdom, settled in the "Black Belt" and constituting the majority of the population, whereas the Negroes in the Northern States are for the most part industrial workers of the lowest categories who have recently come to the various industrial centers from the South (having often even fled from there).

The struggle of the Communists for the equal rights of the Negroes applies to all Negroes, in the North as well as in the South. The struggle for this slogan embraces all or almost all of the important special interests of the Negroes in the North, but not in the South, where the main Communist slogan must be: *The right of self-determination of the Negroes in the Black Belt.* These two slogans, however, are most closely connected. The Negroes in the North are very much interested in winning the right of self-determination for the Negro population of the Black Belt and can thereby hope for strong support for the establishment of true equality of the Negroes in the North. In the South the Negroes are suffering no less but still more than in the North from the glaring lack of all equality; for the most part the struggle for their most urgent partial demands in the Black Belt is nothing more than the struggle for their equal rights, and only the fulfillment of their main slogan, the right of self-determination in the Black Belt, can assure them of true equality.

I. The Struggle for the Equal Rights of the Negroes

2.[51] The basis for the demand of equality of the Negroes is provided by the special yoke to which the Negroes in the United States are subjected by the ruling classes. In comparison with the situation of the other various nationalities and races oppressed by American imperialism, the yoke of the Negroes in the United States is of a peculiar nature and particularly oppressive. This is partly due to the historical past of the American Negroes as imported slaves, but is much more due to the still existing slavery of the American Negro which is immediately apparent, for example, in comparing their situation even with the situation of the Chinese and Japanese workers in the West of the United States, or with the lot of the Filipinos (Malay race) who are under colonial repression.

It is only a Yankee bourgeois lie to say that the yoke of Negro slavery has been lifted in the United States. Formally it has been abolished, but in practice the great majority of the Negro masses in the South are living in slavery in the literal sense of the word. Formally, they are "free" as "tenant farmers" or "contract laborers" on the big plantations of the white landowners, but actually, they are completely in the power of their exploiters; they are not permitted, or else it is made impossible for them to leave their exploiters; if they do leave the plantations, they are brought back and in many cases whipped; many of them are simply taken prisoner under various pretexts and, bound together with long chains, they have to do compulsory labor on the roads. All through the South, the Negroes are not only deprived of all rights, and subjected to the arbitrary will of the white exploiters, but they are also socially ostracized, that is, they are treated in general not as human beings, but as cattle. But this ostracism regarding Negroes is not limited to the South. Not only in the South but throughout the United States, the lynching of Negroes is permitted to go unpunished. Everywhere the American bourgeoisie surrounds the Negroes with an atmosphere of social ostracism.

The 100 percent Yankee arrogance divides the American population into a series of castes, among which the Negroes constitute, so to speak, the caste of the "untouchables," who are in a still lower category than the lowest categories of human society, the immigrant laborers, the yellow immigrants and the Indians. In all big cities the Negroes have to live in special segregated ghettos (and, of course, have to pay extremely high rent). In practice, marriage between Negroes and whites is prohibited, and in the South this is even forbidden by law. In various other ways, the Negroes are segregated, and if they overstep the bounds of the segregation they immediately run the risk of being ill-treated by the 100 percent bandits. As wage-earners, the Negroes are forced to perform the lowest and most difficult work; they generally receive lower wages than the white workers and don't always get the same wages as white workers doing similar work, and their treatment is the very worst. Many AFL trade unions do not admit Negro workers in their ranks, and a number have organized special trade unions for Negroes so that they will not have to let them into their "good white society."

This whole system of "segregation" and "Jim Crowism" is a special form of national and social oppression under which the American Negroes have much to suffer. The origin of all this is not difficult to find: this Yankee arrogance towards the Negroes stinks of the disgusting atmosphere of the old slave market. This is downright robbery and slave-whipping barbarism at the peak of capitalist "culture."

3. The demand for equal rights in our sense of the word means not only demanding the same rights for the Negroes as the whites have in the United States at the present time but also demanding that the Negroes should be granted all rights and other advantages which we demand for the corresponding oppressed classes of whites (workers and other toilers). Thus in our sense of the word, the demand for equal rights means a continuous work of abolishment of all forms of economic and political oppression of the Negroes, as well as their social exclusion, the insults perpetrated against them and their segregation. This is to be obtained by constant struggle by the white and black workers for effective legal protection for the Negroes in all fields, as well as actual enforcement of their equality and combating of every expression of Negrophobia. One of the first Communist slogans is: Death for Negro Lynching!

The struggle for the equal rights of the Negroes does not in any way exclude recognition and support for the Negroes' rights to their own special schools, government organs, etc., wherever the Negro masses put forward such national demands of their own accord. This will, however, in all probability occur to any great extent only in the Black Belt. In other parts of the country, the Negroes suffer above all from being shut out from the general social institutions and not from being prohibited to set up their own national institutions. With the development of the Negro intellectuals (principally in the "free" professions) and of a thin layer of small capitalist business people, there have appeared lately, not only definite efforts for developing a purely national Negro culture but also outspoken bourgeois tendencies towards Negro nationalism. The broad masses of the Negro population in the big industrial centers of the North are, however, making no efforts whatsoever to maintain and cultivate a national aloofness, they are, on the contrary, working for assimilation. This effort of the Negro masses can do much in the future to facilitate the progressive process of amalgamating the whites and Negroes into one nation, and it is under no circumstances the task of the Communists to give support to bourgeois nationalism in its fight with the progressive assimilation tendencies of the Negro working masses.

4. The slogan of equal rights of the Negroes *without a relentless struggle in practice against all manifestations of Negrophobia on the part of the American bourgeoisie* can be nothing but a deceptive liberal gesture of a sly slave-owner or his agent. This slogan is in fact repeated by "socialist" and many other bourgeois politicians and philanthropists who want to get publicity for themselves by appealing to the "sense of justice" of the American bourgeoisie in the individual treatment of the Negroes, and thereby sidetrack attention from the one effective struggle against the shameful system of "white superiority:" from the *class struggle against the American bourgeoisie.* The struggle for equal rights for the Negroes is in fact, one of the most important parts of the proletarian class struggle of the United States.

The struggle for the equal rights for the Negroes must certainly take the form of common struggle by the white and black workers. The increasing unity of the various working-class elements provokes constant attempts on the part of the American bourgeoisie to play one group against another, particularly the white workers against the black and the black workers against the immigrant workers and vice versa, and thus to promote divisions within the working class, which contributes to the bolstering up of American capitalist rule. The Party must carry on a ruthless struggle against all these attempts of the bourgeoisie and do everything to strengthen the bonds of class solidarity of the working class upon a lasting basis.

In the struggle for equal rights for the Negroes, however, it is the duty of the *white* workers to march at *the head* on this struggle. They must everywhere make a breach in the walls of segregation and "Jim Crowism" which have been set up by bourgeois slave-market morality. They must most ruthlessly unmask and condemn the hypocritical reformists and bourgeois "friends of Negroes" who, in reality, are only interested in strengthening the power of the enemies of the Negroes. They, the white workers, must boldly jump at the throat of the 100 percent bandits who strike a Negro in the face. This struggle will be the test of the real international solidarity of the American white workers.

It is the special duty of the revolutionary Negro workers to carry on tireless activity among the Negro working masses to free them of their distrust of the white proletariat and draw them into the common front of the revolutionary class struggle against the bourgeoisie. They must emphasize with all force that the first rule of proletarian morality is that no worker who wants to be an equal member of his class must ever serve as a strikebreaker or a supporter of bourgeois politics. They must ruthlessly unmask all Negro politicians corrupted or directly bribed by American bourgeois ideology, who systematically interfere with the real proletarian struggle for the equal rights for the Negroes.

Furthermore, the Communist Party must resist all tendencies within its own ranks to ignore the Negro question as a national question in the United States, not only in the South, but also in the North. It is advisable for the Communist Party in the North to abstain from the establishment of any special Negro organizations, and in place of this to bring the black and white workers together in common organizations of struggle and joint action. Effective steps must be taken for the organization of Negro workers in the Trade Union Unity League (TUUL)[52] and revolutionary trade unions. Underestimation of this work takes various forms: lack of energy in recruiting Negro workers, in keeping them in our ranks and in drawing them into the full life of the trade unions, in selecting, educating and promoting Negro forces to leading functions in the organization. The Party must make itself entirely responsible for the carrying through of this very important work. It is most urgently necessary to publish a popular mass paper dealing with the Negro question, edited by white and black comrades, and to have all active followers of this paper grouped organizationally.

2. The Struggle for the Right of Self-Determination of the Negroes in the Black Belt

5. It is not correct to consider the Negro zone of the South as a colony of the United States. Such a characterization of the Black Belt could be based in some respects only upon artificially construed analogies, and would create superfluous difficulties for the clarification of ideas. In rejecting this estimation, however, it should not be overlooked that it would be none the less false to try to make a fundamental distinction between the character of national oppression to which the colonial peoples are subjected and the yoke of other oppressed nations. Fundamentally, national oppression in both cases is of the same character, and is in the Black Belt in many respects worse than in a number of actual colonies. On the one hand the Black Belt is not in itself, either economically or politically, such a united whole as to warrant its being called a special colony of the United States, but on the other hand this zone is not, either economically or politically, such an, integral part of the whole United States as any other part of the country. Industrialization in the Black Belt is not, as is generally the case in colonies properly speaking, in contradiction with the ruling interests of the imperialist bourgeoisie, which has in its hands the monopoly of the entire industry, but in so far as industry is developed here, it will in no way bring a solution to the question of living conditions of the oppressed Negro majority, or to the agrarian question, which lies at the basis of the national question. On the contrary, this question is still further aggravated as a result of the increase of the contradictions arising from the pre-capitalist forms of exploitation of the Negro peasantry and of a considerable portion of the Negro proletariat (miners, forestry workers, etc.) in the Black Belt, and at the same time owing to the industrial development here, the growth of the most important driving force of the national revolution, the black working class, is especially strengthened. Thus, the prospect for the future is not an inevitable dying away of the national revolutionary Negro movement in the South, as Lovestone prophesied, but on the contrary, a great

advance of this movement and the rapid approach of a revolutionary crisis in the Black Belt.

6. Owing to the peculiar situation in the Black Belt (the fact that the majority of the resident Negro population are farmers and agricultural laborers and that the capitalist economic system as well as political class rule there is not only of a special kind, but to a great extent still has pre-capitalist and semi-colonial features), the right of self-determination of the Negroes as the main slogan of the Communist Party in the Black Belt is appropriate. This, however, does not in any way mean that the struggle for equal rights of the Negroes in the Black Belt is less necessary or less well founded than it is in the North. On the contrary, here, owing to the whole situation, this struggle is even better founded, but the form of this slogan does not sufficiently correspond with the concrete requirements of the liberation struggle of the Negro population. Anyway, it is clear that in most cases it is a question of the daily conflicts of interest between the Negroes and the white rulers in the Black Belt on the subject of infringement of the most elementary equality rights of the Negroes by the whites. Daily events of the kind are: all Negro persecutions, all arbitrary economic acts of robbery by the white exploiters ("Black Man's Burden") and the whole system of so-called "Jim Crowism." Here, however, it is very important in connection with all these concrete cases of conflict to concentrate the attention of the Negro masses not so much to the general demands of mere equality, but much more to some of the revolutionary basic demands arising from the concrete situation.

The slogan of the right of self-determination occupies the central place in the liberation struggle of the Negro population in the Black Belt against the yoke of American imperialism, but this slogan, as we see it, must be carried out only in connection with two other basic demands. Thus, there are three basic demands to be kept in mind in the Black Belt, namely, the following:

> (1) *Confiscation of the landed property of the white landowners and capitalists for the benefit of the Negro farmers.* The landed property in the hands of the white American exploiters constitutes the most important material basis of

the entire system of national oppression and serfdom of the Negroes in the Black Belt. More than three-quarters of all Negro farmers here are bound in actual serfdom to the farms and plantations of the white exploiters by the feudal system of "sharecropping." Only on paper and not in practice are they freed from the yoke of their former slavery. The same holds completely true for the great mass of black contract laborers; here the contract is only the capitalist expression of the chains of the old slavery, which even today are not infrequently applied in their natural iron form on the roads of the Black Belt (chain-gang work). These are the main forms of present Negro slavery in the Black Belt and no breaking of the chains of this slavery is possible without confiscating all the landed property of the white masters. Without this revolutionary measure, without the agrarian revolution, the right of self-determination of the Negro population would be only a Utopia, or at best would remain only on paper without changing in any way the actual enslavement.

(2) *Establishment of the State Unity of the Black Belt.* At the present time this Negro zone—precisely for the purpose of facilitating national oppression—is artificially split up and divided into a number of various states which include distant localities having a majority of white population. If the right of self-determination of the Negroes is to be put into force, it is necessary wherever possible to bring together into one governmental unit all districts of the South where the majority of the settled population consists of Negroes. Within the limits of this state there will of course remain a fairly significant white minority which must submit to the right of self-determination of the Negro majority. There is no other possible way of carrying out in a democratic manner the right of self-determination of the Negroes. Every plan regarding the establishment of the Negro State with an exclusively Negro population in America (and, of course, still more exporting it to Africa)

is nothing but an unreal and reactionary caricature of the fulfillment of the right of self-determination of the Negroes and every attempt to isolate and transport the Negroes would have the most damaging effect upon their interests; above all, it would violate the right of the Negro farmers in the Black Belt not only to their present residences and their land but also to the land owned by the white landlords and cultivated by Negro labor.

(3) *Right of Self-Determination*. This means complete and unlimited right of the Negro majority to exercise governmental authority in the entire territory of the Black Belt, as well as to decide upon the relations between their territory and other nations, particularly the United States. It would not be right of self-determination in our sense of the word if the Negroes in the Black Belt had the right of determination only in cases which concerned *exclusively* the Negroes and did not affect the whites, because the most important cases arising here are bound to affect the Negroes as well as the whites. First of all, true right to self-determination means that the Negro majority and not the white minority in the entire territory of the administratively united Black Belt exercises the right of administrating governmental, legislative and judicial authority. At the present time all this power here is concentrated in the hands of the white bourgeoisie and landlords. It is they who appoint all officials, it is they who dispose of public property, it is they who determine the taxes, it is they who govern and make the laws. Therefore, *the overthrow of this class rule* in the Black Belt is unconditionally necessary in the struggle for the Negroes' right to self-determination. This, however, means at the same time the overthrow of the yoke of American imperialism in the Black Belt on which the forces of the local white bourgeoisie depend. Only in this way, only if the Negro population of the Black Belt wins its freedom from American imperialism even to the point of deciding itself the relations between its country and other govern-

ments, especially the United States, will it win real and complete self-determination. One should demand from the beginning that no armed forces of American imperialism should remain on the territory of the Black Belt.

7. As stated in the letter of the Polit. Secretariat of the ECCI of March 16th, 1930, the Communists must "*unreservedly* carry on a struggle" for the self-determination of the Negro population in the Black Belt in accordance with what has been set forth above. It is incorrect and harmful to interpret the Communist standpoint to mean that the Communists stand for the right of self-determination of the Negroes only up to a certain point, but not beyond this, for example, to the right of separation. It is also incorrect to say that the Communists are so far only to carry on propaganda or agitation for the right of self-determination, but not to develop any activity to bring this about. No, it is of the utmost importance for the Communist Party to reject any such limitation of its struggle for this slogan. Even if the situation does not yet warrant the raising of the question of uprising, one should not limit oneself at present to propaganda for the demand: "Right to self-determination," but should organize mass actions, such as demonstrations, strikes, tax-boycott movements, etc.

Moreover, the Party cannot make its stand for this slogan dependent upon any conditions, even the condition that the proletariat has the hegemony in the national revolutionary Negro movement or that the majority of the Negroes in the Black Belt adopts the Soviet form (as Pepper demanded), etc. It goes without saying that the Communists in the Black Belt will and must try to win over all working elements of the Negroes, that is, the majority of the population, to their side and to convince them not only that they must win the right of self-determination, but also that they must make use of this right in accordance with the Communist program. But this cannot be made a *condition* for the stand of the Communists in favor of the right of self-determination of the Negro population; if, or so long as the majority of this population wishes to handle the situation in the Black Belt in a different manner from that which we Communists would like, its complete right to self-determination must be recognized. This right we must defend as a free democratic right.

8. In general, the CP of the United States has kept to this correct line recently in its struggle for the right of self-determination of the Negroes even though this line—in some cases—has been unclearly or erroneously expressed.

In particular some misunderstanding has arisen from the failure to make a clear distinction between the demand for "right of self-determination" and the demand for governmental separation, simply treating these two demands in the same way. However, these two demands are not identical. Complete right to self-determination includes also the right to governmental separation, but does not necessarily imply that the Negro population should *make use of this* right under all circumstances, that is, that it must actually separate or attempt to separate the Black Belt from the existing governmental federation with the United States. If it desires to separate it must be free to do so; but if it prefers to remain federated with the United States it must also be free to do that. This is the correct meaning of the idea of self-determination and it must be recognized quite independently of whether the United States are still a capitalist state or if a proletarian dictatorship has already been established there.

It is, however, another matter if it is not a case of the *right* of the oppressed nation concerned to separate or to maintain governmental contact, but if the question is treated on its merits; whether it is to work for state separation, whether it is to struggle *for this* or not. This is another question, on which the stand of the Communists must vary according to the concrete conditions. If the proletariat has come into power in the United States, the Communist Negroes will not come out for but *against* separation of the Negro Republic federation with the United States. But the *right* of the Negroes to governmental separation will be *unconditionally realized* by the Communist Party, it will unconditionally give the Negro population of the Black Belt freedom of choice even on this question. Only when the proletariat has come into power in the United States the Communists will carry on propaganda among the working masses of the Negro population against separation, in order to convince them that it is much better and in the interest of the Negro nation for the Black Belt to be a free republic, where the Negro majority has complete right of self-determination but remains governmentally federated with the great proletarian republic of the United States. The bourgeois counterrevolutionists on the other hand will then be interested in boosting the separation tendencies in the ranks of the various nationalities in order to utilize separatist nationalism as a barrier for the bourgeois counterrevolution against the consolidation of the proletarian dictatorship.

But the question at the present time is not this. As long as capitalism rules in the United States the Communists cannot come out against governmental separation of the Negro zone from the United States. They recognize that this separation from the imperialist United States would be preferable from the standpoint of the national interests of the Negro population, to their present oppressed state, and therefore, the Communists are ready at any time to offer all their support if only the working masses of the Negro population are ready to take up the struggle for governmental independence of the Black Belt. At the present time, however, the situation in the national struggle in the South is not such as to win mass support of the working Negroes for this separatist struggle; and it is not the task of the Communists to call upon them to separate without taking into consideration the existing situation and the desires of the Negro masses.

The situation in the Negro question of the United States, however, may undergo a radical change. It is even probable that the separatist efforts to obtain complete State independence of the Black Belt will gain ground among the Negro masses of the South in the near future. This is connected with the prospective sharpening of the national conflicts in the South, with the advance of the national revolutionary Negro movement and with the exceptionally brutal fascists aggressiveness of the white exploiters of the South, as well as with the support of this aggressiveness by the central government authority of the United States. In this sharpening of the situation in the South, Negro separatism will presumably increase, and the question of the independence of the Black Belt will become the question of the day. Then the Communist Party must also face this question and, if the circumstances seem favorable, must stand up with all strength and courage for the struggle to win independence and for the establishment of a Negro republic in the Black Belt.

9. The general relation of Communists to separatist tendencies among the Negroes, described above, cannot mean that Communists associate themselves at present, or generally speaking, during capitalism, indis-

criminately and without criticism with all the separatist currents of the various bourgeois or petty-bourgeois Negro groups. For there is not only a national revolutionary, but also a reactionary Negro separatism, for instance, that represented by Garvey; his Utopia of an isolated Negro State (regardless if in Africa or America, if it is supposed to consist of Negroes only) pursues the only political aim of diverting the Negro masses from the real liberation struggle against American imperialism.

It would be a mistake to imagine that the right of self-determination slogan is a truly revolutionary slogan only in connection with the demand for complete separation. The question of power is decided not only through the demand of separation, but just as much through the demand of the right to decide the separation question and self-determination in general. A direct question of power is also the demand of confiscation of the land of the white exploiters in the South, as well as the demand of the Negroes that the entire Black Belt be amalgamated into a State unit.

Hereby, every single fundamental demand of the liberation struggle of the Negroes in the Black Belt is such that—if once thoroughly understood by the Negro masses and adopted as their slogan—it will lead them into the struggle for the overthrow of the power of the ruling bourgeoisie, which is impossible without such revolutionary struggle. One cannot deny that it is just possible for the Negro population of the Black Belt to win the right to self-determination already during capitalism; but it is perfectly clear and indubitable that this is possible only through successful revolutionary struggle for power against the American bourgeoisie, through wresting the Negroes' right to self-determination from the American imperialism. Thus, the slogan of right to self-determination is a real slogan of national rebellion which, to be considered as such, need not be supplemented by proclaiming struggle for the complete separation of the Negro zone, at least not at present. But it must be made perfectly clear to the Negro masses that the slogan "right to self-determination" includes the demand of full freedom for them to decide even the question of complete separation. "We demand freedom of separation, real right to self-determination"—wrote Lenin: "certainly not in order to 'recommend' separation, but on the contrary, in order to facilitate and accelerate the democratic rapprochement and unification of nations." For the same purpose, Lenin's Party, the CP of the Soviet Union, bestowed after its seizure of power on all the peoples hitherto oppressed by Russian Tsarism the full right to self-determination, including the right of complete separation, and achieved thereby its enormous successes with regard to the democratic rapprochement and voluntary unification of nations.

10. The slogan for the self-determination right and the other fundamental slogans of the Negro question in the Black Belt does not exclude but rather presupposes an energetic development of the struggle for concrete partial demands linked up with the daily needs and afflictions of wide masses of working Negroes. In order to avoid, in this connection, the danger of opportunist back-slidings, Communists must above all remember this:

> (a) The direct aims and partial demands around which a partial struggle develops are to be linked up in the course of the struggle with the revolutionary fundamental slogans brought up by the question of power, in a popular manner corresponding to the mood of the masses. (Confiscation of the big landholdings, establishment of governmental unity of the Black Belt, right of self-determination of the Negro population in the Black Belt.) Bourgeois-socialist tendencies to oppose such a revolutionary widening and deepening of the fighting demands must be fought.

> (b) One should not venture to draw up a complete program of some kind or a system of "positive" partial demands. Such programs on the part of petty-bourgeois politicians should be exposed as attempts to divert the masses from the necessary hard struggles by fostering reformist and democratic illusions among them. Every positive partial demand which might crop up is to be considered from the viewpoint of whether it is in keeping with our revolutionary fundamental slogans, or whether it is of a reformist or reactionary tendency. Every kind of national oppression which arouses the indignation of the Negro masses can be used as a suitable point of departure for the development of partial struggles, during which the abolition of such oppression, as well as their prevention through revolution-

ary struggle against the ruling exploiting dictatorship must be demanded.

(c) Everything should be done to bring wide masses of Negroes into these partial struggles—this is important—and not to carry the various partial demands to such an ultra-radical point, that the mass of working Negroes are no longer able to recognise them as *their own*. Without a real mobilization of the mass movements—in spite of the sabotage of the bourgeois reformist Negro politicians—even the best Communist partial demands get hung up. On the other hand, even some relatively insignificant acts of the Ku Klux Klan bandits in the Black Belt can become the occasion of important political movements, provided the Communists are able to organize the resistance of the indignant Negro masses. In such cases, mass movements of this kind can easily develop into real rebellion. This rests on the fact that—as Lenin said—"Every act of national oppression calls forth resistance on the part of the masses of the population, and the tendency of every act of resistance on the part of oppressed peoples is the national uprising."

d) Communists must fight in the *forefront* of the national-liberation movement and must do their utmost for the progress of this mass movement and its revolutionization. Negro Communists must *clearly dissociate* themselves from all bourgeois currents in the Negro movement, must indefatigably oppose the spread of the influence of the bourgeois groups on the working Negroes, and in dealing with them must apply the Communist tactic laid down by the Sixth Comintern Congress with regard to the colonial question, in order to guarantee the *hegemony of the Negro proletariat* in the national liberation movement of the Negro population, and to coordinate wide masses of the Negro peasantry in a steady fighting alliance with the proletariat.

e) One must work with the utmost energy for the establishment and consolidation of *Communist Party orga-*

nizations and revolutionary *trade unions* in the South. Furthermore, immediate measures must be taken for the organization of proletarian and peasant *self-defense* of whites and blacks against the Ku Klux Klan; for this purpose, the CP is to give further instructions.

11. It is particularly incumbent on Negro Communists to criticize consistently the halfheartedness and hesitations of the petty-bourgeois national-revolutionary Negro leaders in the liberation struggle of the Black Belt, exposing them before the masses. All national reformist currents as, for instance, Garveyism, which are an obstacle to the revolutionization of the Negro masses, must be fought systematically and with the utmost energy. Simultaneously, Negro Communists must carry on among the Negro masses an energetic struggle against nationalist moods directed indiscriminately against all whites, workers as well as capitalists, Communists, as well as imperialists. Their constant call to the Negro masses must be: *revolutionary struggle against the ruling white bourgeoisie, through a fighting alliance with the revolutionary white proletariat!* Negro Communists must indefatigably explain to the mass of the Negro population that even if many white workers in America are still infected with Negrophobia, the American proletariat, as a class, which owing to its struggle against the American bourgeoisie represents the only truly revolutionary class, will be the only real mainstay of Negro liberation. In as far as successes in the national-revolutionary struggle of the Negro population of the South for its right to self-determination are already possible under capitalism, they can be achieved only if this struggle is effectively supported by proletarian mass actions on a large scale in the other parts of the United States. But it is also clear that "only a victorious proletarian revolution will *finally* decide the agrarian question and the national question in the South of the United States, in the interest of the predominating mass of the Negro population of the country." (Colonial Theses of the Sixth World Congress.)

12. The struggle regarding the Negro question in the North must be linked up with the liberation struggle in the South, in order to endow the Negro movement throughout the United States with the necessary effective strength. After all, in the North as well as in the South, it is

a question of the real emancipation of the American Negroes which has in fact never taken place before. The Communist Party of the United States must bring into play its entire revolutionary energy in order to mobilize the widest possible masses of the white and black proletariat of the United States, not by words, but by deeds, for real effective support of the struggle for the liberation of the Negroes. Enslavement of the Negroes is one of the most important foundations of the imperialist dictatorship of USA capitalism. The more American imperialism fastens its yoke on the millions strong Negro masses, the more must the Communist Party develop the mass struggle for Negro emancipation, and the better use it must make of all conflicts which arise out of national differences, as an incentive for revolutionary mass actions against the bourgeoisie. This is as much in the direct interest of the proletarian revolution in America. Whether the rebellion of the Negroes is to be the outcome of a general revolutionary situation in the United States, whether it is to originate in the whirlpool of decisive fights for power by the working-class, for proletarian dictatorship, or whether on the contrary, the Negro rebellion will be the prelude of gigantic struggles for power by the American proletariat, cannot be foretold now. But in either contingency, it is essential for the Communist Party *to make an energetic beginning already now* with the organization of *joint mass struggles* of white and black workers against Negro oppression. This alone will enable us to get rid of the bourgeois white chauvinism which is polluting the ranks of the white workers of America, to overcome the distrust of the Negro masses caused by the inhuman barbarous Negro slave traffic still carried on by the American bourgeoisie—in as far as it is directed even against all white workers—and to win over to our side these millions of Negroes as active fellow fighters in the struggle for the overthrow of bourgeois power throughout America.

SECTION 01

HISTORY

About Section One: History

The selections in this section provide historical context for the Black Belt Thesis.

In 1915, Lenin analyzed the data on US agriculture, in order to better understand the nature of US capitalism at that moment. Finding that the "survivals of slavery" in the southern US established a concrete similarity with the survivals of feudalism in Russian society, particularly in the form of sharecropping, Lenin insisted that Black peoples' struggles for land were central to revolutionary processes in North America.

George Padmore, in two selections, provides further historical context. In a 1930 essay, he charted the primary mechanisms of "white ruling class terrorism" in the Black Belt, including peonage, police violence, criminalization and imprisonment. In 1931, Padmore analyzed the oppression of Black workers as a class, and as a nation, situating the struggle in the Black Belt in an international context of Black struggles against racism, colonialism, and class exploitation. The struggle of Black workers in the US, he argued, was a counterpart to the struggle of the Black masses in the colonies.

A 1932 article from the CPUSA newspaper, *Negro Worker*, provides a materialist analysis of lynching, as "the most open and violent expression" of "boss terror against an oppressed national minority." It situates the Scottsboro case in the context of fascistic attacks by sheriffs, landlords, and groups like the Ku Klux Klan.

A selection from Harry Haywood's book *Negro Liberation* examines "the curious anomaly of a virtual serfdom in the very heart of the most highly industrialized country in the world." Haywood situates the Great Migration in relation to "the profound economic and historical causes which have shaped the Black Belt as the main region of Negro concentration in this country."

In a 1953 article, originally published in *Monthly Review*, W. E. B. Du Bois analyzes the "newest South" as "a paradise for the investor," which built its prosperity "on the poverty and ignorance of its disfranchised lowest masses." Assessing the concrete conditions of Black people in the US, Du Bois concluded that "White North America beyond the urge of sound economics is persistently driving black folk toward socialism."

'CAPITALISM AND AGRICULTURE IN THE UNITED STATES OF AMERICA'*

V. I. LENIN
1915

3. The Former Slave-Owning South

The United States of America, writes Mr. Himmer, is a "country which has never known feudalism and is free from its economic survivals" (p. 41 of his article). This is the very opposite of the truth, for the economic survivals of *slavery* are not in any way distinguishable from those of feudalism, and in the former slave-owning South of the USA these survivals *are still very powerful.* It would not be worthwhile to dwell on Mr. Himmer's mistake if it were merely one in a hastily written article. But all liberal and all Narodnik writings in Russia show that the very same "mistake" is being made regularly and with unusual stubbornness with regard to the Russian labor-service system, our own survival of feudalism.

The South of the USA was slave-owning until slavery was swept away by the Civil War of 1861–65. To this day, the Negroes, who make up no more than from 0.7 to 2.2% of the population in the North and the West, constitute from 22.6 to 33.7% of the population in the South. For the USA as a whole, the Negroes constitute 10.7% of

---

* V. I. Lenin, "PART ONE—Capitalism and Agriculture in the United States of America," in *New Data on the Laws Governing the Development of Capitalism in Agriculture* (Moscow, 1964), https://www.marxists.org/archive/lenin/works/1915/newdev/index.htm.

the population. There is no need to elaborate on the degraded social status of the Negroes: the American bourgeoisie is in no way better in this respect than the bourgeoisie of any other country. Having "freed" the Negroes, it took good care, under "free," republican-democratic capitalism, to restore everything possible, and do everything possible and impossible for the most shameless and despicable oppression of the Negroes. A minor statistical fact will illustrate their cultural level. While the proportion of illiterates in 1900 among the white population of the USA of 10 years of age and over was 6.2%, among the Negroes it was as high as 44.5%! More than seven times as high! In the North and the West illiteracy amounted from 4 to 6% (1900), while in the South it was from 22.9 to 23.9%! One can easily imagine the complex of legal and social relationships that corresponds to this disgraceful fact from the sphere of popular literacy.

What then is the economic basis that has produced and continues to support this fine "superstructure"?

It is the typically Russian, "purely Russian" *labor service system*, which is known as *sharecropping*.

In 1910, Negroes owned 920,883 farms, i.e., 14.5% of the total. Of the total number of farmers, 37% were tenants; 62.1%, owners; the remaining 0.9% of the farms were run by managers. But among the whites 39.2% were tenant farmers, and among the Negroes—75.3%! The typical white farmer in America is an owner, the typical Negro farmer is a tenant. The proportion of tenants in the West was only 14%: this section is being settled, with new lands unoccupied, and is an El Dorado (a short-lived and unreliable El Dorado, to be sure) for the small "independent farmer." In the North, the proportion of tenant farmers was 26.5%, and in the South, 49.6%! Half of the Southern farmers were tenants.

But that is not all. These are not even tenants in the European, civilized, modern capitalist sense of the word. They are chiefly semi-feudal or—which is the same thing in economic terms—semi-slave *sharecroppers*. In the "free" West, sharecroppers were in the minority (25,000 out of a total of 53,000 tenants). In the old North, which was settled long ago, 483,000 out of 766,000 tenant farmers, i.e., 63%, were sharecroppers. In the South, 1,021,000 out of 1,537,000 tenant farmers, *i.e., 66%*, were *sharecroppers*.

In 1910, free, republican-democratic America had 1,500,000 sharecroppers, of whom *more than 1,000,000 were Negroes*. And the proportion of sharecroppers to the total number of farmers is not decreasing, but is on the contrary steadily and rather rapidly increasing. In 1880, 17.5% of the farmers in the USA were sharecroppers, in 1890, 18.4%; in 1900, 22.2%; and in 1910, 24%.

American statisticians draw the following conclusions from the 1910 returns:

> In the South the conditions have at all times been somewhat different from those in the North, and many of the tenant farms are parts of plantations of considerable size which date from before the Civil War." In the South, "the system of operation by tenants—chiefly colored tenants—has succeeded the system of operation by slave labor. . . . The development of the tenant system is most conspicuous in the South, where the large plantations formerly operated by slave labor have in many cases been broken up into small parcels or tracts and leased to tenants. . . . These plantations are in many cases still operated substantially as agricultural units, the tenants being subjected to a degree of supervision more or less similar to that which hired farm laborers are subjected to in the North.[53]

To show what the South is like, it is essential to add that its population is fleeing to other capitalist areas and to the towns, just as the peasantry in Russia is fleeing from the most backward central agricultural gubernias, where the survivals of serfdom have been most greatly preserved, in order to escape the rule of the notorious Markovs, to those areas of Russia which have a higher level of capitalist development, to the metropolitan cities, the industrial gubernias and the South (see *The Development of Capitalism in Russia*[54]). The sharecropping area, both in America and in Russia, is the most stagnant area, where the masses are subjected to the greatest degradation and oppression. Immigrants to America, who have such an outstanding role to play in the country's economy and all its social life, shun the South. In 1910, the foreign-born formed 14.5% of the total population of America. But in the South the figure was only l%–4% for the several divisions, whereas in the other divisions the proportion of incomers ranged from not less than 13.9% to 27.7% (New England). For the "emancipated" Negroes, the American South is a kind of prison where they are hemmed in, isolated and deprived of fresh air. The South is distinguished by the immobility of its population and by the greatest "attachment to the land:" with the exception of that division of the South, which still has considerable homesteading (West South Central), 91%–92% of the population in the two other divisions of the South resided in the same division where they were born, whereas for the United States as a whole the figure was 72.6%, i.e., the mobility of the population is much greater. In the West, which is a solid homestead area, only 35%–41% of the population lived in the division of their birth.

Negroes are in full flight from the two Southern divisions where there is no homesteading: in the 10 years between the last two censuses, these two divisions provided other parts of the country with almost 600,000 "black" people. The Negroes flee mainly to the towns: in the South, 77%–80% of all the Negroes live in rural communities; in other areas, only 8%–32%. Thus it turns out that there is a startling similarity in the economic status of the Negroes in America and the peasants in the heart of agricultural Russia who *"were formerly landowners' serfs."*

4. Average Size of Farms, 'Disintegration of Capitalism' in the South

Having examined the chief distinctive features of the three main sections of the USA, as well as the general nature of their economic conditions, we can now proceed to an analysis of the data most commonly referred to. These are primarily data on the average acreage of farms. It is on the basis of these data that a great many economists, including Mr. Himmer, draw the most categorical conclusions (see chart, top of next page).

On the whole, there seems at first glance to be a reduction in the average acreage of all farmland and an uncertain fluctuation—upward and downward—in the average improved acreage. But there is a distinct break in the 1860–70 period and this I have indicated by a line. During that period there was an enormous *decrease* in the average acreage of all farmland by 46 acres (from 199.2 to 153.3) and the greatest change (from 79.8 to 71.0), also a reduction, in the average acreage of improved land.

What was the reason? Obviously, the Civil War of 1861–65 and the abolition of slavery. A decisive blow was dealt at the latifundia of

Average acreage per farm in the USA		
Years	All farmland	Improved land
1850	202.6	78.0
1860	199.2	79.8
1870	153.3	71.0
1880	133.7	71.0
1890	136.5	78.3
1900	146.2	72.2
1910	138.1	75.2

the slave-owners. Further on we shall see repeated confirmation of this fact, but it is so generally known that it is surprising that it needs any proof at all. Let us separate the returns for the North and those for the South.

	Average acreage per farm			
	South		North	
Years	All farmland	Improved land	All farmland	Improved land
1850	332.1	101.1	127.1	65.4
1860	335.4	101.3	126.4	68.3
1870	214.2	69.2	117.0	69.2
1880	153.4	56.2	114.9	76.6
1890	139.7	58.8	123.7	87.8
1900	138.2	48.1	132.2	90.9
1910	114.4	48.6	143.0	100.3

We find that in the South the average improved acreage per farm between 1860 and 1870 greatly *decreased* (from 101.3 to 69.2), and that in the North it slightly *increased* (from 68.3 to 69.2). This means that the cause lay in the specific conditions of evolution in the South. There we find even after the abolition of slavery, a reduction in the average acreage of farms, although the process is slow and not continuous.

Mr. Himmer's deduction is that in the South "the small-scale family farms are extending their domination, while capital is leaving agriculture for other spheres of investment.... Agricultural capitalism is rapidly disintegrating in the South Atlantic states...."

This is an amusing assertion likely to be matched only in the arguments of our Narodniks on the "disintegration of capitalism" in Russia after 1861 in consequence of the landlords abandoning corvée for the labor-service (i.e., semi-corvée!) system of economy. The breakup of the slave-worked latifundia is called the "disintegration of capitalism." The transformation of the unimproved land of yesterday's slave-owners into the small farms of Negroes, half of whom are sharecroppers (it should be borne in mind that the proportion of sharecroppers has been steadily *growing* from census to census!), is called the "disintegration of capitalism." It is hardly possible to go any further in distorting the fundamental concepts of economics!

Chapter Twelve of the 1910 Census supplies information on typical Southern "plantations"—not of the old slave period, but of our own day. On the 39,073 plantations there are 39,073 "landlord farms" and 398,905 tenant farms, or an average of 10 tenants per landlord or "master." Plantations average 724 acres, of which only 405 acres is improved, more than 300 acres being unimproved, not a bad reserve for the gentlemen who were the slave-owners of yesterday to draw on in extending their plans of exploitation....

Land on the average plantation is distributed as follows: "landlord" farm—331 acres, of which 87 is improved. "Tenant" farms, i.e., the parcels of the Negro sharecroppers, who continue to work for the master and under his eye, average 38 acres, of which 31 is improved land.

As the population and the demand for cotton increase, the former slave-owners of the South begin to parcel out their vast latifundia, nine-tenths of the land on which is still unimproved, into small tracts which are either sold to the Negroes or, more frequently, leased to them on a half-crop basis. (From 1900 to 1910, the number of farmers in the South who were full owners of all their farmland increased from 1,237,000 to 1,329,000, i.e., 7.5%, while the number of sharecroppers went up from 772,000 to 1,021,000, i.e., 32.2%.) And yet an economist has appeared who says this is "disintegration of capitalism." ...

I designate as latifundia farms with an area of 1,000 acres and over. In 1910, the proportion of such farms in the USA was 0.8% (50,135 farms), and they added up to 167.1 million acres, or 19.0% of the total amount of land. This is an average of 3,332 acres per latifundium. Only 18.7% of their acreage was improved while for all farms the figure was 54.4%. The capitalist North has the smallest number of latifundia: 0.5% of the total number of farms accounting for 6.9% of the land, 41.1% of which is improved. The West has the greatest number of latifundia: 3.9% of the total number of farms accounting for 48.3% of the land; 32.3% of the land in the latifundia is improved. But it is in the former slave-owning South that the latifundia have the *highest* proportion of unimproved land: 0.7% of the farms are latifundia; they account for 23.9% of the land; *only 8.5% of the land* in the latifundia is improved! Incidentally, these detailed statistics clearly show that there is really no foundation for the common practice of classifying the latifundia as capitalist enterprises, without a detailed analysis of the specific data for each country and each area.

During the 10 years from 1900 to 1910, the total acreage of the latifundia, but only of the latifundia, showed a *decrease*. The reduction was quite substantial: from 197.8 million to 167.1 million acres, i.e., 30.7 million acres. In the South, there was a reduction of 31.8 million acres (in the North, an increase of 2.3 million, and in the West, a reduction of 1.2 million). Consequently, it is in the South, and in the slave-owning South alone, that the latifundia, with their negligible proportion (8.5%) of improved land, are being broken up on a really vast scale.

The inescapable conclusion is that the only exact definition of the economic process under way is—a transition from the slave-holding latifundia, nine-tenths of which remained unimproved, to small *commercial* agriculture. It is a transition to commercial farms and not to farms worked by family labor, as Mr. Himmer and the Narodniks, together with all the bourgeois economists who sing cheap hymns to "labor," love to say. The term "family labor" has no politico-economic meaning and is indirectly misleading. It is devoid of meaning because the small farmer "labors" under any social system of economy, be it slavery, serfdom or capitalism. The term "family labor" is just an empty phrase, pure oratory which serves to cover up the *confusion* of entirely different social forms of economic organization—a confusion from which the bourgeoisie alone stands to gain. The term "family labor" is misleading and deceives the public, for it creates the impression that hired labor is not employed.

Mr. Himmer, like all bourgeois economists, evades just these statistics on hired labor, although they are the most important data on the question of capitalism in agriculture and although they are to be found in the 1900 Census report, as well as in the 1910 *Abstract—Farm Crops, by States*, which Mr. Himmer himself quotes (note on p. 49 of his article).

The nature of the staple crop of the South shows that the growth of small-scale agriculture in the South is nothing but the growth of commercial farming. That crop is cotton. Cereals yield 29.3% of the total crop value in the South; hay and forage, 5.1%; and cotton, 42.7%. From 1870 to 1910, the production of wool in the USA went up from 162 million lbs. to 321 million lbs., i.e., it doubled; wheat, increased from 236 million to 635 million bushels, i.e., less than threefold; corn, from 1,094 million to 2,886 million bushels, also less than threefold; and cotton, from 4,000,000 bales (of 500 lbs. each) to 12,000,000, i.e., threefold. The growth of the crop that is primarily commercial was faster than that of other, less commercialized, crops. In addition, there was in the main division of the South, the South Atlantic, a rather substantial development of tobacco production (12.1% of the crop value in the State of Virginia); vegetables (20.1% of the total crop value in the State of Delaware, 23.2% in the State of Florida); fruits (21.3% of the total crop value in the State of Florida); etc. The nature of all these crops implies an intensification of farming, a larger scale of operations on smaller acreages, and greater employment of hired labor.

I shall now proceed to a detailed analysis of the returns on hired labor; let us note only that the employment of hired labor is also growing in the South, although in this respect it lags behind the other sections—*less* hired labor is employed because of the *wider* practice of semi-slave sharecropping.

'LIFE AMONG NEGRO FARMERS IN AMERICA'
GEORGE PADMORE
FROM *THE NEGRO WORKER*
MAY 1, 1930

There are about 12,000,000 Negroes in the United States. The vast majority of these blacks are on the land, either as agricultural wage laborers, sharecroppers or poor farmers. They live in certain sections of America known as the Southern States. In some of these states they are so thickly concentrated that they form a sort of black country of their own called "The Black Belt." And strange to say, it is in these very territories that the Negroes suffer the most brutal oppression.

White ruling class terrorism is so widespread throughout "the Black Belt," that from time to time whole communities of Negro workers move away and seek new homes in the Northern States and other parts of America, where they are able to buy arms and thereby protect themselves against mob law.

The most widespread method of terrorism practiced in the South among the black farming population is what is known as Peonage. This is the most brutal and demoralizing form of economic exploitation. It has its basis in the rent and profit system which grew out of chattel slavery. After the Negroes were "freed" from slavery, they had no land of their own, or the means whereby to gain a livelihood, so

---

* George Padmore, "Life Among Negro Farmers in America," *The Negro Worker* 3, no. 7 (May 1, 1930): 12–14.

they were compelled to remain on the plantations of their masters. Some of them sold their labor power for wages, while others entered into a sort of feudal contract relationship which bound them to the land like serfs. The landlords allotted a certain quantity of land to each black family, and supplied tools, seed, and food to the tenants until the harvest was reaped. The crop is then taken over by the landlord, who sells it and afterwards made an account to the tenant. The tenants always given less than what the crop was sold for, and in this way is continually indebted to the landlord. For example, if a Negro cultivated a hundred bales of cotton which fetched $800 on the market, the landlord will present him with an account of $800 for supplies alleged to have been rendered during the year, so even if the Negro paid $600, he should still owe the landlord $200 which he would be compelled to pay off by planting another crop under similar conditions as before.

This is repeated year after year. Even if the Negro took the landlord to court his statement of the facts would not be believed, because the word of the white man can not be refuted by a black. Furthermore, the Southern landlords are not only the overseers and bookkeepers of their plantations, but are the political dictators of the community as well; and when they make a statement it becomes the law of the court. It is always the prerogative of the ruling class of the South to determine when Negro workers should leave their service, or under what conditions they are bound.

Negroes who rebel against these outrages and run away are arrested by the police and other uniformed thugs with the aid of blood hounds especially trained for this purpose. They are brought back to the plantations and turned over to the landlords either as vagrants or as runaways.

Another method by which labor is recruited is through the chain gang. Whenever the landlords need labor they simply go to the local judge and arrange that the police be ordered to arrest the required number of workers. In this way whole communities of able-bodied blacks are commonly apprehended. All kinds of form-up charges are made against them. When fined in court they have to agree to enter the service of the landlords who pay a small fine for the opportunity to reduce the Negroes to involuntary servitude. In this way the judges and the police get the court fees, and the landlords cheap labor.

A brief account from one of the peonage districts is sufficient to illustrate this point. Passing along the street where a Negro had been mistreated by his white master, an observer inquired of the worker: "Why do you stand this?" "That is just the damned trouble down here" responded the black. "I once complained to the court when another white man beat me, the man denied it and the judge believed his story imposed upon me a fine which I could not pay, so I have to work it out in the services of this man who was present in the court at that time and paid it in order to get the opportunity to force me to work for him."

Whenever there is a shortage of labor the Southern capitalists carry out these repressive measures. Thousands of blacks are still being held as slaves in the coal mines and on road construction work in the state of Alabama, Mississippi, Texas, and Georgia. A new law was enacted in the State of Florida in 1919 to the effect, that whenever a Negro is unable to pay his debts he is to be imprisoned, and the jailer has the right to rent him out to a farmer until such time as the farmer is satisfied to release him.

Just a few days ago a white man by the name of Wilson, who owns a 7,000 acre farm near Greenwood, Mississippi, went into the country of Moxubee, scouting for Negro farm laborers. He had signed up 25 colored workers and had chartered two freight cars for their transportation to Greenwood, when the businessmen and plantation owners in Moxubee discovered Wilson's activities. They immediately organized a small band of 100 men and drove Wilson out of the town. The Negroes who had dared to sign up to leave were stripped naked and most brutally flogged in public as a warning to other blacks never to attempt to migrate.

There is a special law in Mississippi which makes it a criminal offense punished by fine or imprisonment for agents to enter the State and contract for labor. This law was enacted in order to prevent Negro tenants and agricultural laborers from leaving their masters no matter how badly they were treated, or how high the wage offered by other employers outside of the State.

A recent investigation has disclosed the existence of large peonage farms in the extreme Southern part of Florida. Over 5,000 Negroes have been collected from various parts of the State and lured away to toil in the turpentine camps where they are forced to work day and night under armed guards. Life in these places is indescribable hell holes. The workers are huddled together in shacks, given a minimum amount of food of the worst quality, and denied the most elementary sanitary conveniences. Conditions are more primitive than in some colonial countries. As a result, disease is very rampant in these barbed-wire compounds. Hundreds of blacks die annually from starvation and exposure, while others meet a quicker and more welcome death at the hands of their cruel task masters.

Negro farmers and agricultural laborers are completely segregated from all forms of social intercourse with whites in the South. They are not even allowed to ride in the same coaches with the whites. Wherever railroad companies agreed to permit them to travel they are provided with small dirty wooden compartments, for which they have to pay the same fare as the white passengers, who enjoy the most up-to-day railroad conveniences. In streetcars, Negroes, get in and off from the rear end, while the white enter from the front and have priority to the best seats. In those places where Negroes are admitted to the theaters they are huddled together in filthy balconies far removed from the stage.

Black farmers are not permitted to patronize restaurants which cater to whites; neither are they allowed to use the same public bathing beaches, or entrances to buildings as other people. Negroes are barred at libraries, museums, art galleries, and other centers of culture. Very limited educational opportunities are offered them. In most places they are compelled to send their children to separate schools and as to be expected the capitalist State expends by far more money on the education of white children than black ones, although the Negro workers are made to pay the same taxes for the maintenance of the public school system.

Politically, Negroes in the South are completely disfranchised. This is done with open violence and terror. On election days, armed white mobs, agents of the capitalists, keep the Negroes away from the polls in the Southern States. Certain enactments known as the "Black Laws," have been incorporated in the Statutes of some States in order to more effectively deprive the Negroes of their political rights. These laws are chiefly based on property and educational qualifications. As the majority of Negroes are propertyless, and their standard of literacy is a matter to be determined by the capitalist politics, it becomes very easy for them to be ruled off the ballot.

Wherever one goes in the South one sees a striking similarity in the appearance of black communities derisively called "Nigger Towns." The outstanding feature of these ghettos are their very unsanitary conditions. For the bourgeois politicians although they impel the Negroes to pay the same amount of taxes as the whites, they never spend any money to improve the standard of life among the black workers. Epidemics frequently break out in these settlements, taking heavy toll among the workers, especially their children. The death rate among Negro farmers is in some cases 50 percent higher than whites. This is especially so in the case of contagious diseases such as tuberculosis, typhus, etc.

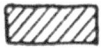 # SELECTIONS FROM
THE LIFE AND STRUGGLES
OF NEGRO TOILERS
GEORGE PADMORE
1931

Introduction

It has been estimated that there are about 250 million Negroes in the world. The vast majority of these people are workers and peasants. They are scattered throughout various geographical territories. The bulk of them, however, still live on the continent of Africa—the original home of the black race. There are, nevertheless, large populations of Negroes in the *New World*. For instance, there are about 15 millions in the United States, 10 millions in Brazil, 10 millions in the West Indies, and 5 to 7 millions in various Latin American countries, such as Colombia, Honduras, Venezuela, Nicaragua, etc., etc.

The oppression of Negroes assumes two distinct forms: on the one hand they are oppressed as a class, and on the other as a nation. This national (race) oppression has its basis in the social-economic relation of the Negro under capitalism. National (race) oppression assumes its most pronounced forms in the *United States of America*, especially in the Black Belt of the Southern States, where lynching, peonage, Jim-Crowism, political disfranchisement, and social ostracism is widespread; and in the *Union of South Africa*, where the blacks, who form the majority of the entire population have been robbed of their

---

* George Padmore, *The Life and Struggles of Negro Toilers* (London: Red International of Labour Unions Magazine, 1931), https://www.marxists.org/archive/padmore/1931/negro-toilers/index.htm.

lands and are segregated on Reserves, enslaved in Compounds, and subjected to the vilest forms of anti-labor and racial laws (Poll, Hut, Pass taxes) and color bar system in industry.

The general conditions under which Negroes live, either as a national (racial) group or as a class, form one of the most degrading spectacles of bourgeois civilization.

Since the present crisis of world capitalism begun the economic, political, and social status of the Negro toilers are becoming ever worse and worse. The reason for this is obvious: the imperialists, whether American, English, French, Belgian, etc., etc., are frantically trying to find a way out of their difficulties. In order to do so, they are not only intensifying the exploitation of the white workers in the various imperialist countries by launching an offensive through means of rationalization, wage cuts, abolition of social insurance, unemployment, etc., but they are turning their attention more and more towards Africa and other black semi-colonies (Haiti, Liberia), which represent the last stronghold of world imperialism. In this way the bourgeoisie hope to unload the major burden of the crisis on the shoulders of the black colonial and semi-colonial masses.

Furthermore, as the majority of the Negro workers in the United States and the colonies are still largely unorganized, thanks to the treachery and betrayal of the *American Federation of Labor* and the so-called progressive Mustie group in the United States, the social-fascist labor bureaucrats of the *Amsterdam International*, the *II International*, and the black reformist trade union leaders (Kadalie and Champion in South Africa, Randolph and Croswaith in the United States), as well as the national reformist misleader, Marcus Garvey, the Negro toilers are experiencing great difficulties today in withstanding the ruthless offensive of the international imperialists. Despite these handicaps the Negro masses, goaded into desperation by the inhuman conditions forced upon them on the one hand, and inspired by the revolutionary movement on the other, are beginning to wake up and assume the counteroffensive against their oppressors.

We can already see the beginnings of a conscious effort on the part of these Negro masses to consolidate their fighting forces, and to bring them into closer contact with the advanced ranks of the international revolutionary proletariat, by the holding of a conference in *Hamburg, Germany*, in July 1930.

Selections from *The Life and Struggles of Negro Toilers*

This was the first *International Conference of Negro Workers* which had ever been convened. At this conference Negro delegates from different parts of Africa, the United States, West Indies, and Latin America not only discussed trade union questions, but dealt with the most vital problems affecting their social and political conditions, as for example the expropriation of land by the imperialist robbers in Africa; the imposition of Head and Poll taxes; the enslaving of toilers through Pass laws and other anti-labor and racial legislation in Africa; lynching, peonage and segregation in the United States; as well as unemployment, which has thrown millions of these black toilers on the streets, faced with the specter of starvation and death.

In view of the present world situation, it is necessary to describe the *Life and Struggles of the Negro Toilers*, so that the workers in the metropolitan countries under whose imperialism these masses live will be better able to make themselves acquainted with some of the methods which the capitalists of the "mother" countries adopt to enslave the black colonial and semi-colonial peoples. For it is only by knowing these facts will the revolutionary working classes in Europe and America realize the danger ahead of them.

It is also necessary for the workers in the capitalist countries to understand that it is only through the exploiting of the colonial workers, from whose sweat and blood superprofits are extorted, that the imperialists are able to bribe the reformist and social-fascist trade union bureaucrats and thereby enable them to betray the struggles of the workers.

The purpose of this pamphlet is threefold:

(1) Briefly to set forth some of the conditions of life of the Negro workers and peasants in different parts of the world; and

(2) To enumerate some of the struggles which they have attempted to wage in order to free themselves from the yoke of imperialism; and

(3) To indicate in a general way the tasks of the proletariat in the advanced countries so that the millions of black toilers might be better prepared to carry on the struggles against their white imperialist oppressors and native

(race) exploiters, and join forces with their white brothers against the common enemy—World Capitalism.

FROM PART ONE: 2. BLACK SLAVES IN THE NEW WORLD

Besides the 200 million Negroes estimated inhabiting the Continent of Africa, there are between 40 to 50 million Negroes scattered throughout the New World—the United States, the West Indies and Latin America. They are the descendants of the slaves who were brought from Africa to work upon the plantations and the mines in the territories which they now occupy. Therefore, unlike their black brother in Africa, the Negroes in the New World have had centuries of contact with the white capitalist civilization. But like the Negroes in Africa, they are subjected to the same barbarous methods of imperialist plunder and exploitation.

I. THE UNITED STATES OF AMERICA

Even in the United States, which the apologists for bourgeois democracy consider the "land of the free and the home of the brave," we find 15 million Negroes brutally enslaved. The story of the oppression of Negroes in the United States forms one of the darkest pages in the history of capitalism. In no other so-called civilized country in the world are human beings treated as badly as these 15 million Negroes. They live under a perpetual regime of white terror, which expresses itself in lynchings, peonage, racial segregation, and other pronounced forms of white chauvinism.

The vast majority of the 15,000,000 Negroes in the United States are toilers—industrial workers and poor peasants. The bulk of them are still on the land, either as agricultural laborers, sharecroppers or tenant farmers. They live in certain sections of the Southern States, where they are so thickly populated that they form a sort of compacted territory of their own, known as the "Black Belt." Here the Negroes are in the majority.

There are some 219 counties in the South where the population is nearly half or more Negroes. The State of Georgia, which covers an area of 52,265 square miles with a population of 2,895,832, has the largest black population of any state in the American Union while the State of Mississippi, which is 46,865 square miles with a total population of 1,790,618, the blacks number 52.2 percent (census of 1920).

And, strange to say, it is in these thickly populated territories that the Negroes suffer most oppression. They are absolutely at the mercy of every fiendish mob incited by the white landlords and capitalists. Bands of business and professional men make periodical raids upon the black countryside, where they lynch Negroes, burn homes and destroy the crops and other property belonging to the blacks. In most cases of lynching the Negroes are burned to death after their bodies have been soaked in gasoline, while others are hanged from trees. On these occasions the entire white community turned out to witness the bloody spectacles, which were made "Roman Holidays."

White ruling class terrorism becomes so vicious at times that entire Negro communities move away and seek new homes in the North and other parts of the country where they are better able to defend themselves. It is estimated that over two million Negroes left the South for industrial cities during the war and post-war period.

White Chauvinism and the Labor Movement

Race prejudice or white chauvinism is one of the chief weapons in the hands of the capitalist class in order to oppress and enslave the black workers. In the United States the working class is made up of different nationalities and races which are grouped into white and black. In order to prevent these workers from uniting together in militant struggle against the bourgeoisie who rob them all alike, the employers and their agents in the Labor movement (reformists and social-fascists), encourage the workers to hate each other by playing up racial and national differences.

As a general rule Negroes are not permitted to join the reformist trade unions, which are under the control of social fascist leaders like William Green and Matthew Woll, of the American Federation of Labor. As a result of this policy of discrimination, the black workers in the North, like those in the South, are compelled to do the hardest and dirtiest work for the lowest wages and in periods of economic depression such as the present they are always the first to be discharged from their jobs. With the seven million unemployed in the United States today, the Negroes are feeling its effects more severely than any other section of the working class. Millions of them are now walking the streets of every big city of the North and the rural districts of the South faced with the specter of starvation and death.

The only trade unions of America which admit Negro workers on the basis of *full political, economic, and social equality* are the revolutionary unions affiliated with the Trade Union Unity League, the American Section of the Red International of Labor Unions. These unions are under the influence of Communist leadership and conduct intensive national campaigns calling upon the black and white workers to unite against the American bourgeoisie, and their labor agents, the reformist trade union leaders of the American Federation of Labor, as well as the socialists, whose policy it is to divide the workers on the basis of color in order that they may be exploited more effectively. In this the capitalists have been fairly successful in the past, but the workers are now beginning to see the folly and danger of racial antagonism and are starting to unite into militant trade unions and unemployed councils, under the leadership of the Communist Party and the revolutionary trade union center, the TUUL.

Southern Oppression

The Southern bourgeoisie and landlords are largely the descendants of the former slave-owning class. They are the most oppressive of the American ruling class. Trained in all the vicious practice of chattel slavery, they torture and brutalize their workers in the most barbarous fashion. Living in constant fear of the Negro masses, the capitalists, who exploited them to the very limit, maintain a reign of fascist terrorism through the State apparatus (court, police, militia), as well as the Church. Some of the most active agents of the oppressors are the preachers, who go around the countryside stirring up racial hatred and mob law against the Negroes.

The most widespread forms of economic, political and social oppression of Negroes are: *(a)* peonage, *(b)* slavery, *(c)* lynching, *(d)* Jim Crowism.

Most of these terrorist practices against Negroes are perpetuated by specially created fascist organizations, such as the Ku Klux Klan, the American Legion, the Black Shirts, the Caucasian Crusaders, etc., etc. These organizations are supported by the bourgeoisie and reactionary middle class elements. They invade the sections where the Negroes live, burn homes and crops, kill off livestock, poison drinking water wells, murder and lynch unarmed men, women and children who dare to offer resistance to their pogroms.

Selections from *The Life and Struggles of Negro Toilers*

A few words about each of these forms of socioeconomic oppression:

(a) Peonage. Peonage is the most brutal and demoralizing form of economic exploitation. It has its basis in the rent and profit system which grew out of chattel slavery. After the Negroes were "freed," they had no land of their own or the means whereby to gain a livelihood, so most of them were compelled to remain on the plantations of their masters. Some of them sold their labor power for wages, while others entered into a sort of feudal contractual relationship which bound them to the land like serfs. The landlords allot a certain quantity of land to each black family, and supplied tools, seed and food to the tenants until the harvest has been reaped. The crop is then taken over by the landlords, who sell it and afterwards make an account to the tenants. The tenants are always given less than what the crop sells for, and in this way they continually find themselves indebted to the landlords. For example, if a Negro cultivated a hundred bales of cotton which fetched $600 on the market, the landlord will present him with an account of $800 for supplies alleged to have been rendered during the year, so even if the Negro paid the $600 he would still owe the landlord $200, which he would be compelled to pay off by planting another crop under similar conditions as before. This is repeated year after year. Even if the Negro took the landlord to court, his statement of the facts would not be believed, because the word of a white man cannot be refuted by a black. Furthermore, the Southern landlords are not only the overseers, bookkeepers of their plantations, but are the political dictators of the community as well, and when they make a statement it becomes the law of the court. It has always been the prerogative of the ruling class of the South to decide when the Negro workers should leave their service, or under what conditions they are bound. Negroes who rebel against these outrages and run away are hunted down by the police and other uniformed thugs, with the aid of bloodhounds which are especially employed for this purpose. They are brought back to the plantations and turned over to the landlords either as vagrants or as runaways.

Another method by which labor is recruited is through the chain gang. Whenever the landlords need labor they simply go to the local judge and arrange that the police be ordered to arrest the required number of workers. In this way whole communities of able-bodied blacks are commonly apprehended. All kinds of frame-up charges are made against them. When fined in court they have to agree to enter the service of the landlords, who pay a small fine for the opportunity to reduce the Negroes to servitude. In this way the judges and the police get the court fees, and the landlords cheap labor.

A brief account from one of the peonage districts is sufficient to illustrate this point. Passing along the street where a Negro had been mistreated by his white master, an observer inquired of the worker: "Why do you stand this?" "That is just the damned trouble down here" responded the black, "I once complained to the court when another white man beat me. The man denied it and the judge, who believed his story, imposed upon me a fine which I could not pay, so I have to work out in the service of this man who was present in the court at the time and paid it in order to get the opportunity to force me to work for him."

Whenever there is a shortage of labor the Southern capitalists do not only resort to these repressive measures, but also commandeer the use of child labor. For example, by order of the white county superintendent (Memphis, Tennessee), 8,000 Negro students enrolled in schools of Shelby county were taken out of the schoolrooms and placed in cotton fields during the season of 1930. The "cotton recesses" affect only Negro students. Colored schools are always closed until after the cotton crops are gathered. Negro rural schools in the South are run for an average of six months, with two suspensions, one for the planting and the second for the picking of cotton. White schools are open for the usual nine-month term. Compulsory child labor is widespread throughout the South.

(b) Slavery. Thousands of blacks are still being held as slaves in the coal mines and on road construction work in the States of Alabama, Mississippi, Texas and Georgia. A law was enacted in the State of Florida in 1919 to the effect that, whenever a Negro is unable to pay his debts, he is to be imprisoned, and the jailer has the right to rent him out to a farmer until such times as the farmer is satisfied to release him. There is a special law in Mississippi which makes it a criminal offense, punished by fines or imprisonment, for agents to enter the State and contract for labor. This law was enacted in order to prevent Negro tenants and agricultural laborers from leaving their masters, no matter how badly

they are being treated or how high the wage offered by other employers outside of the State.

A white man by the name of Wilson, who owns a 7,000 acre farm near Greenwood, Mississippi, went into the county of Moxubee scouting for Negro farm laborers in 1930—he had signed up 25 colored workers and had chartered two freight trucks for their transportation to Greenwood when the business men and plantation owners in Moxubee discovered Wilson's activities. They immediately organized a band of 100 men and drove Wilson out of the town. The Negroes who had dared to sign up to leave were stripped naked and most brutally flogged in public as a warning to other blacks never to attempt to migrate.

Investigations have disclosed the existence of large slave farms in the extreme Southern part of Florida. Over 5,000 Negroes have been collected from various parts of the State and lured away to toil in the turpentine camps, where they are forced to work day and night under armed guards. Life in these places are indescribable hell holes. The workers are huddled together in shacks, given a minimum amount of food of the worst quality, and denied the most elementary sanitary conveniences. Conditions are more primitive than in some colonial countries. As a result, disease is very rampant in these barbed-wire compounds. Hundreds of blacks die annually from starvation and exposure, while others meet a quicker and more welcome death at the hands of their cruel task masters.

(c) Lynching. Hand in hand with peonage is mob rule, which expresses itself in lynchings. These outrages, although chiefly perpetrated in the South, occur in other parts of the United States of America.

Over 3,256 Negro farmers and workers have met their death at the hands of white lynching mobs between 1885 and 1930. Georgia heads the list of lynching States with a record of 441 Negroes and 256 whites during the period of 35 years. There is hardly a month which does not bring its tidings of this form of class outrage and racial terrorism.

The circumstances under which a Negro named Henry Lowry, about forty years of age, was lynched typifies the practice as it has developed in the United States. The story of this outrage was written on the scene of the lynching by a reporter of a capitalist newspaper, who describes the incident as follows:

More than 500 people stood by and looked on while the Negro was slowly burnt to a crisp. A few women were scattered among the crowd of Arkansas planters who directed the gruesome work. Not once did the slayed beg for mercy despite the fact that he suffered one of the most horrible deaths imaginable. With the Negro chained to a log, members of the mob placed a little fire of leaves around his feet. Gasoline was then poured on the leaves, and the carrying out of the death sentence was under way.

Inch by inch the Negro was fairly cooked to death. Every few minutes fresh leaves were tossed on the funeral pyre until the blaze had passed the Negro's waist. As the flames were eating away his abdomen, a member of the mob stepped forward and saturated the body with more gasoline. It was then only a few minutes until the Negro had been reduced to ashes.

Even after the flesh had dropped away from his legs, and the flames were leaping towards his face, Lowry retained consciousness. Not once did he whimper or beg for mercy. Once or twice he attempted to pick up the hot ashes in his hands and thrust them into his mouth in order to hasten death.

A correspondent of the *Memphis News Scimitar*, another Southern bourgeois paper, wrote the following description of the lynching of a young Negro worker in Tennessee:

I watched an angry mob chain a Negro to an iron stick. I watched them place wood around his helpless body. I watched them pour gasoline on this wood. And I watched the men set this wood on fire I stood in a crowd of 600 people as the flames gradually crept nearer and nearer to the helpless Negro. I watched the flames climb higher and higher, encircling him without mercy. I heard his cry of agony as the flames reached him and set his clothes on fire.

Selections from *The Life and Struggles of Negro Toilers*

"Oh, God!" he shouted. "I didn't do it. Have mercy!" The blaze leaped higher. The Negro struggled. He kicked the chain loose from his ankles, but it held his waist and neck together against the iron that was becoming red with intense heat. "Have mercy, I didn't do it—I didn't do it!" he shouted again and again.

Soon he became quiet. There was no doubt that he was dead. The flames jumped and leaped about his head. An odor of burning flesh reached my nostrils. I felt suddenly sickened. Through the leaping blaze I could see the Negro sagging and supported by the chains.

When the first odor of the baking flesh reached the mob, there was a slight stir. Several men moved nervously.

"Let's finish it up," someone said. Instantly about twelve men stepped from the crowd. They piled wood on the fire that was already blazing high. The Negro was dead, but more wood was piled on the flames. They jumped higher and higher. Nothing could be seen now for the blaze encircled everything.

Then the crowd walked away. In the vanguard of the mob I noticed a woman. She seemed to be rather young, but it is hard to tell about a woman of her type, strong and healthy, apparently a woman of the country. She walked with a firm even stride. She was beautiful in a way.

The crowd walked slowly away.

"I am hungry," someone complained, "let's get something to eat."

Thus ended another act of the great drama of American civilization! Of the ten lynchings which occurred in 1929, the last one took place in the State of Kentucky on Christmas Day—the occasion on which the bishops and priests and the other "holy men of God," who carry on a campaign of lies and slander against the Soviet Union, were chanting their hymns to their God and shouting *"Peace on Earth, Goodwill to Men!"*

Since the beginning of 1930, 36 lynchings have already taken place. One of the victims was a Negro woman about sixty years old, the mother of four children. The woman worked for a white farmer in North Carolina. He refused to pay her wages and she threatened to report him to the police. That same night the farmer organized a group of business men and landlords, led them to the woman's house and took her to a nearby field where she was hanged from a tree.

After the lynching of two Negroes, Shipp and Smith, at Marion, Indiana, pictures of their charred bodies were sold in the shops of the city of Terre Haute, where bloodthirsty capitalists bought these stocks up as souvenirs of "how to keep the 'niggers' in their place."

However, one of the most fiendish and atrocious outrages committed against a Negro worker occurred in Jacksonville, Florida, on Christmas Eve in 1930. A Negro youth by the name of Timothy Rouse, employed as an orderly in a municipal hospital, was accused of carrying on amorous relations with a white fellow worker. The physicians at the hospital became so infuriated over the idea of a white woman being in love with a Negro that they called a meeting of the business men of the city who demanded that Rouse be immediately dismissed. Shortly afterwards the Negro was arrested and thrown into prison. A few days later a mob, headed by the petty bourgeois elements of Jacksonville broke into the jail, placed the youth into an automobile and took him to the outskirts of the city where he was placed under anesthetics and castrated by doctors who were part of the mob. The hooligans then returned to the city and ordered an ambulance to go to the spot where the victim was left and remove him to a Negro hospital. As usual the State officials, many of whom participated in the outrage, made no attempt to discover the culprits, giving as the excuse that the inhuman operation was performed "by unknown parties."

As barbarous as this outrage is, let it be known that Rouse is not the first Negro to be subjected to this form of atrocity. A number of similar cases occurred in other sections of the South, where the ruling classes—in their determination to prevent any relationship between the white and black workers—resorted to the most barbarous and savage assaults upon Negro men suspected of having any personal relationship with white women.

(d) Segregation, better known in America as Jim-Crowism, is the most widespread form of social oppression in the United States. Wherever Negroes live, whether in the North or South, they are segregated in their social relationships from the whites. This applies most generally in public utility service, schools, hospitals, recreation centers, and other places of amusement, etc. In some States Negroes are not even allowed to ride in the same coaches with the whites. Wherever railroad companies agreed to permit them to ride they are provided with small dirty wooden compartments for which they have to pay the same fare as the white passengers, who enjoy the most up-to-date railroad conveniences. On Southern streetcars, Negroes get in and off from the rear while the whites enter from the front and have priority to the best seats. In those places where Negroes are admitted to the theaters they are forced to enter through back doors, and inside the theaters are huddled together in filthy balconies far removed from the stage.

Black workers are not permitted to patronize restaurants which cater to whites, neither are they allowed to use the same public bathing beaches or entrances to buildings as other people. Negroes are debarred from libraries, museums, art galleries, and other centers of culture. Very limited educational and cultural opportunities are offered to them. In most places they are compelled to send their children to separate schools, and, as is to be expected the capitalist State expends by far more money on the education of white children than black, although the Negro workers are made to pay the same taxes for the maintenance of the public schools system. A few figures will illustrate the marked disproportion in the educational budget for blacks and whites in the South (see chart, top of next page).

In the face of this marked discrimination for the education of the two races, one can easily appreciate the tremendous handicaps which the children of Negro workers and peasants are confronted with in acquiring education and culture. Nevertheless, through great personal sacrifices, the Negroes have themselves carried on the struggle to liquidate illiteracy.

State	For white child	For Negro
South Carolina	60,12	5,90
Georgia	48,00	7,00
Mississippi	32,57	6,00
Louisiana	74,24	8,20
Alabama	40,92	8,70
Arkansas	32,23	9,00
Florida	78,22	12,00

(e) Disfranchisement. Politically, Negroes in the South are completely disfranchised; this is done with open violence and terror. On election days there are armed white mobs, agents paid by the capitalist politicians to keep the Negroes away from the polls in the Southern States. Furthermore, certain enactments, known as the "Black Laws," have been incorporated in the Statutes of some States in order to more effectively deprive the Negroes of their political rights. These laws are chiefly based on property and educational qualifications. As the vast majority of Negroes are propertyless, and their standard of literacy is a matter to be determined by the politicians (Republicans and Democrats), it becomes very easy for them to be ruled off the ballot. During every election campaign in America, Negro workers who attempt to vote are openly shot down before the polling stations by armed thugs and gangsters, specially hired by the various capitalist parties to prevent the blacks from taking part in the elections. *The Republican, Democratic* and *"Socialist"* parties are all hostile to the Negroes. Only the Communist Party fights for their full economic, social and political equality, and champions the right of self-determination for the Negro masses who inhabit the *Black Belt*.

(f) Ghetto Life. Wherever one goes in America one sees a striking similarity in the appearance of black communities derisively called *"Nigger Towns."* The outstanding feature of these ghettos are their very unsanitary conditions. For the bourgeois politicians, although they compel the Negroes to pay the same amount of taxes as the whites, never spend any money to improve the standard of life among the black workers. Epidemics frequently break out in these black settlements, taking heavy

toll among the workers, especially their children. The death rate among the Negro workers in America is in some cases 50 percent higher than whites. This is especially so in the case of contagious diseases, such as tuberculosis, typhus, etc. Even in the North, where Negroes are supposed to be better off than in the South, they are still the victims of varied forms of social oppression. First of all they are isolated from the rest of the working class by traditional social codes imposed upon the workers by the bourgeoisie, in order to maintain an ideological influence over the white workers, who are taught to hate and despise their black comrades. Therefore, we find that the less class-conscious white workers, like the capitalists, have the tendency to consider the Negro workers as social outcasts—members of a pariah race.

FROM PART TWO:
4. THE AWAKENING OF NEGRO TOILERS

Now that we have described some of the conditions under which Negro toilers live in various parts of the world, all of which glaringly expose the brutal and inhuman policies adopted by the various capitalist exploiters in order to extract superprofits out of the labor of these toilers, we shall now attempt briefly to chronicle some of the recent revolts, uprisings and strikes, which have occurred in the different sections of the Black world. These counter-offensives against the imperialists are of great significance, for they demonstrate the tremendous revolutionary potentialities of the Negro toiling masses, and show their readiness to wage a relentless struggle against European and American imperialism as well as their own native and racial oppressors who are the agents and lackeys of the white imperialists.

VII. THE UNITED STATES

The revolutionary spirit among the Negro toilers is not only confined to the black colonial masses, but is also manifesting itself among the Negro proletariat in the United States.

Thanks to the economic crisis, which has worsened the standard of living of these workers to a very marked degree, the Negro masses are becoming more and more radicalized. This leftward swing of the Negro masses is bringing them into closer and closer alliance with the class-conscious white workers under the leadership of the *Communist Party and Trade Union Unity League*, the revolutionary trade union center in the USA. In order to break up this alliance between the whites and blacks, and thereby weaken the counter-offensive of the workers against the capitalists, the bourgeoisie, with the aid of their social-fascist lackeys of the Socialist Party and the American Federation of Labor, as well as the open fascist organizations like the *Ku Klux Klan*, the *Black Shirts*, the *American Legion*, etc., have launched a new wave of white terror (lynching) against the Negro masses. The bourgeoisie hope that, by playing up social prejudice and inciting lynchings and race riots, they will be able to distract the attention of the workers from their common class interests in fighting against the widespread misery and starvation. The Negro workers are showing their determination not to permit themselves to be led astray and thereby breaking up the united front between themselves and the white workers against their oppressors.

The most striking expressions of solidarity between the toilers of both races are to be seen in the united struggles of the Unemployed.

For example, on the 6th of March 1930, the first *International Day of Struggle against Unemployment*, organized and led by the Communist Party and the TUUL, thousands of Negro workers not only participated in the monster demonstrations which took place in all the big industrial centers of the country, but played a leading role.

Since then the Negro workers, together with their class-conscious white allies, have carried on repeated struggles in various parts of the United States. A demonstration of over three thousand workers, about two-thirds Negroes, took place in Birmingham, Alabama, on December 21st, 1930, under militant slogans demanding work or relief.

The same applied to the Hunger March which took place in Toledo, Ohio, on December 22nd, 1930—while in Charlotte, North Carolina, and Denver, Colorado, thousands of Negro and white workers carried on militant struggles against the police who attempted to break up their demonstration. In the course of all these demonstrations the police and other capitalist agents have directed most vicious attacks upon the blacks, in order to break up the interracial solidarity and to intimidate the Negroes from taking an active part in the struggles of their class.

Apart from these joint struggles of the white and black unemployed, the Negroes themselves have organized many spontaneous strikes and demonstrations. In Chicago, Negro women, by means of a successful campaign of picketing white capitalist enterprises (Woolworth Stores) won the right to be employed in places that attempted to discriminate against them. Spontaneous manifestations of struggle are becoming widespread in the South. In Georgia, Tennessee, Alabama, etc., Negro tenants and farm laborers are breaking into the warehouses of the white farmers and landlords and helping themselves to food. Agricultural workers in Tennessee called a number of strikes in 1930. The same applies to New Orleans, where Negro dockers went on a spontaneous strike. Besides these cases of spontaneous demonstrations, there has been a wave of resistance by the Negro workers in the South in the form of armed defense. Landlords attempting to terrorize Negroes and attack them and their families have been shot. In December 1930, an unemployed demonstration of 300 Negroes with banners *"We want work or food"* was organized in Shreveport, Louisiana, which developed into a clash between the workers and the police. Wherever we turn in America Today we find an increasing spirit of revolutionary consciousness among the Negro masses.

FROM PART FOUR: 6. REVOLUTIONARY PERSPECTIVES

I. THE ROLE OF THE RILU IN THE STRUGGLES OF THE NEGRO TOILERS

The Red International of Labor Unions (RILU, also Profintern) celebrated its Tenth Anniversary in 1930. Having been organized in the very heat of the acute postwar economic and political crisis in the most important European countries, the Profintern came to be the militant revolutionary headquarters of the world trade union movement, rallying to its banner all the class-conscious proletarian elements of the whole world.

Today the Profintern is in the thick of its struggle for winning over the working class. In spite of its fine successes in extending its influence the Profintern cannot yet say that it embraces the majority of the working class. The Profintern is still obliged to wage a relentless struggle for freeing the workers from the influence of the bourgeoisie, the reformists and anarcho-syndicalists. The greatest enemy of the Profintern in the struggle for influence over the working class is the International Trade Union Federation, the so-called Amsterdam International.

The Amsterdam International was organized one year prior to the Profintern. In spite of its high-sounding name of "International Federation," Amsterdam is, in the main, an association of European trade unions, owing to the fact that out of the 28 organizations affiliating with it 23 are in Europe and only 5 organizations are non-European. Besides, the Amsterdam International is a white chauvinist international. The Amsterdamites reflect the interests of the upper strata of the working class in the imperialist countries, and look down upon the trade union movement of the colonial and colored peoples. Amsterdam's first and most important task is to preserve and reinforce capitalism and imperialism, and to strengthen the position of the bourgeoisie by suppressing the revolutionary movement in the imperialist countries and the national liberation movements in the colonies and semi-colonial countries.

The Profintern is the first real International of Trade Unions, because the workers of all nationalities and races, regardless of color or creed, have rallied to its banner. The Profintern has its sections in practically all countries in the world, in the form of independent trade unions and opposition groups and minorities inside the reformist trade unions. Besides these trade unions, which are organizationally connected with the Profintern, there are a whole number of trade union federations which adhere to the ideological leadership of the Profintern. Two very powerful organizations are among these—the Pan-Pacific Trade Union Secretariat and the Latin American Confederation of Labor.

The Red International of Labor Unions is the first Trade Union International which furthered the development of the trade union movement among the colonial peoples, and succeeded in rallying a great part of them to its banner. It is the only international which conducts a consistent and permanent struggle against white chauvinism for equal rights for the labor movement in the colonial and semi-colonial countries, for the correct solution of the national-race problem. This struggle has only just begun. The problem of national equality has not been sufficiently appraised even by many of the Profintern supporters, while in the ranks of those sections of the working class which still follow the reformist and the reactionary leadership the "race struggle" in most cases, we regret to say, overshadows the class struggle. The Profintern has, however, mapped out a correct line for solving the national-race problem. It has indicated the path for waging the struggle against race chauvinism, against all color bars, for uniting the workers of all races and nations.

A very vivid example of the national-race policy of the Profintern is its fight for strengthening and extending the trade union movement among the Negro workers. The Negro workers are the most exploited, the most oppressed in the world. It was the fate of the Negro workers to pay the horrible tribute to slavery, which served to destroy millions upon millions of black toilers. The Negro workers even now are actually slave-bound to their white conquerors. Different forms of forced labor, peonage, expropriation of their lands, extraordinary laws and unbearably heavy taxes, lynchings, segregation, etc., etc., are up till now the fate of the Negro toiling masses languishing under the yoke of imperialism. Tens of thousands of Negro workers are still groaning under the lash of their enslavers.

The Negro workers, however, exploited and oppressed by the imperialists, have not received the necessary support of the organized labor movement. The white worker, in many cases even today, still regards the Negro as a pariah, and scornfully refuses to stretch out a helping hand to his black brother. Even in the ranks of the revolutionary workers numerous examples of white chauvinism can be recorded. A long and bitter struggle has been waged by the Profintern against this psychology of "white superiority." Day in and day out, year after year, the Profintern has raised the Negro problem before its affiliated sections in the USA, South Africa, England, France, Belgium, Portugal, etc., sharply condemning any and all manifestations of white chauvinism and underestimation of winning the black workers for the class struggle, pointing out the necessity of paying the most serious attention to the organization of the Negro workers into revolutionary trade unions together with the white workers.

In order to strengthen and stimulate trade union activities among the Negro masses, the Profintern finally established a Negro Trade Union Committee composed of Negro workers from the United States, South, East, West, and Equatorial Africa, the British and French West Indies, and Latin America.

Since the establishment of the Committee, the Profintern has to some extent succeeded in overcoming white chauvinism in its ranks, and has corrected the mistakes of its American section, which formerly ignored work among the Negroes. The Profintern will continue its fight until it completely eradicates all traces of white chauvinism from its ranks and unites all workers—white black, yellow, brown—in one revolutionary trade union movement.

II. WHAT MUST BE DONE?

In order to help the Profintern and its revolutionary trade union sections in the United States and South Africa to carry out the task of building up strong unions by strengthening the bonds of solidarity between the white and black workers, two things must be done.

(1) The class-conscious white workers must take the initiative of drawing the Negro workers into the revolutionary unions and the movement of the unemployed, guaranteeing to them every opportunity of actively participating in shaping the policies of the workers' organizations and leading the united front struggles of the working class against the offensive of the capitalists.

In this connection it is the special task of the revolutionary unions to bring the white workers into the struggle on behalf of the Negro demands. It must be borne in mind that the Negro masses will not be won for the revolutionary struggles until such time as the most conscious section of the white workers show, by action, that they are fighting with the Negroes against all racial discrimination and persecution. Every class-conscious worker must bear in mind that the age long oppression of the colonial and weak nationalities by the imperialist powers has given rise to a feeling of bitterness among the masses of the enslaved countries, as well as a feeling of distrust toward the oppressing nation in general and toward the proletariat of those nations. This point was particularly emphasized in the resolution of the Communist International on the Negro Question in USA.

It is absolutely necessary to pursue this policy. No retreat before white chauvinism must be tolerated, for only by *deeds and not words* will we be able to dispel the distrust which the more backward sections of the Negro toiling masses have towards the whites, a suspicion which has developed among them as a result of the traditional policy of the white reformist trade union leaders (Green, Mathew Woll, John L. Lewis, etc.). These AFL fakers not only refuse to organize the Negroes, but, when compelled to do so in order to safeguard the privileged position of the white labor aristocrats, invariably "Jim-Crow" the Negroes into separate unions and leave them at the mercy of the capitalists. Furthermore, the white workers must realize that in the present condition of world capitalism one of the aims of the imperialists is to find a way out of their difficulties by using the Negro workers, especially in the colonies, to worsen the already low standard of the white workers. Because of this the struggles of the Negro workers against the capitalist offensive must be made part and parcel of the common struggle against imperialism.

The emancipation of the white workers from the yoke of capitalism can only be achieved by making a decisive break with all reformist tendencies, which are the ideologies of the bourgeoisie within the ranks of the working class. They must come forward boldly in support of the program of the Communist International and the RILU, which alone struggle for the overthrow of capitalism and the liberation of the toiling masses of all races and color. The workers of the imperialist countries must not forget the memorable words of Marx that "labor in the white skin cannot free itself while labor in the black is enslaved."

(2) The Negro workers must also take a more active part in the revolutionary struggles of the working class as a whole. They must make a decisive break with all bourgeois and petty-bourgeois reformist movements. They must not permit themselves to be misled by the "left" phrases of the American Negro petty-bourgeois reformists, such as Du Bois, Moton, Depriest, etc., etc., who are merely office-seekers and demagogues paid by the ruling class to befuddle the Negro masses in order to direct their attention away from revolutionary struggle into reformist channels.

The Negro workers must also conduct a more relentless struggle against the Negro trade union lackeys of the reformists, whose chief task is to betray the struggles of the Negroes on the economic front. This has been glaringly revealed both in the USA and in South Africa. For example, A. Phillip Randolph and his henchman, Frank Croswaith, "leaders" of the Pullman Porters' Union and members of the Socialist Party, are the most outstanding examples of Negro reformists. Some years ago the Pullman Porters' Union was the biggest mass organization among Negro workers, but thanks to the opportunist policies pursued by Randolph and his supporters the organization is almost bankrupt. Today it is largely a dues-paying organization and sick and death benefit society, completely under the domination of the bureaucrats of the AFL, whose last act of betrayal of the Negro workers was openly to sabotage their struggles against the Pullman Company in 1928.

The same role of treachery has been played by the Negro reformists and other misleaders in the Union of South Africa. The natives must therefore conduct a sharper struggle against the tactics of Kadalie and Champion, as well as Ballinger, the British Independent Labour Party leader, who are the chief disrupters and splitters of the working-class movement among the blacks.

These agents of Amsterdam can boast of an unparalleled record of betrayals of the struggles of the natives of South Africa. The most recent example of Kadalie's hypocrisy was during the railroad strike in East London in 1930. After hundreds of native railroad workers downed tools and went out on strike Kadalie entered into a secret conference with the agents of the Government, who owned the railroads, and then appealed to the men to go back in order that they might get a few shillings to pay their dues from which Kadalie could secure his salary.

Again during the heroic struggles of the natives on Dingaan's Day (December 16th, 1930) Kadalie and Champion attempted to sabotage the demonstrations of the workers, who openly fought with the police for the right to protest against the vicious slave laws of the Hertzog's Government by burning their passes at monster mass meetings. Kadalie told the workers to be submissive and obey their oppressors. He promised to send a petition to Hertzog asking him to abolish the Pass laws, failing which he would call upon the workers to demonstrate in 1934. This shows the bankruptcy of Kadalie and company.

The struggle against Garveyism represents one of the major tasks of the Negro toilers in America and the African and West Indian colonies.

Why must we struggle against Garveyism? As the "Program of the Communist International" correctly states: "Garveyism is a dangerous ideology which bears not a single democratic trait, and which toys with the aristocratic attributes of a nonexistent 'Negro kingdom!' It must be strongly resisted, for it is not a help but a hindrance to the mass Negro struggle for liberation against American imperialism."

Garvey is more than a dishonest demagogue who, taking advantage of the revolutionary wave of protest of the Negro toilers against imperialist oppression and exploitation, was able to crystallize a mass movement in America in the years immediately after the war. His dishonesty and fraudulent business schemes, such as the *Black Star Line*, through which he extorted millions and millions of dollars out of the sweat of the Negro working class, soon led to his imprisonment. After his release Garvey was deported back to Jamaica, his native country. Isolated from the main body of the organization, Garvey has been unable to maintain his former autocratic control over the movement, as a result of which there has been a complete disintegration of the organization, which is now under the control of a number of warring factional leaders. Garvey, who was formerly in the service of American imperialism, has now switched his allegiance to the British, who are utilizing him in order to keep the Negro toilers in the British colonies under submission. With this object in view the imperial Government has permitted Garvey to open his headquarters in London.

Despite the bankruptcy of the Garvey movement the ideology of Garveyism, which is the most reactionary expression in Negro bourgeois nationalism, still continues to exert some influence among certain sections of the Negro masses. The black landlords and capitalists who support Garveyism are merely trying to mobilize the Negro workers and peasants to support them in establishing a Negro Republic in Africa, where they would be able to set themselves up as the rulers in order to continue the exploitation of the toilers of their race, free from white imperialist competition. In its class content Garveyism is alien to the interests of the Negro toilers. Like *Zionism* and *Gandhism*, it is merely out to utilize racial and national consciousness for the purpose of promoting the class interests of the black bourgeoisie and landlords. In order to further their own aims, the leaders of Garveyism have attempted to utilize the same demagogic methods of appeal used by the leaders of Zionism. For example, they promise to "free" the black workers from all forms of oppression in reward for supporting the utopian program of "Back to Africa," behind which slogan Garvey attempts to conceal the truly imperialist aims of the Negro bourgeoisie.

The Negro workers must not be deceived by the demagogic gestures of Garvey and his supporters. They must realize that the only way in which they can win their freedom and emancipation is by organizing their forces millions strong, and in alliance with the class-conscious white workers in the imperialist countries, as well as the oppressed masses of China, India, Latin America, and other colonial and semi-colonial countries, deliver a final blow to world imperialism.

'LYNCH JUSTICE IN AMERICA'
FROM *THE NEGRO WORKER*
JULY 15, 1932

In the midst of the intense worldwide fight for the freedom of the Scottsboro victims, it is well to get a perspective view of the larger issues involved in the case. The Scottsboro frame-up is not an isolated instance of persecution; it is part and parcel of a huge, cold-blooded system of oppression and terrorization of millions of Negro toilers—a system that has well nigh then reduced to a science by the boss class that imposes it.

This boss terror against an oppressed National minority finds its most open and violent expression in lynching, an institution which is rooted deeply in the damnable economic system which gives it birth and nourishes it. The present economic crisis, the growing capitalist offensive against the mounting struggle of the workers of all races reveals more clearly than ever before the economic class basis of Negro lynching. It can no longer be denied that lynching and lynch frame-ups are invariably the direct result of developing class struggles. Lynch Law is the threat facing the Negro workers who attempt or dare to struggle against wage cuts and evictions or for unemployment insurance; the Negro sharecropper or farm laborer who protests against the virtual peonage imposed upon him by the landlords and loan sharks. These lynchings of recent occurrences, chosen at random, amply illustrate the class background of the infamous practice.

---

* "Lynch Justice in America," *The Negro Worker* 2, no. 7 (July 15, 1932): 12–14.

A Bloody Record

The murder of Ralph Grey at Camp Hill, Alabama, by a posse of sheriffs and landlords for his activity in the organization of the Croppers Union. The lynch frame-up of Willie Peterson, disabled and unemployed Negro war veteran, avowedly as part of the reign of terror intended to suppress the forward movement towards organization among the Negro and white workers and sharecroppers of Alabama.

The murder of the three Negro workers in Chicago and of two in Cleveland shot down by policemen in connection with the struggle against evictions.

Added to these instances are the wanton murders of individual Negro unemployed workers by sheriffs and police in every part of the country for nonpayment of rent. Recently a large number of destitute workers suffering from cold and starvation were shot down by company detectives in various towns for picking up coal or fuel along railroad tracks.

Two tendencies are evident in this systematic persecution of Negro workers. First we find that more and more the boss class is supplementing open lynching—i.e. with rope, faggot, and gun, etc.—with its newly perfected device of "legal lynching"—i.e. lynching by "due process of (capitalist) law." Legal lynching is just as effective as stringing the victim up a tree, the capitalists think. It is safer, less "scandalous," being covered with the respectable cloak of capitalist "justice" and is invariably accompanied by the praises and thanks of such bootlicking, reformist organizations as the National Association for the Advancement of Colored People.

The Scottsboro Frame-Up

The Scottsboro case, the most outstanding example of legal lynching contains all the typical elements of the damnable frame-up system—the trumped-up charges and lying testimony of State witnesses, the speedy mockery of a trial in a carefully whipped up atmosphere of lynch mania, the handpicked jury and prejudiced judge, denial of the most elemental rights to the Negro victims who are doomed to death in advance etc.

Other notable examples of the legal lynching system are the cases of Euel Lee (Orphan Jones) in Maryland, Willie Brown in Philadelphia,

Willie Peterson in Birmingham, Jess Jollins in Oklahoma and Bonny Lee Ross in Texas. In refusing to grant a stay of execution to young Ross, who was railroaded to the electric chair, Governor Ross Sterling of Texas brazenly admitted the role of lynching as a weapon in the boss campaign of suppression of the Negro masses in stating that, "it may be that this man is innocent but it is sometimes necessary to burn a house in order to save a village."

The Black Hundreds

Another dangerous trend in the present growth of boss-inspired lynch mania is the passing from the stage of individual lynchings to armed terroristic attacks against whole communities by organized bands of fascist lynchers—Ku Kluxers, Black Shirts, Legionnaires, etc. This tendency was apparent in the mass slaughter and disarming of Negroes in the Birmingham district at the time of the Willie Peterson frame-up and in the ruthless terrorization of Negro comrades along the Eastern Shores of Maryland during the recent lynch fever, particularly in connection with the lynching of Matthew Williams in Salisbury, which was accompanied by a series of the most provocative acts against the Negro masses in that vicinity. In this instance the body of the dying Williams was dragged through the streets of the Negro neighborhood, his fingers and toes were cut off and thrown on the porches of Negro houses and the lynchers shouted threats to the whole Negro population.

The contemptible Ku Klux practice of "night riding" has been resumed in some parts of the south, as illustrated in the very recent incident at Greenfield, Tenn., where a band of cowardly fascists rode down on a Negro community during the night, hurling threats at the workers and burning several shacks.

Divide and Rule Policy

The ruling class has a two-fold purpose in fostering this vicious campaign of terror against the Negro toilers—(1) by whipping up lynch hysteria, it aims to divide the workers, and thus to weaken them; (2) it aims by this means to keep in terrorized subjection the Negro masses who constitute a great portion of the American working class.

Against this growing lynch terror, the workers of the whole world, Negro and white, must carry on a wide relentless struggle. It is absolutely essential for all workers to realize that the sharpening of the lynch terror is an integral factor in the general campaign of capitalist reaction against the toilers as a whole, aimed particularly to strike at the growing unity of Negro and white workers.

'CHAPTER 1: THE PROBLEM'
HARRY HAYWOOD
FROM *NEGRO LIBERATION*
1948

The Negro Question in the United States is agrarian in origin. It involves the problem of a depressed peasantry living under a system of sharecropping, riding-boss supervision, debt slavery, chronic land hunger, and dependency—in short, the plantation system, a relic of chattel slavery.

It presents the curious anomaly of a virtual serfdom in the very heart of the most highly industrialized country in the world. Slave-whipping barbarism at the center of "enlightened" twentieth-century capitalist cultures—that is the core of America's "race" problem.

The Black Belt

Today, long after the abolition of slavery, about five million southern Negroes of the fifteen million total Negro population of the country still live in the Black Belt, historically a continuous area of Negro majority. It holds a Negro population equal to that of the whole Negro population of the North and West, and almost a third of the entire country's Negro inhabitants. This Negro population is larger than the total population of such countries as Switzerland or Norway. Embracing the central cotton-growing region of the South, the Black Belt is

---

* Harry Haywood, "Chapter 1: The Problem," in *Negro Liberation* (New York: International Publishers, 1948), 11–20.

the area in which plantation economy is most firmly rooted; the peon farms of today correspond to the slave plantation of yesterday.

The Black Belt shapes a crescent through twelve Southern states. Heading down from its eastern point in Virginia's Tidewater section, it cuts a strip through North Carolina, cuts into Florida, passes through lower and central Georgia and Alabama, engulfs Mississippi and the Louisiana Delta, wedges into eastern Texas and southwest Tennessee, and has its western anchor in southern Arkansas.

The Black Belt is the center of America's Negro problem, the core of its greatest concentration. Here is the seat of the infection from which the virus of Negro persecution spreads throughout the country, contaminating all phases of Negro life. Here, in the status of the Black Belt Negro, is the clue to the economic, social, and cultural inequality of America's black millions. To quote Arthur F. Raper, well-known southern scholar:

"The Black Belt sketches the section of the nation where the smallest proportion of adults exercise the franchise and it defines the most solid part of the Solid South." Here is the stronghold of white supremacy, where the Negro is excluded from political life and his children are denied adequate educational opportunities; all institutions are designed to keep the Negro "in his place," and violence and the threat of violence always hang over his head.

The Black Belt is likewise the matrix of the nation's number one economic problem—the cradle of southern economic and cultural lag. And, as a growing body of southern white liberal opinion is coming to understand, its depressing influence bears down fully upon the white population of the South. Says Raper:

> Human relations in Atlanta, Birmingham, Montgomery, Memphis, New Orleans, and Dallas are determined largely by the attitudes of the people of the Black Belt plantations from which many of their inhabitants, white and Negro, came. The standard of living in these cities does not escape the influence of this area of deterioration. No real relief can come to the region so long as the planter, who wants dependent workers, can confound the situation by setting the white worker over against the black worker, and so long as the industrialist, who wants cheap labor, can

achieve his end by pitting urban labor against rural labor. There are literally millions of farm laborers in the Black Belt who are eagerly awaiting an opportunity to work for wages even smaller than are now being paid textile and steel workers in southern cities.

It is not surprising, therefore, that wages in the traditionally "lily white" textile industry "grow progressively lower the further one penetrates into the Deep South."

The County System

The Black Belt is arbitrarily broken up by a mass of state or county boundaries and administrative, judicial, and electoral subdivisions. These divisions in no way correspond with the economic and political needs of the oppressed majority population and are artificially maintained and gerrymandered by the real rulers of the South. Their avowed purpose is to perpetuate the political impotence of the region's predominant Negro population.

The role of the country government as an instrument of governmental power for Bourbon planter interests and the decisive influence of the county in the state politics of the region were dramatically brought out in the results of Georgia's gubernatorial primaries of July 1946. Through a county unit system of voting, in which elections are rigged in favor of downstate planter, the rabid Ku Kluxer, Eugene Talmadge, was nominated, despite a statewide popular vote majority for his opponent, James V. Carmichael.

The Skeleton in the Closet

Shackled by a common slavery and bound by a common history, ethnic origin and aspirations, the Negro people have problems which are matters of growing import, not alone to the South but to the whole country.

The explosive political material in this condition has never been ignored by the leaders of southern Bourbonry, and it is the skeleton in the closet of the rabid "white supremacists" of the Talmadge-Bilbo breed. Here is a condition which their obscene racism is designed to hide. Political power in the hands of the black majority, the same specter that haunted their slave-trading forbears, dogs them today; for even a breath of genuine freedom for the millions of black bondsmen would change the social face of the South.

One can only marvel at the cynicism of our erstwhile Secretary of State, James F. Byrnes who, in the name of "free elections," attacks the peoples' democracies of eastern Europe. If applied to his own Black Belt state of South Carolina, "free elections" would mean the end of the stolen power of the Bourbon clique which Mr. Byrnes really represents. Let it be remembered that the first milestone in the meteoric political career of our eminent ex-Secretary of State was in 1922, when he was elected to Congress with only 4,163 votes cast in a congressional district with a population of 300,000!

The great mass of American people remain in deep ignorance of the existence of the huge vassal Negro community in the Black Belt, and of its blighting influence on our country's democracy. The truth concerning the Black Belt, so essential to any serious analysis of the Negro problem, remains buried in the works of authors not widely read by the general public. Vital statistical facts are unstated, distorted, or obscured in a mass of inconsequential minutiae by federal and state agencies (the United States Census Bureau not excepted), from which they can be extracted only by the most painstaking research. As Karl Brandt, a critic of agricultural statistics, pointed out in *Social Research* a decade ago:

> In counting farm operators the census makes no distinction between the sharecropper on the one hand, and, on the other hand, the farmer who operates his property either personally or with the aid of a manager and the tenant who operates a rented farm. By this procedure the census has erased from the whole picture one of the most distinctive features in the constitution of agriculture in this and in many other countries. *Strange as it may seem, in current American agricultural statistics the plantation does not exist.* (Italics mine –H. H.)

The Negro Community

In order fully to understand the Negro question as a whole, one must first see clearly that, despite state and county borders, the Black Belt is an entity in itself, comprising a population chiefly Negro and constituting a stable community of Negro Americans.

According to the 1940 United States Census, the Black Belt contains 180 counties of proved Negro majority, ranging from 50 to 85 percent. The total population of the counties of absolute Negro Majority in 1940 was 4,237,739. Of this total, 2,642,808 (or 63 percent) were Negroes.

The extent of this Negro concentration is, however, by no means limited to those counties having a clear Negro majority. Such counties constitute only the core of the community.

Obviously, population concentrations do not stop short at state or county lines. The compact Negro community overflows such lines into neighboring counties. This is borne out by the 1940 Census which lists some 290 counties having populations which are from 30 to 50 percent Negro.

The area of concentration of the Negro population spans about 470 counties with an overall average Negro population of 48.7 percent of the total. We make no attempt rigidly to fix the boundaries of the Black Belt. However, anyone not completely blinded by the present arbitrarily erected state and county lines can see that within the territory embraced by these counties there is a well-defined, compact and stable Negro community.

In 1940 the population of the entire Black Belt area (including both Negro majority counties and peripheral areas) totaled 10,256,289, of which 4,993,612 (or 48.7 percent) were Negroes.

The following table, compiled from US Bureau of Census population statistics for Black Belt countries from 1860 to 1940 by James Allen, in an article in Political Affairs, clearly indicates the existence of an historically continuous Negro community (see chart at top of next page).

The 'Mass Exodus' Theory

It has been asserted that this Negro majority in the Black Belt is rapidly disintegrating as a result of "huge migrations"—a veritable "mass exodus" of Negroes, especially during the late war. This contention is refuted by the table of figures shown, and also by the latest estimates on these Negro migrations.

Census Year	Total Population	Negro Population	Percent Negro of total
1940	10,256,289	4,993,612	48.7
1930	9,525,865	4,790,049	50.3
1920	8,968,132	4,806,565	53.6
1910	8,387,958	4,842,766	57.7
1900	7,498,900	4,448,992	59.9
1890	6,465,307	3,866,792	59.8
1880	5,750,410	3,466,924	60.3
1870	4,431,597	2,560,263	57.8
1860	4,362,009	2,461,099	56.4

It is true that there has been a decrease in the ratio of Negro to total population in the Black Belt area over the years, a trend which has been in evidence since the Civil War. It is also true that there has been a steady, and even sharp, decrease in the number of counties of Negro majority, particularly between 1900 and 1940, when it declined from 300 in the former year to 180 in the latter, or 37 percent. Despite these facts, however, the total Negro population did not decline; in fact, it even increased, although the increase was slight as compared to that of the white population. And as for the area of Negro majority, although its shrinkage has continued, its rate of decline fell off sharply in the decade of 1930–40 which also showed an increase in the total Negro population for the first time since 1900.

While these facts indicate the necessity of going beyond bare statistics for an understanding of what is happening to the Negro community in the Black Belt, they do not indicate a disintegration of the Negro concentration in this area. The figures in our table show a decline in the total Negro population during the decades 1910–30 only, the period during which there was also the sharpest decline in the number of counties of Negro majority. This was the era of "the great migration" connected with the industrial boom of World War I and the prosperity period of the 'twenties. This decline clearly registered the "flight" of those elements of the population who were able to break away from a backward, depressed agricultural area and, in response to the needs of capitalistic industrial expansion, war and postwar prosperity gave way to the great crisis and depression of 1930–40, there occurred an absolute growth of the total Negro population in the Black Belt and a marked slowing up of the rate of decline of the counties of Negro majority.

It is obvious, therefore, that the movements of decline and growth of the Negro population and its concentration in the Black Belt have been conditioned by the economic fluctuations accompanying the development of monopoly capitalism in the United States. Any substantial disintegration of this concentrated Negro community would depend entirely upon a continuous and uninterrupted process of industrial expansion and prosperity in the country as a whole. But there is absolutely nothing in the perspective of capitalist development to warrant such an assumption. If therefore, we confine ourselves to the facts rather than to wishful thinking, the feature that stands out is not the breaking up of the Negro concentration in the Black Belt, but its stubborn persistence.

Migration during the Second World War

Have the migratory movements of World War II affected the stability of this region? According to a special wartime survey (1940–44), released by the Bureau of the Census in 1945, the non-white resident population in "ten congested war production areas included less than 300,000 Negroes moving into these areas." Three of these cities were in the South.

Even if generous allowance is made for migration to other commercial and industrial centers not included in this survey, there is no evidence of a major decrease in the total Negro population of the Black Belt below that of 1940, that is, of a breakup of the concentration there. Moreover, the factors responsible for such a possible decline have clearly come to an end with the close of the war, and have been replaced by the immobilizing influences of coming crisis and depression. Monopoly capital, which is responsible for the conditions encouraging mass migration, at the same time imposes an automatic check on these migrations through the "busy" which follows the "boom."

The latest census figures available show that even during the war-dominated years of 1940–47, with their impetus to large-scale migration, the total Negro population of the South remained essentially stationary (a total of 9,530,000 in 1947 as compared with 10,007,323 in 1940).

The main wartime shift was away from agriculture into other occupations. The extent of this shift was largely a matter of conjecture until a January 1948 release of the Census Bureau (*Series P-20*, No. 9) brought to light the fact that 60 percent of the nation's non-white population (96 percent of which are Negroes) had become urban by April 1947, as compared to about 48.0 percent in 1940. In spite of the fact that the non-white population was expanding at a rate of 50 percent more rapidly than the white (11.6 percent increase in seven years as compared to 7.5 percent increase of the white inhabitants), the rural-farm Negro population declined by an estimated total of 1,270,000, or by more than 26.0 percent, while the urban population increased by 2,550,000, or by about 40 percent. There was some movement from the farm to rural villages.

The survey of 1940–44 further shows that not all the Negro migration was from the Black Belt, or even from the rural areas of the South alone. In fact, it revealed a change in the direction of Negro migration which had prevailed from 1870–1941. The migrations of World War II broke away from the purely South-to-North pattern which characterized the early migrations. Thus, although the latest movements had their origin in the South, three of the ten terminal areas mentioned in the survey were in the Black Belt itself: Charlestown, S.C.; Hampton Roads, Va.; and Mobile, Ala., or in the periphery of the Black Belt.

On the whole, there was no northward migration of Negroes during the recent war comparable in size and significance to that of World War I. The entrance of Negroes into war industries was considerably delayed, because of a tremendous reserve of unemployed white workers in the cities, both North and South, and because of the age-old policy of employers which decrees that the Negro must be the "last hired."

In 1942 Charles S. Johnson reported that:

> When placements through the US Employment Service reached the highest peak, Negroes and other non-whites composed only 3 percent of the placements in 20 large war industries, and they were less than 3 percent of the referrals

for pre-employment training courses. They are at present about 1 percent of the total in those pre-employment and refresher courses. In one city ... with two large shipbuilding concerns, there were nationwide requests for shipyard workers, in spite of the fact that the US Employment Service reported 6,000 Negro workers available in the active file of the Employment Service in that city.

Plainly, those in search of an easy solution of the Negro question in the South—through peaceful out-migration of the Negro people—have "overlooked" the profound economic and historical causes which have shaped the Black Belt as the main region of Negro concentration in this country—*forces which still operate to maintain it as such.*

The explanation—and solution—is not to be found in dry statistical data lone. The explanation lies, on the one hand, in the overall operation of monopoly capital which closes the door to out-migration as quickly as it opens it, and, on the other hand, in the plantation economy which dominates the Black Belt region and its relation to the economy of the country as a whole.

'NEGROES AND THE CRISIS OF CAPITALISM IN THE US'
W. E. B. DU BOIS
FROM *MONTHLY REVIEW*
APRIL 1953

How "free" was the black freedman in 1863? He had no clothes, no home, tools, or land. Thaddeus Stevens begged the government to give him a bit of the land which his blood had fertilized for 244 years. The nation refused. Frederick Douglass and Charles Sumner asked for the Negro the right to vote. The nation yielded because only Negro votes could force the white South to conform to the demands of Big Business in tariff legislation and debt control. This accomplished, the nation took away the Negro's vote, and the vote of most poor whites went with it.

A fantastic economic development followed. In the South the land was rich and the climate mild. There was sun and rain for grain, fruit, and fiber. There were natural resources in rivers, harbors, and forests. In the bosom of the earth lay coal, iron, oil, sulfur, and salt. All this either already belonged to or was practically given by the government to the landholder and capitalist. Only a small part of it went to labor, black or white.

Capital was needed to develop this economic paradise. Government furnished much of this capital free to the landholder and employer.

---

* W. E. B. Du Bois, "Negroes and the Crisis of Capitalism in the U.S.," *Monthly Review*, April 1953.

Railroads were subsidized, and rivers and harbors improved; private wealth largely escaped taxation. The North, fattened on tariff legislation, money control, and cheap immigrant labor, poured private capital into the South. When Southern labor lost half its vote, landholders and capitalists filled the state legislatures and Congress with servants of exploitation. This gave all the powerful chairmanships in Congress to the South under the Democrats, and large influence under Republicans. During World War I, a large part of the military training program was located in the South, and the government overpaid interested landlords and merchants and contractors to the tune of hundreds of millions of dollars—a performance which was to be largely repeated in World War II. During the depression, most relief money paid out in the South went to landlords, not to workers.

During and after World War II, Southern industry moved into high gear. The Federal government poured billions of grants-in-aid into the South. Washington was lavish with "Certificates of Necessity" to build new factories, and owners of oil wells were given tax rebates for depletion of the oil which God gave the nation; and today they seek to grab the $80 billion worth of oil underseas.

Above all, the South furnished and boasted of one of the largest pools of cheap, docile, unorganized labor, skilled and unskilled, in the civilized world. This mass of labor was historically split into white and black, each hating and fearing each other to a degree that persons unfamiliar with the region cannot begin to imagine. Southern labor was further split into organized and unorganized groups; and finally, all American labor was split by red-baiting and the smear of "Communism."

Here was a paradise for the investor, which the state governments improved. Labor laws in the South were lax and carelessly enforced; company towns arose under complete corporate control; the police and militia were organized against labor. Race hate and fear and scab tactics were deliberately encouraged so as to make any complaint or effort at betterment liable to burst into riot, lynching, or race war.

The result has been startling. In 1919, the South turned out less than a fifth of our mining products; by 1946, the proportion had risen to nearly half. The value of manufactures in the South has risen in thirty years from a tenth to nearly a fifth of the national total. Many of the new and promising industries are seeking the South; since

World War II, no less than $11 billion has been invested there in new industrial plants. The Southeast already has 80 percent of the nation's cotton mills and virtually all the new chemical fiber industry. It is drawing the woolen and worsted mills, and the textile machinery mills will soon follow. Paper and pulp mills and plastics represent hundreds of millions in new investments. The Southwest is perhaps the fastest-growing chemical empire in the world.

This newest South, turning back to its slave past, believes its present and future prosperity can best be built on the poverty and ignorance of its disfranchised lowest masses—and these low-paid workers now include not only Negroes, but Mexicans, Puerto Ricans, and the unskilled, unorganized whites. Progress by means of this poverty is the creed of the present South.

The Northern white worker long went his way oblivious to what was happening in the South. He awoke when the black Southern laborer fled North after World War I, and he welcomed him by riots. Slowly, however, the black man has been integrated into the unions, except those in whose crafts he was not skilled and had no chance to learn. One of these was the textile unions. They excluded Negroes. It is taking a long time to prove to them that their attitude toward Negroes was dangerous. If Negro wages were low in the South, what business was that of New England white labor? Today the union man sees that it was his business. The factories are moving out of New England and the North into the South. One hundred thousand textile workers are idle. This illustrates a paradox of capitalism: in the South, the nation, and the world, the workers are too poor to buy the textiles they need; while machinery is able to make more textiles than its owners can sell at the prices they demand.

Wages in the South are 20 percent lower than in the North, and Negro wages as a legacy from [the National Industrial Recovery Act], are at least 20 percent below white wages. This wage differential between North and South represents increased profits of $4 to $5 billion a year. Small wonder that the Negro population in the rural South decreased by 50,000 in the last decade, and that the number of Negroes in the North increased by 55 percent. Of nine million industrial workers in the South, less than three million are unionized. Last year 40,000 members of the Congress of Industrial Organizations (CIO) Textile Workers Union, which excludes Negroes, struck in the

South, and spent $1,250,000 in five weeks. They lost, and their membership fell from 20 to 15 percent of the operatives. The carpetbaggers today are the vast Northern corporations which own the new Southern industry, and the scalawags are the Southern politicians whom they send to state legislatures and Congress.

The organized effort of American industry to usurp government, surpasses anything in modern history, even that of Adolf Hitler from whom it was learned. From the use of psychology to spread truth has come the use of organized gathering of news to guide public opinion and then deliberately to mislead it by scientific advertising and propaganda. This has led in our day to suppression of truth, omission of facts, misinterpretation of news, and deliberate falsehood on a wide scale. Mass capitalistic control of books and periodicals, news gathering and distribution, radio, cinema, and television has made the throttling of democracy possible and the distortion of education and failure of justice widespread. It can only be countered by public knowledge of what this government by propaganda is accomplishing and how.

In the nation as a whole we have full employment and high wages for most skilled workers, but this state of affairs is maintained by manufacturing arms and ammunition which rapidly deteriorate in value, and by giving it away and paying for it by taxes which lower high wages, and by high prices. How long can we maintain this merry-go-round?

What now must American Negroes say to this situation? This question raises another: what is the real nature of this group today?

There are nearly 15 million persons of known Negro descent in this country; two-thirds of these are in the former slave states, somewhat fewer than a third are in the North, and a half million are in the far West. This distribution marks a notable change from the recent past: in 1860, nine-tenths of the Negroes were in the slave South; in 1900, there were only 900,000 in the North.

The group is not homogeneous and is in process of rapid change. From a predominantly rural group in 1900, it is today mainly urban. As late as 1940, 7 million Negroes in the United States lived on farms and 6.5 million in cities. In 1950, 6 million were on farms and 9 million lived in cities! These large-scale shifts, of course, create great strains on family and social life.

These Negroes are closely integrated into the industry of the nation, but the character of that integration is rapidly changing.

From being predominantly farm laborers, today 83 percent are in nonagricultural occupations and only 17 percent on farms. Of the former, 40 percent are servants and 19 percent are laborers; skilled and semi-skilled workers represent 30 percent. A little over a tenth of the employed Negro population is in business and the professions.

This indicates a group of poor people, especially those remaining in the South, where their median wage is about $1,000 a year. The Southern farm laborers are even poorer. For example, in South Carolina, nearly half the Negroes on farms earn less than $500 a year. Southern whites have a median wage of $2,000, and Northern whites $3,000.

Most American Negroes are as a mass ignorant. Perhaps two-thirds can read and write, if we depend on draft statistics which are lower than the census report of 11 percent illiteracy. This naturally follows from the poor, segregated Negro school system. In the South, adult Negroes have had on the average half as many years of schooling as whites. Most colored adults in the North had their education in the South, and show it in lack of training.

The proportion of the Negro population that has attained middle- or upper-class status can only be guessed at. Some surveys indicate that in cities like New York and Chicago, perhaps seven to ten percent of Negro families have incomes of over $5,000 a year, and 20 percent receive from $3,000 to $5,000; while from five to ten percent are in the slums, earning under $1,000. On account of continued disfranchisement in the South, only 40 percent of Southern Negroes vote; but in the North, Negroes wield political power and hold some important offices.

What now is the attitude of this upper group toward the present capitalistic crisis in America? For the most part they are capitalists in thinking, believing in "making money," in saving and investing. When they hire labor they exploit it as do their white neighbors. In businesses, like insurance, they employ the same methods as white insurance companies, within the protection of color discrimination. The colored landlord is no different from the white. Many Negro fortunes have been gained in antisocial activities like gambling.

Negro Americans, like whites, are subject to the mass propaganda by which monopoly of news gathering and distribution; concentrated ownership of radio, cinema, and television; and financial control of publication, make democratic government nearly impossible today by denying knowledge of the truth to the average man. But Negroes are repelled by the custom of calling agitation for Negro rights "Communism." This has caused some sudden reversals of snap judgment by officials in high places, but it makes the average black man suspicious, and this suspicion may increase.

Today any Negro leader who is willing to testify to the "free and equal" position of Negroes in America can get free travel to Asia, Europe, or Africa, with no passport difficulties. Even if he will not testify but is willing to keep still, a variety of perquisites, including scholarships, are available.

Some Negro leaders with much to lose in property, credit, or reputation have yielded to panic; two colored authors in recent new editions of their books have deleted references to Paul Robeson and myself in order to appease the witch-hunters. Much time and thought of misguided intellectuals has been devoted to helping deprive American Negroes of natural leadership or to scaring them into silence by threat of imprisonment, loss of work, or by smearing them as "Communists." Negro colleges especially are silenced and influenced by funds raised by Big Business and visits from distinguished capitalists. Their courses in sociology, economics, and history are carefully watched.

This kind of suppression and censorship, however, does not solve anything; it but complicates the situation. For a time it may deprive Negroes of some of their best-trained and wealthiest leaders, but despite this, the color bar, will not release the main mass of the group. The bar may bend and loosen. Rich Negroes may travel with less annoyance; they may stop in the higher-priced hotels and eat in the more costly restaurants; the theaters and movie houses in the North and border states may let down the bars. Beyond that, because of constitutional law and mounting costs, the wall of segregation in education may be breached. But with all this, what results? The color bar in this nation will not soon be broken. Even as it yields in places the insult of what remains will be more deeply felt by the still half free.

When the whole caste structure finally does fall, Negroes will be divided into classes even more sharply than now, and the main mass will become a part of the working class of the nation and the world, which will surely go socialist.

As long as caste remains, the Negro leaders are bound to their own group. This group, despite its class differences in income property, education, and type of work, is still bound together by a certain unity usually called racial, but really cultural. It has an art and literature and intricate ties of social intercourse. Negroes intermarry with each other almost exclusively and live largely in the same neighborhoods. They gain information about themselves and about Africa and the West Indies only from some 200 weekly newspapers and various magazines which also have something of a special interpretation of the facts as relating to this group. These periodicals, to attract white advertising and political dole, are becoming timid and suppressing news; yet they cannot become too timid or they will lose readers.

The Negro group is continually pushed toward socialistic experiment; the churches try it in recreation and relief; the fraternal orders' experiment in insurance; the fraternities give scholarships; there have been trials of consumers' cooperation. In time, this group with any increase in pressure, might become a veritable school of socialism.

A Negro of talent, education, and money may not live in a Negro ghetto; he may not attend a Negro church, and he may welcome whites to his home and table. Less often, but now and then, his children or friends may marry white persons. He may be elected to public office with the help of white votes and be referred to in the public press without being carefully designated as "colored." But such cases will be exceptional. For the most part, the educated well-to-do American Negro is firmly bound to his powerful group. His memories are memories of its oppressions, insults, and repressions. He rejoices in its victories. He cannot break off from the Negro church entirely and the Negro vote will be his chief dependence in elections. His family will chiefly marry Negroes, and Negroes will constitute the main body of his friends and acquaintances. Consequently no matter how self-centered he may be, he will not be able to avoid exercising some leadership in the group of which he is a part, not only by inner attraction but also by outer force.

In the white world he will not be a member of any church or social club; he will not be nominated to public office except in a Negro district. He may be endured in an exclusive neighborhood but not welcomed. His reception in hotels, restaurants, and public entertainments in the North will vary according to locality. In the South and border states he will almost invariably be excluded. If he tours the nation in his car, most of the "motels" will exclude him. In his leadership and social thinking, therefore, he must consider the future of his race or he will neglect himself and his family.

What this paper is considering is the question of the critical place which this segregated group of Negroes will occupy as the crisis of capitalism in the United States develops. This crisis of American capitalism could be rendered more serious than it is if the leadership of a tenth of the nation should fail in its responsibilities. The crisis arises from the fact that this nation under the control of Big Business is trying stubbornly, and in defiance of the clear historical development of the world since World War I, to oppose state socialism. This Negro group is at present far from being revolutionary. Its fault rather has hitherto been yielding to pressure and bowing in fatal humility when resistance and retaliation would have been best not only for the Negroes themselves but for their oppressors as well.

What will American Negroes answer to the challenge of socialism? What part will they think the State should play in future industry and development? The Negro must see that his advance so far has depended on federal action rather than on states rights or individual initiative. Federal action emancipated him from slavery and is his lone hope for stopping lynching, enacting a Fair Employment Practices Committee (FEPC), and getting justice in the courts.

But far beyond this is the inevitable relation of the colored folk of the United States to the colored peoples of America, Africa, Asia, and the world. When a great nation like the Soviet Union not only refuses to draw the color line but cannot conceive of such barbarism, in the face of the color prejudice which nearly every white nation of Europe and North America practices—what can, what must Negroes think? When China went Communist the impact on the Negro race was tremendous, and no amount of yelling and shrieking will change this. Russia taught her peasants to read and write in a generation. The United States leaves a third of her Negroes illiterate after 90 years of half-hearted effort. If the darker world gradually finds that socialism is the only answer to the color line, then the colored peoples of the world will go socialist and black Americans will perforce march in the ranks. They will not so much lead as be pushed by their own people.

The United States, with its existing social structure, cannot today abolish the color line despite its promises. It cannot stop injustice in the courts based on color and race. Above all, it cannot stop the exploitation of black workers by white capital, especially in the newest South. White North America beyond the urge of sound economics is persistently driving black folk toward socialism. It is the United States which is straining every effort to enslave Asia and Africa, and educated and well-to-do black Americans are coming to know this just as well as anybody. They may delay their reaction; they may hold ominous silence. But in the end, if this pressure keeps up, they will join the march to economic emancipation, because otherwise they cannot themselves be free.

SECTION 02

ORGANIZATION

About Section Two: Organization

The texts in this section provide a window into how the Black Belt Thesis was practically applied, to build the working-class movement in the US South.

In a series of articles in *The Communist,* the CPUSA's theoretical journal, Cyril Briggs outlines the work involved in building the National Textile Workers Union, against the disintegrating tendency of white chauvinism, and against the "lynching spirit" that had been whipped up in Gastonia, North Carolina.

Articles from the *Negro Worker* provide further context for the conditions under which Trade Union Unity League organizers worked against the "fascist methods" employed in the South.

Eugene Gordon, writing in *New Masses,* reported on the efforts of sharecroppers and agricultural workers to organize in Alabama. Black people in rural Alabama had been reading the *Southern Worker,* and they were committed to building the Sharecroppers Union, to the extent of armed defense from armed attacks from the police and landlord-organized vigilante mobs.

A selection from Angelo Herndon's autobiography, *Let Me Live,* provides further details on the scale of violence that communist militants faced down in their practical efforts towards building independent working-class political power. No less, Herndon provides a perspective on the kinds of individual conversations involved with poor Black and white workers in the South which forged working-class consciousness.

Writing in *The Crisis,* Louise Thompson [Patterson] reported on the combination of racism and anti-communism that fueled fascist reaction in Southern courts, police system, and media, the conditions under which thousands of militant workers organized in the Black Belt.

In a selection from his autobiography *Black Bolshevik,* Harry Haywood detailed a visit to the South during the 1930s, reporting on the conditions for political work in Birmingham, Alabama and Atlanta.

In a "reply to a misled worker," the editors of the *Southern Worker,* the CPUSA's regional newspaper in the South, insisted on the centrality of the fight against supremacism among white workers, and the ironclad necessity of organizing working-class unity, across racial divisions.

A 1932 pamphlet from the German communist Clara Zetkin gives perspective of how the Black Belt Thesis shaped the international communist movement of the time, beyond North America.

'FURTHER NOTES ON NEGRO QUESTION IN SOUTHERN TEXTILE STRIKES'
CYRIL BRIGGS
FROM *THE COMMUNIST*
JULY 1929

S ince writing the article on "The Negro Question in the Southern Textile Strikes," which appeared in the June number of *The Communist*, certain developments have occurred which necessitate an elaboration of the subject.

Significant of the change which has been wrought in the minds of the white strikers and concrete proof of the correctness of the Union's policy of organizing the Negroes together with the white workers on a basis of full equality is the fact that following the unprovoked police attack on the strikers' tent colony, the shooting of the chief of police and the arrest of the strike leaders, the white strikers themselves took action to save Otto Hall, Negro organizer for the union, from the lynching fate prepared for him by the local mill owners and the police. The fact that Hall had been absent in Bessemer City at the time of the attack on the strikers' tent colony, and could have had no part in its defense, made no difference to the mill bosses and their business allies and police tools who saw in Hall's connection with the union an opportunity to whip up a lynching spirit against the strikers and

---

* Cyril Briggs, "Further Notes on the Negro Question in Southern Textile Strikes," *The Communist*, July 1929, Marxists Internet Archive

their leaders. They planned to use the Negro question to mobilize the community against a cause so unpopular to the white ruling class as the organization of Southern workers against capitalist rationalization and starvation wages. It would not have been the first time that the Negro question had been utilized by the Southern bourgeoisie against an unpopular cause. Had the police succeeded in laying their hands on Hall it is certain that not only would Hall have been lynched but it is highly likely that with the Negro question to serve as a fuse there would have been a tremendous emotional explosion and other lynchings that night. The Gastonia newspapers did their best to work up a lynching spirit, but lacking the Negro issue which the capture and lynching of Comrade Hall would have furnished, fell far short of actual success. However, these newspapers are now busy mobilizing sentiment for a legal lynching via the capitalist courts and the electric chair of the fifteen strike leaders under arrest on the charge of murder in connection with the killing of the chief of police, and it behooves our Party to exert every ounce of its strength in defense of these fifteen victims of one of the most murderous frame-ups in the history of the labor movement.

Unaware that there had been trouble in Gastonia and that the stage was even then set for his lynching, Comrade Hall was on his way back from Bessemer City. The white strikers were up against a test. Deprived of the guidance of their leader, all of whom, with the exception of Beal who was away, had been rounded up by the police, they faced a situation calling for quick thinking, quick action and a spirit of loyalty to their Negro organizer, based upon an acceptance of the Negro policy of the Union. They responded magnificently! Breaking through the police cordon thrown about the roads leading into Gastonia, a committee of white strikers succeeded in intercepting the car in which Comrade Hall was returning to Gastonia and, warning him of his danger, rushed him to a railroad station forty miles from Gastonia where they raised sufficient money for his fare and put him on a train for New York City. Also, even before this, the white strikers had furnished Comrade Hall with a body guard in his movements about the strike area, giving notice to the world in general and to the mill bosses and their police thugs in particular that they accepted him as an organizer and leader of their union and were prepared to protect him. It seems that we had less trouble in convincing the Southern white strikers of the correctness of our policy than with some of our own comrades in the strike area!

That men who a few months before would have willingly and avidly responded to any proposal of the white ruling class for the lynching of a Negro, should have risked their liberty and even their lives in breaking through the police cordon to save the life of a Negro union organizer is both significant of the change which has come over the first section of the Southern white working class to come under our leadership and indicative of what can be accomplished with the actual launching of a broad ideological campaign among the Southern white working masses against white chauvinism.

In the light of this change in the attitude of these white strikers toward the Negro, the capitulation of some of our comrades to white chauvinism becomes all the more inexcusable. For this retreat before white chauvinism it is my opinion that Comrade Jack Johnstone was mainly responsible. Comrade Johnstone was several times severely censured by the Party Secretariat for his attitude on the Union's Negro policy, his statement that the Union had no policy for the South (tantamount to saying that the Union's Negro policy for the South must be different to its policy for the North), his wrong interpretation of RILU and Comintern decisions to "set up special unions for these Negro workers who are not allowed to join the white unions" as authority for setting up Jim Crow locals in the left wing unions we ourselves are organizing, and for his opportunist proposal that "if we found that the Negro workers did not want to join the regular locals that special Negro locals be formed." Also, Comrade Johnstone, as the CEC representative in the strike area, committed a serious breach of Party discipline in his failure to fight in the fraction for the line of the Party, confining himself to a mere presentation of that line with the declaration that he had opposed it in the meetings of the Secretariat at which he was present. Comrade Johnstone based opposition to the Party line on his opinion that any effort to organize Negroes and white in the South in the same locals and on a basis of full equality for the Negro would militate against the opportunity to organize the white workers and, if persisted in, would amount to an abandonment of the white workers.

Comrade Karl Reeve appears to have had much the same attitude on the Union's Negro policy as Comrade Johnstone. He particularly took the attitude that the putting into effect of the Union's Negro policy would mean the destruction of the Union. Comrade Reeve must share with Comrade Johnstone the responsibility for the disgraceful retreat before white chauvinism.

Comrade George Pershing was the organizer in charge of the mass meeting at Bessemer City at which a Jim-Crow wire was stretched across the hall to divide the Negroes from the white strikers. Comrade Pershing did not give instructions to put up this wire. His responsibility lies in the fact that he did not discourage and prevent such an insult to the Negro strikers. But this is hardly surprising when we take into account Comrade Pershing's inexperience, plus the confusion in the fraction, plus the wavering of older and more experienced comrades like Reeve and Johnstone.

That there are still large sections of the rank and file that have not yet fully orientated themselves on the Negro decisions of the Communist International, the RILU and the Party was evident even before the Southern retreat occurred to dramatize our weakness on the Negro question. That leading comrades like Johnstone could be so confused was not, however, to be expected.

That there is still a good deal of confusion on this issue on the part of responsible comrades is evidenced even in the treatment of my article in the June *Communist*. My caption for that article "The Negro Question in the Southern Textile Strikes" although correct in the title was made to read in the page heads as "The Negro Problem, etc." And worse yet, an unauthorized and wholly impermissible change was made in a sentence of the article in which the words "the Negro Question in the South" were changed to read "Our Negro Problem in the South."[55]

It should be crystal clear to any Communist who gives this question the serious consideration it deserves that the Communist Party can have no Negro problem, South or North. Our problem is rather a problem of white chauvinism among the working class and in the very ranks of the Communist Party itself.

Communists must be careful not to fall into the error of accepting the capitalist estimation of the Negro as a problem. Even viewing the country as a whole the correct Communist viewpoint would be that there is at worst a race problem, not a Negro problem. And certainly our problem is not what to do with the Negro, but rather how to overcome the capitalist ideology of race separation and racial hatred in order that we may, as the Party equally of the Negro and white workers, achieve complete working-class unity in the furtherance of our struggle for the overthrow of capitalism.

Note

Comrade Otto Hall has sent in the following note of correction in connection with some remarks made by Comrade Briggs in his article in the June issue of the Communist:

> *At the time Comrade Briggs wrote his article I was still in Gastonia and therefore all the facts were not fully available. I did not make the motion to organize the Negro workers into the American Negro Labor Congress. What I did propose was to organize those Negro workers who could not be organized into the National Textile Workers' Union (NTWU) into the Labor Congress, that is those Negro workers who were not working in the textile industry. This is quite a different thing. My mistake was in not making this motion clear enough and in not keeping a copy of it.*

'A NEGRO TUUL ORGANIZER IN THE SOUTH OF THE USA'
GILBERT LEWIS
FROM *THE NEGRO WORKER*
MAY 1, 1930

The bourbon capitalists of the South have been able to maintain their semi-feudal sway over the millions of brutally oppressed and bitterly exploited Negro and white toilers solely because of their ability to keep these workers unorganized and divided. About this the Southern ruling class has no illusions. It knows that these workers and especially the Negro workers, when organized under the militant leadership of the Communist Party and the revolutionary trade unions can be but a battering ram for the smashing of the entire capitalist system, breeder of all forms of economic, social and political inequalities.

Thus they will do all in their power, resort to all forms of terror to keep these workers unorganized. This is shown in the bitter attacks upon the National Textile Workers Union and the Communist Party in Gastonia, the International Labor Defense in Charlotte and Norfolk, the NTWU and Communist Party in Atlanta, the Trade Union Unity League, and especially the Negro organizer of the Trade Union Unity League, in Chattanooga.

I, along with four other workers, two of them white organizers for the TUUL, were arrested on March 5, while holding an open-

---

* Gilbert Lewis, "A Negro T.U.U.L. Organizer in the South of the U.S.A.," *The Negro Worker* 3, no. 7 (May 1, 1930): 9–12.

air meeting. This meeting, the final mobilization of workers for the great March 6 demonstration, was held on the corner where most of the unemployed gather. The police, after a vain attempt to drive the workers from the streets and our meeting, arrested us and charged us with "blocking traffic" and refusing to move on "when ordered to do so by a police officer."

Use of Fascist Methods

From the moment of my arrest until the time of my release fascist methods were employed against me, "lynch him, lynch the black bastard!" cried a group, identified as Ku Kluxers, who gathered around the police when I was seized. Noticing, however, the militancy of the Negro and white workers who had also gathered around in my defense they thought better of the matter.

"You got a helluva nerve," said one big Southern detective, "to get upon these streets to make a speech. Stick up your damn hands before I blackjack you."

In the courtroom little effort was made by the capitalist judge, Martin A. Fleming, to conceal the true class against class issue of the case. I was charged with blocking traffic; the following are the major questions that were asked:

"Do you believe in the Christian religion?'"

"Didn't you get up in a meeting and advise the workers to stay away from church and stop giving money to the preachers?"

"Isn't it true that your organization is trying to smash the American Federation of Labor?"

"Where did you come from?"

"Were you sent here to organize the Negroes?"

"Where did you get that fancy talk from? You didn't learn it in the South."

An open hand for all terror against me even in the courtroom, had been given the bosses' thugs.

"Why in hell don't you stand still before I kick hell out of you!" one big thug said to me as I, becoming tired of the long proceedings, shifted from one foot to the other.

I was given a fine of fifty dollars cash or 112 days on the chain gang. A cowardly lawyer refused to appeal the case and I was led away to a cell.

Southern Lynch Law

Before reaching the cell, however, several things occurred to me. Three detectives took me into a private room, locked the door and made an attempt to change my accent.

"You're a fresh Nigger," one of them said. "I am going to change that fancy talk of yours and make you talk like a real Chattanooga Nigger," and with this he landed a blow on my jaw. Another came to his aid and the two of them rained blows upon my head and face.

After convincing themselves that my speech could not be changed from that of a militant TUUL organizer to that of a cringing, Uncle Tom type of Negro, with his "Yessir" and "Nosir" and abject servility, they turned me over to another, who weighed and fingerprinted me.

Five o'clock in the afternoon, no lawyer having been found who would take the case, I was taken from the city jail to the workhouse. On entering the workhouse the driver of the patrol said to the guard, (pointing to me): "Here is a fellow who swears he can't be made to work, but wants to overthrow the government and believes in social equality for Niggers. (In the South social equality means only one thing—intermarriage). I guess you know what to do with him."

In the workhouse a steel ring 3.5 inches in diameter was riveted on each of my legs. These were joined together by a steel chain 14 inches long, the chains are placed on your legs on entering the prison and are not removed until the day you leave.

The next morning along with 44 other prisoners, I was taken out to a large slag (rock pile) and set to work digging rock with a sixteen-pound rough-handled pick. My hands began to grow blisters. One of them burst and the blood shot out. I paused for a moment to wipe it away.

"Go on there, you," shouted the burly guard. "A little blood of your own will do you Reds good."

A little later, while attempting to drive the pick through a three-foot mass of solid rock, I became exhausted and stopped to blow. The guard yelled at me to keep going, stating that Reds would find no picnic on the chain gang as long as he was around. He stood over me, gun in hand, the whole time I was there, watching my every move. About eleven-thirty, workers and sympathizers came forward and paid my fine. The guard showed his disappointment in being cheated of the chance to work a "Red" to death or shoot him should he offer the least resistance.

These bitter attacks upon the revolutionary organizations of the workers by the bosses is being met with increasing resistance from the workers. On the very day that I was being sentenced to one hundred and twelve days on the chain gang for organizing the workers to struggle for work or wages, workers throughout the world were demonstrating millions strong against starvation. Right in Chattanooga, though all the leaders were in jail, rank and file workers of the Unemployed Council held a mass meeting and would have marched on City Hall but for a fierce rain storm that made it impossible. The attacks of the bosses are bearing fruit but not the kind of fruit counted upon by these bosses.

 # 'A SOUTHERN TEXTILE WORKER: LETTER TO THE FIFTH CONGRESS OF THE RED INTERNATIONAL OF LABOR UNIONS'
FROM *THE NEGRO WORKER*
NOVEMBER 1, 1930

Comrades, I bring to you greetings to the Fifth Congress of the Red International of Labor Unions (RILU) in the name of the seven Gastonian prisoners, in the name of thousands of exploited workers in the South.

You hear of the prosperity that we have in America. That is all right for the capitalists. The prosperity for the workers is 12 long hours of hard slavery in the textile and steel mills. We work from 10 to 12 hours a day. But, comrades, we, the workers of the South, are awakening to the fact that the way to fight the capitalists—we have woke up that the only way to fight the capitalists is with the RILU. Our answer of the working class in the South you can see today will be in the wind-up. The workers in the South will answer the capitalists with the sword of the RILU.

In the South children go to work at the age of 9 to 12 years old. I went to work 12 long hours in the mill when I was 12 and have been working for 14 years in a textile plant.

---

* "A Southern Textile Worker: Letter to Fifth Congress of the Red International of Labor Unions," *The Negro Worker*, November 1, 1930, 25.

These workers, the white workers, have always been told to hate the colored workers, but the Black and white workers are putting their shoulders to the wheel in solidarity to fight together to win better conditions for their living. The workers have learned that it is not a race question but a bread-and-butter question. They have learned very well to fight. Now the workers in many plants of the Southern States are meeting in solidarity and demanding unemployment relief. Before if the white workers had been told to sit in a hall with colored workers they would have thought they would have been discredited for life. The reason the bosses divided the workers was so that they would not come together to fight capitalists.

Us, workers in the South, appreciate what the national Textile Workers' Union woke us up to and educated the South and learned us to fight. Before we had organizations of the American Federation of Labor which refused to organize the colored and low-paid workers, but with the NTWU entering the South we found the only way to better conditions was organizations of all the workers.

Note

This comrade is a Southern-born white worker. He has been employed since his childhood days in the sweat-mills of North Carolina for the paltry sum of $15 per week.

When the National Textile Workers' Union, a left-wing organization affiliated to the Trade Union Unity League entered the South in 1929 and began to organize the black and white textile workers together, our comrade was one of the first white workers to join the union. He took an active part in all of the struggles of the workers, and was arrested during the Gastonia strike and charged with the "crime" of organizing Negroes into the same union with the whites. For this the comrade along with six others has been sentenced to twenty years in jail. The Social-Fascist leaders of the American Federation of Labor actively aided the textile barons in railroading these militants to the dungeons of capitalism.

Despite all the attempts of the capitalists and their agenda—the American Federation of Labor bureaucrats and the socialists—to crush the spirit of the workers, the struggle continued to spread throughout the South arising thousands and thousands of black and white workers to organize and fight for better conditions.

'ALABAMA MASSACRE'
EUGENE GORDON
FROM *NEW MASSES*
JULY 1931

A few months ago a small group of Negro sharecroppers and farm hands of Alabama, driven to desperation by hunger and the sense of the futility of appealing to Southern ruling class "justice," met and discussed means of organizing. Most of these men were illiterate. They met without any definite idea as to precisely what form their purposed organization would take. They were woefully ignorant of the stencils and the catchphrases of the intellectual economist. They knew only that they were starving; that their families were indentured slaves at the mercy of the ruling class whites of that community; that there was no efficacy in prayers to an all-wise and all-white god; that if they did not move to fight against the terrors of their new slavery they would be exterminated. But they met and they talked among themselves. They decided in their meeting, and in subsequent meetings, that they must be the nucleus of a permanent organization, the purpose of which would be to fight for the relief of the present-day slaves of the South. Out of that small beginning there grew an organization of from 700 to 800 black sharecroppers and farm workers.

Hearing of their revolutionary efforts to organize, the Southern branch of the League of Struggle for Negro Rights (LSNR) consulted with them and offered them such assistance as they seemed to need.

---

* Eugene Gordon, "Alabama Massacre," *New Masses*, August 1931, Marxists Internet Archive.

One of the startling facts revealed to the LSNR was that some of these black backwoodsmen had regularly been reading the *Southern Worker*, and, reading it, had experienced a flaring up of their smoldering revolutionary fires. Since most of the men could not read, it is evident that their knowledge of what the *Southern Worker* said came from discussions with those who could read a little. Many of the older men doubtless saw in this experience a revival of the rebel spirit of sixty-five and seventy years ago, when an occasional rebel who had been taught to read at the "big house" shared his precious knowledge with the ignorant men and women of the fields; ignorant men and women who were nevertheless wise enough to know that they would be mercilessly beaten if their masters or the overseer caught them looking at any kind of printed matter.

The more literate among the Camp Hill sharecroppers and farm hands read the revolutionary messages from the *Southern Worker*, and a sense of the degradation that had been forced upon them by the greedy and heartless landowners flared into their consciousness. But what is more important than that, they realized that sporadic and individual assaults upon their oppressors would bring them nothing but defeat and death. It was not their intention to organize guerrilla bands to harass the wealthy land-owner-oppressor by ambuscade attacks; it was their purpose only to organize so that the force of their demands for "justice" would have the keener effect. They were astute enough to know that the South has never respected anything but organized force.

They had not been meeting very long before the landowners learned of the organization. That is to say, the landowners learned that the Negroes were coming together regularly and that all these meetings were not designed to the glory of God and the white bosses. Some of the meetings were held in the church; some of them, in order that suspicion might be diverted, were held at the houses of members of the organization. By this time the organization had been officially named the Sharecroppers Union, and it is here that the League of Struggle for Negro Rights further assisted. The white landowners, now thoroughly frightened at these mysterious goings on of the black peasantry, assumed that plans were being laid to attack them.

On Wednesday night, July 15, about 150 of the 800 or so members of the Negroes organization met to formulate the demands they had been discussing. The landowners must have been on the lookout, for the meeting was no sooner under way than a number of them appeared, accompanied by the chief of police and scores of landowners sworn in temporarily as "deputies." On the outside of the meeting house, located in a lonely and isolated spot, Ralph Gray, one of the active organizers of the Sharecroppers Union, stood on guard. He was one of the two armed Negroes. The Sheriff's party fired wounding Gray. They invaded the meeting, and were momentarily halted by the revolver of the chairman. Outnumbered by armed and murderous landowners backed by southern "justice," the sharecroppers strategically gave way. Some of them rescued the wounded man in the dark. They called in a physician to attend his wounds, and the physician tattled to the mob. As a consequence a larger force of "deputies," led by the gallant sheriff, set out a night or two later to finish Gray, whom they looked upon as the leader. But the sharecroppers had been reading the *Southern Worker* and so knew something about organized resistance to capitalist thug attack. They were expecting a counter attack and were prepared. Displayed about the house in the woods, they lay waiting. When the sheriff's gang of two hundred or more approached the house, it began immediately to fire. It fired round after round into the shack where the wounded man lay. It was surprised by an answering fire from the woods. The leader of the gang, Sheriff J. Kyle Young, was (according to the *Birmingham News*) "critically wounded," and one of his deputies was "slightly wounded." The *News* makes no mention of the others in the gang who were wounded. Several of the sharecroppers were wounded and four were accounted "missing" after the fight. Gray was finally killed and his wife's skull fractured by members of the gang.

Perhaps no better summing up could be made than that which was written by a correspondent for the International Labor Defense (ILD), which immediately assumed defense of the 32 sharecroppers who were locked up. The ILD statement says: "The sharecroppers union has been in process of organization during the past few months against miserable starvation wages. The plantation owners planned to cut off the sharecroppers from all food advances, giving a small number the alternative of working in the fields or sawmills at wages of sixty to ninety cents a day. The organized lynchers were after the members and leaders of the union. The sharecropper's demands as formulated up to the time of the massacre were: (1) Food advances to continue until settlement time; (2) Settlement to be made in full by cash payment; (3) The sharecroppers to have the right to sell their crops where they saw fit; (4) To have the right of a garden for their home use; (5) A three-hour midday rest."

These miserable crumbs are what the black farm workers were planning to ask for; these miserable crumbs were what some of them died for.

The white sharecroppers of that section are secretly with the Negroes; their confusion of mind prevents their being actively with them. But they have been awakened. The blacks have shown them how to die like free men. They themselves being less than free.

EXCERPT FROM *LET ME LIVE*
ANGELO HERNDON

CHAPTER FIFTEEN

For weeks I walked about with my head swathed in bandages—my wounds were deep and they caused me excruciating pain. The police-lynchers had done a good job on me. Upon the order of my doctor I was forced into a long period of idleness. I almost made myself ill with impatience; so much important work still had to be done and there was I twiddling my thumbs behind the lines, so to speak. The feeling of relief which I experienced when I finally resumed my assignments as organizer for the Unemployment Council among Negro and white workers in Atlanta cannot adequately be described. I am of an active nature and have always led a busy life. Next to the fear of hanging, a state of prolonged idleness affords me the greatest pain.

2

The acute unemployment situation in the South in 1932 created the acid soil in which the "American Fascisti Order of the Black Shirts" blossomed out in all its exotic rankness. The "American Fascisti" grew luxuriantly in Tennessee, Alabama and Georgia. To Atlanta's eternal shame may it be recorded that it was one of the principal centers in the country for these whites. Fully twenty-one thousand white jobless joined the Order there. What made their joining so pathetic, beyond even the possibility of being regarded as contemptible, was the motive

---

*   Angelo Herndon, *Let Me Live* (Ann Arbor: University of Michigan Press, 2007).

behind it. The cheap Fascist demagogues had seduced them into the organization with the tempting assurance that they would be given jobs once they became members. The human scavengers fattened upon the misery and despair of these men who moved heaven and earth to scrape together the large initiation fee and membership dues. The leaders even opened a plant where they manufactured the black shirts which their followers were obliged to buy from them at an exorbitant price.

The Fascist racketeers were no fools. They understood the psychology of their starving victims. Their appeal to them was irresistible. It went something like this:

> Run the niggers back to the country where they came from—Africa! They steal the jobs away from us white men because they work for lower wages. Our motto is therefore: America for Americans! And Americans don't mean niggers either! Old Glory waves over our white man's country and no real white man will work for nigger wages.

The Fascists drew to them two kinds of followers. There were the common hoodlums and social outcasts who found a profitable outlet in the Order for their criminal activities. There were also misguided white workers, the so-called poor white trash, the rejected, the poverty stricken, who in their bitterness and unreflective rebellion, fell into the maw of the Fascist monster. To these my heart went out, for they were workers like myself and had suffered so bitterly at the hands of our common exploiters.

For months the Fascists terrorized the Negro population of Atlanta. Instance upon instance of mob violence against Negro workers who had jobs mounted swiftly into an orgy of hysteria. The whole Negro population of the city lived in constant fear of their lives. The Hooded night riders now had an excellent opportunity to carry on their imbecilic mummery. They were "Knights" in regalia; they rode smartly on horseback and could delight themselves in delusions of grandeur. Like ghouls in a nightmare, they clattered through the streets in the dark, terrifying the Negro population with threats against life and limb and making babies cry with their blood-curdling yells.

Like the traditional knights of old, they too displayed matchless chivalry. They would swoop down on factories, railroad yards and hotels, and drag out all the Negro workers into the streets. Then the fun would begin. Bravely masked so that no one could recognize them, the "Knights" carried on their reign of terror over the whimpering Negro men and women.

One thing all lynch acts have in common: their unmentionable sexual degeneracy. It is indeed significant to note that every flogging, every beating and every lynching has as its point of emphasis the defilement or the mutilation of the sex organs of the victim! . . .

While the Fascists were carrying on their campaign of terror, the Unemployment Council and the Communist Party did not remain idle. They arranged educational meetings and issued leaflets by the thousands, warning the white workers of Atlanta that "they were being taken for a ride" by men who had no conscience, by common gangsters. Patiently they explained that the Negro workers were not the enemies of white workers, but that, on the contrary, both were being exploited, starved, and abandoned by the same white oppressors. Because of our efforts at enlightenment, hundreds of workers were spared the degrading experience of becoming members of lynch mobs.

Things finally turned out as we Communists had warned, and our ranks became swollen with the disillusioned "Knights."

3

One of the most stirring experiences I had during my stay in Atlanta was my friendship with Jim, a white carpenter who at one time had been a member of the Black Shirts.[56] I met him in a very original way. That should not be any cause for surprise, for everything Jim did was done in an original way. He was honest and blunt and he had a happy knack of saying the right thing at the wrong time. Needless to say, he livened things up a bit.

One day, as I was paying a visit to the Post Office, I heard myself addressed in the following words:

"Say, buddy, can you give a fellow the price of a cup of coffee?"

I looked up and saw a timid little man. He was as lean as a bean pole. His face was emaciated; his skin was wrinkled like a dried apple. I noticed with surprise that he wore the black shirt of the Fascist Order.

Misinterpreting my look of surprise as meaning that I did not believe that he was actually in need, he turned upon me his sad eyes, tearing with hunger, and in a tremulous voice said:

"Believe me, buddy, I'm hungry. I haven't eaten in days and my stomach feels like a lead pipe."

I, who knew so well what hunger and despair meant, would be the last person on earth to trifle with anyone down on his luck. But I felt that merely to fill this man's empty belly would not be enough. I wished to do something constructive for him and therefore I wanted first to understand him clearly. So I said to him without too much friendliness:

"I don't understand you. You can see that I am a Negro and I can also see that you're wearing a black shirt. Your kind hates and tortures my kind. What do you want of me?"

He was visibly taken aback and at a loss to answer. He finally muttered:

"I know. You're right, buddy—and yet, you're all wrong. You can see how it is: If I'm wearing a black shirt, it's because it's the only shirt I've got. If you got a white shirt to spare, buddy, I'll be just as glad to wear it as this black one!"

It was now my turn to become embarrassed, and as I slipped him some money, he muttered hurriedly something about Fascists:

"They not only picked my pockets clean, but they stole my pants as well."

And he cursed out loud with a fervor that I respected and understood.

Before leaving me he told me that he had a large family, and what was one to do with a large family when one could not feed it? He said almost in a wail: "No job—no money—no future—no nothing! Hell and damnation!"

A few days later I saw Jim again. He looked just as miserable and hungry as when I saw him last. He told me that he was still out of a job. I again offered him some money for food. But this time he refused point blank. His face had actually turned scarlet. I was upset by his display of pride, for I well understood its origin. There is no pride so saddening as that of a starving worker.

To ease the embarrassment for both of us, I quickly changed the subject. I tried to do a little bit of missionary work on him. I told him all about the Unemployment Council and tried to prove to him how it was to his best interests that he become a member. He listened in grave silence and nodded his head in agreement. But it struck me that his agreement was not altogether wholehearted. He was accepting it with mental reservations. I sensed that there was something wrong somewhere. So I went exploring.

"What's the matter, Jim?" I asked. "What's troubling you, what's holding you back?"

Was it necessary for me to ask the question? I guessed the answer the minute I noticed his secret embarrassment.

But Jim was hardly the kind of man to leave a direct question unanswered. He said in his blunt and smiling way:

"See here, buddy, I think you're a swell fellow, even though you're a 'nigra.' So don't get me wrong when I say that God never intended white folks and 'nigras' to mix together and organize into one union and what the devil else you may think of."

I saw that arguing about God's racial intentions would do neither Jim nor me any good. So I left the divine plan of things behind us and turned to a subject that in my experience always struck a sympathetic chord in every worker I ever spoke to. I said:

"Please tell me, Jim, when you had a job as a carpenter, did you get as much pay as a carpenter would in the North for the same kind and quality of work?"

"No."

"Did you ever try to figure out why?"

"No."

"Well, I'll tell you why. It's because the bosses have got us all split up down here. The Northern workers are not a bit better than we are and yet they get higher wages. And why is that? Because, Jim, they are united. They fight together. But we Southern workers are dumbbells. We remain divided. It does us no good, but it delights our bosses. It's easier to keep us down that way. Take, for instance, a strike down South. When the whites down tools, the bosses call in the Negroes to scab. When the Negroes strike the bosses call in the whites to scab. What are we doing? We are only cutting off each other's nose to spite each other's face. If you think there's sense in that you're a smarter man than I am.

"Did you ever try to figure out why the unions in the South are so weak? It's because the whites refuse to belong in the same union with Negroes. On the other hand, the Negroes don't trust the whites. Do you blame them? We are deprived of the most elementary human rights down in these parts. If we try to organize we are beaten up and thrown into jail on framed charges. If we hold our meetings, it is in secret and at the risk of our very lives. We Southern workers, both black and white, are like a house that is divided against itself; we are like an army marching out to engage the enemy, but on our way we get to fighting among ourselves and altogether forget the enemy. When we fight each other we grow weaker, and as we grow weaker, our enemy, the bosses, grows stronger. If you see any logic in continuing this condition, you're welcome to it."

I noticed that Jim was listening admiringly to my eloquence.

"You're damn smart for a 'nigra,' Angelo," he said to me.

I ignored the flattery and continued:

"I am not trying to show you that I am smart, Jim. I am talking to you seriously. Take this relief, now. The government authorities are passing the buck all the time. The Commissioners keep on telling you white folks that they cannot give any more relief than you are getting because they have to feed so many Negroes. Then they turn around and tell the Negroes that the grand old USA is a white man's country and that whites come first on relief. Hail Columbia! Now what is the upshot of all this? Both whites and Negroes feel they have a just cause to hate each other, and so while they are busy fighting each other, the government and the big bosses get away with the loot which they divert from relief. Now suppose all of us suckers, whether white unemployed or Negro unemployed, went down to the Commissioners and talked turkey to them:

"'Look here, we are all starving. You have been making both ends of us fight against our middle: our stomachs. Now we have seen through your bluff and have decided to organize together into one big, powerful union. You cannot put us off now with lies and racial hatred with which you think you can cover up your real, shameful plot against the masses of the people. We'll make you listen to our demands!'

"Jim, don't you see how foolish it is to go into the fight with half an army when we could have a whole one? Don't you see that our bosses are bribing you into a state of helplessness with their wretched flattery, tricking you to believe that you are a big shot, a member of a superior race, a white man! How long can you continue being drunk on this poppycock? You wish to march to battle strong, but how can you march if one of your two good feet, the foot that represents the Negro workers, is chained to the ground?"

Jim looked flabbergasted. All he could say was:

"Funny, I never saw it that way! Well, you've given me food for thought. I'll go home and think it over and if I come to see things your way, I'll come back and look you up."

I was therefore not at all surprised when one week later Jim approached me on the street. Externally I noticed that he had gone through an astonishing transformation. The timid, haunted look was no longer there. His feet no longer dragged. A curious nervous energy marked his movements. Why, he even smiled in a weak, apologetic way, an expression of jollity that he was not at all used to. I sensed something unusual was coming, so I stopped short and waited for him to open the conversation. He did not disappoint me. He went straight to the attack with the following words:

"*Mister* Herndon, I am calling a meeting for the unemployed in my house. If you care to come, I'll be very glad to see you."

When I heard the word "Mister," and noted the emphasis he placed on it, I understood fully what had happened inside of him. I was very happy for his sake because I knew that at last he was cured of that racial dry rot. I clasped his hand and shook it warmly and assured him that nothing would give me more pleasure than to come to his meeting.

When I came to the meeting I was pleasantly surprised to see that Jim had brought two other Negroes. It happens occasionally that when a decent white man finds a Negro whose manners and address are pleasing to him, he condescends to make an exception in his case and to treat him as an equal. Such a Negro usually is honored in the private conversations of white men with the inelegant description of "white nigger," something which in itself shows a deep racial prejudice. I must confess that I was ungenerous for a moment in believing that Jim had made an exception of me because he liked me personally. But when I saw the other two Negroes at the meeting, workers who certainly possessed no social graces of any kind to flatter a white man's interest, I recognized with pleasure that Jim was fully grown into a civilized man.

4

There was nothing unique in my experience with Jim. If I have taken the trouble to tell of the manner of his transformation from a Fascist to a class-conscious worker, it is only because he represents in type and experience a large mass of white American workers. During my stay in Atlanta as organizer for the Unemployment Council, I had many similar experiences with other white Jims. And I am somewhat vainglorious at the success I had in drawing them as active workers into the Council.

My friend Jim tried to make up for lost time. He was busy as a bee helping in the preparations for an open-air meeting of the Council. The meeting took place in a vacant lot where the neighborhood scalawags played their baseball games. More than three hundred Negro and white workers attended.

Before the meeting adjourned, a committee was elected to investigate the cases of those families which had been denied aid by the county and Federal relief agencies. There were thousands of such cases. It was a gigantic task that we set ourselves. And as men whom bitter experience had taught to look at things soberly and realistically, we did not try to minimize the enormous difficulties we would have face. Systematically and calmly we went about building Unemployment Council Committees, block by block, street by street and section by section. We held dozens of public meetings. Frequently all of us went without dinner to pay for the leaflets and other essential expenses. It is a miracle how with no visible funds at our command we would carry on such a lively and successful campaign. "Moscow gold!" charged our enemies. We who tightened our belts and made personal sacrifices of the most fantastic nature only smiled.

Why hide the fact? The officials of the county and Federal relief agencies did not like us a bit. We did nothing but embarrass them at every turn. And their tender governmental sensibilities could not endure the strain of our rough tactics. We harassed them at every opportunity and brazenly learned how to reject "no" for an answer. We had a partiality for the word "yes." And the authorities preferred the word "no." So we were deadlocked practically all the time.

Particularly offensive to the relief authorities was our handling of the Brandon case. We pressed the matter very vigorously and made ourselves a nuisance morning, noon and night. Mr. Brandon's story was as pathetic as any I've ever heard. It aroused wide sympathy among all those sufficiently human to be capable of sympathy.

Mr. Brandon was an elderly, sedate white worker who had given the best years of his life to increase the profits of the textile and railroad companies in Atlanta. He was always a model citizen. He never questioned the why and wherefore of things, minded his own business, went to church regularly, contributed to the Red Cross and the Community Chest and was a member in good standing of the Democratic Party. Mr. Brandon was not like many other workers who spent their pay before they even earned it on getting drunk on Saturday night and in card playing. He was scrupulously sober and respectable. Concern over his wife and his seven children, whom he dearly loved, made him a hard worker and a thrifty saver. Penny by penny he put his money by until he had several hundred dollars tucked safely away against a "rainy day."

That "rainy day" finally arrived. But it did not come the way he had expected. The bank in which he kept his hard-earned savings closed down. He now found himself old and decrepit, with no possibility of obtaining a job, for millions of other men, younger and stronger than he, were obliged to go without work. Unable to pay his rent, his landlord finally threw his few sticks of furniture out into the street. He had no friends and he was too proud to ask for charity. So he and his family dragged their belongings on a borrowed wheelbarrow into the woods just outside of the city. When members of the Unemployment Council found him he was living in a hole which he and his children had dug in the side of a hill. He had covered the inside with boards and got his water from a rain barrel.

I volunteered to go with a delegation of Negro and white workers to intercede for him. The dispensers of public charity received us with hostility. The supervisor said to me:

"What are you butting in for? Are you related to Mr. Brandon?"

"Certainly!" I answered with conviction. "He's my class brother."

Jim now lost his temper. He spoke with bitterness:

"It's all right for you, mister, to be so high and mighty. Your belly is full. You have a fat job, for which we citizens pay. But not everybody is as fortunate as you. Hungry people have as much right to live as you who live off the fat of the land. One would think that a man like Mr. Brandon, who has lived a useful life, would now in his old age be treated with some concern by you whose job it is to look after him. Just go and take a look at the way he lives—like an animal in a hole in the ground, only unlike an animal he can no longer fight to keep alive. He's too old and tired and sick."

The face of the supervisor became flushed with anger. In a loud voice, feeling secure because of the presence of squad of hastily summoned policemen, he said:

"I'm not interested to listen to your speeches, Mister Bolshevik. We are perfectly capable of taking care of the business of this office without your assistance. You better mind your own business and don't come nosing in on other people's affairs."

All the while he spoke, excitable Jim was vainly trying to calm himself. I could see that the thing nearest his heart at the moment was the desire to punch the supervisor in the nose, I understood his feelings. But I pulled at Jim's sleeve.

"Let me answer him," I whispered.

And addressing the relief official, I said in a determined voice:

"You say it's none of our business. Well, whether you like it or not, it is our business. No human being is going to die like a dog while we are around, just because heartless officials like you handle the people's funds. Rest assured, mister, this matter is so much our business that if you will refuse to help Mr. Brandon immediately, we promise you on our word as workers and citizens that, within one hour's time, we'll hold a demonstration in front of the Governor's mansion and we'll plaster your name on every placard we can get."

My words had the desired effect. I saw that the supervisor had broken into a cold sweat. The prospect of being so flatteringly advertised by us before the whole city did not appeal to him very much. In fact, the thought of it made him a changed man. It was quite astonishing. From a snarling, contemptuous bully, he now had turned into a polite, sugary gentleman. He offered us cigarettes. . . .

"Calm yourselves, calm yourselves, boys, I am afraid you have misunderstood me! Please be reasonable! Please try to understand my position. Is it my fault that Washington doesn't send me any money? Complain to them and not to me. They've got the power. I haven't. Believe me, my heart bleeds for all the poor unfortunates in the city. But what am I to do? I am not a mint."

Excerpt from *Let Me Live*

We could clearly see that he was stalling and trying to pass the buck. We were determined not to let him get away with it. And so I said to him:

"We don't care where you get the money from. My fellow workers here on the delegation are agreed that if you don't immediately come to the aid of Mr. Brandon, we'll demonstrate before the Governor's mansion."

"All right, all right," muttered the relief supervisor wearily. "You win."

In our presence he called in a relief investigator and ordered her to move Mr. Brandon and his family into a house and to supply them with food regularly.

Our delegation left the supervisor's office in high spirits. Jim seemed overawed by our extraordinary success. He said to me in the incredulous voice of a man who had just witnessed a miracle:

"Do you know what, Angelo, nothing succeeds like success."

"You mean nothing succeeds like organization," I answered.

5

When the news of the Brandon victory circulated through the city, hundreds of letters from workers poured into the office of the Unemployment Council, requesting information on how to organize block committees. About a month later, another incident occurred which further added to the prestige of the Council.

On a certain day a Negro worker and his family were evicted from their home. As they had no place to go, they sat down on their household goods and abandoned themselves to their grief. Suddenly a car drove up and stopped near by. A drunken white man and woman got out and began tinkering with the motor. They fumed and cursed and despite all their efforts could not get the car started. The evicted Negro worker, who was an obliging fellow, volunteered his help. As he busied himself over the motor, the white owner of the car continued his cursing out loud. At that moment two police officers passed by, and, hearing the blasphemy, stopped and arrested the Negro worker for using "abusive language in the presence of a white woman."

The Negro worker protested his innocence. The white man kept chivalrous silence and his drunken woman companion complained out loud about those "filthy-mouthed niggers." Obviously, she wished to protect her male companion.

After the police had mauled up the poor Negro worker, they locked him up in jail. Later they came back and performed a similar service for his wife. They beat her up black and blue and also locked her up. The two were later found guilty of using blasphemous language, and as they could not pay their fine of twenty dollars, they received a twenty-day sentence.

When I told Jim about the incident, he grew hot under the collar. Righteous indignation turned the former lamb into a roaring lion. He looked ready to storm the city hall single-handed. But I calmed him down and assured him that an organized effort would be more effective than any individual act. So Jim immediately went to work and formed a shock brigade of volunteer movers to carry the furniture of the evicted Negro worker back into his house. As they were doing this, the landlord came by. He was threatening and overbearing and promised the committee on his honor as a white gentleman that he would see them, the "poor, white trash" and the "dirty niggers" hang by the neck by the time he got through with them.

He proceeded to padlock the house. And as he began to walk away, he turned without warning on Jim and, throwing all of his heavy weight into his arm, punched him in the jaw, felling him to the ground. For a man of Jim's spindly architecture, the drubbing he gave the landlord after he got to his feet again was truly astonishing. The landlord had to be treated by a doctor on the spot after the skirmish.

When later I saw Jim, I congratulated him heartily upon his victory.

"Oh, that was nawthing," he drawled modestly. "It wasn't my strength, but the anger in me that knocked that blankety blank landlord cold."

6

That same day Jim headed a delegation of white workers to the mayor of Atlanta. But His Honor refused to be seen. Instead, his secretary preached them a sermon on the dignity of the white race.

"You ought to be ashamed of yourselves," she rebuked them sternly. (So Jim reported to me later.) "How can you be interested in niggers and call yourselves white men and women?"

Jim who was the spokesman for the delegation answered her:

"Now, when you want to flatter us you call us white men, but behind our backs, what do you call us? 'Poor white trash,' no? Well, we poor white trash have learned that being white does not make us any different from the Negro worker. We are no more the dumbbells that we were. We have learned our lesson from bitter experience. Today we are organizing Negro and white workers, and although you may not like our company, you and the mayor are going to see a lot of us from now on."

A few days later Jim came to me with a beaming face and told me breathlessly that by the mayor's order, the two framed Negro workers had been released from jail.

"Nothing succeeds like success, does it, Jim?" I asked, banteringly. Jim thumbed his nose at me, playfully.

"You mean nothing succeeds like organization!"

7

About this time the World War veterans were preparing for their historic Bonus Expeditionary Force (BEF) march on Washington. Kenneth Murrel, a notorious Red-baiter, who was Commander of the Atlanta American Legion, took charge of the local contingent. He issued an order that no veterans belonging to the "Communistic Unemployment Council" would be allowed to march to the capital. However, the veterans in our organization were no mollycoddles. They appealed to the rank and file of the American Legion not to fall into the hysteria of Red-baiting that their Commander was whipping up.

The Atlanta BEF called a meeting at the state capital one night. The Negro-hating Murrel saw to it that no Negro veterans were invited. As he could not possibly overlook the Negro veterans, he and other officials of the Legion had called for a special Negro veterans' meeting the following Sunday.

That Sunday night I was one of the most interested spectators at the Negro meeting. Kenneth Murrel presided. He gave us the typical demagogic applesauce about how much concern he had for the Negro veteran. As the first speaker, he introduced a certain suave gentleman without mentioning his name, but referring to him merely as "a member of the State Legislature." This "statesman" immediately launched into a tirade against Communistic and subversive elements that were trying to stir up trouble among the classes with the avowed aim of overthrowing the United States government. He warned the assembled veterans that they must not allow the paid agents of Moscow to talk them into seditious acts against their government.

I noticed with gratification that the audience remained silent and hostile to these warnings. There was something unpleasant and slimy about the "legislator's" heart-warming concern "for the law-abiding poor Negroes."

It would have taken very little encouragement for the audience to have given him the classic razzberry.

After he had ended speaking, I went up to him and, with an ingenuous air, said:

"You're right, Mr. Speaker, about those Communists. They are just a bunch of foreigners who want to set up their Soviet dictatorship here. But as long as there are men like you, that will never happen."

He beamed at me benignly and said:

"You've said a mouthful, boy. The Jew Reds have been trying to cause us trouble down here by stirring up members of your race against white people all on account of that damn Scottsboro rape. Now, look here, you're an intelligent boy, admit that those nine niggers raped them white girls. Do you think they would have been arrested for nothing, now do you?"

"Right you are, mister," I agreed hypocritically. "By the way, I did not catch your name when the chairman introduced you. Won't you be so good as to tell it to me so that I can tell other Negroes about the inspiring speech you made here tonight?"

The speaker was touched.

"Sure, sure, you bet I will. My name is James Barksdale."

"Thank you, Mr. Barksdale."

I made a careful investigation the following day and discovered, not to my surprise, that the benign Mr. Barksdale, who loved the Negro people so touchingly, was no "member of the State Legislature." What he really was—I laugh with amusement when I think of it—a Kleagle of the KKK!

8

The following day the Communist Party of Atlanta issued ten thousand leaflets bearing the title: "Who are the Reds and what do they stand for?" Needless to say, this leaflet was an exposé of the "legislator" Barksdale. We distributed these leaflets to the War veterans. They succeeded in tearing the blinders from the eyes of many. The best gauge of their success was the intensive campaign which the

Atlanta Georgian, the Hearst yellow sheet, and other local newspapers, suddenly unleashed against the Communists. They quoted from the leaflet very freely, in fact so freely, that there was not a word of similarity between their quotations and our own original statements. This did not surprise us. The most degraded journalistic prostitute of the world was capable of the most revolting perversions of truth that it was possible to imagine.

The *Atlanta Georgian* was not the kind of newspaper to do things by halves. Before long the effects of its howling the Red scare from the rooftops got the police all warmed up. They began to stir up muddy waters in order that they might be able to fish. They went in search of all those suspected of Red activity. And Red activity to the police meant anything from reading the Declaration of Independence in public to eating candy manufactured in the Soviet Union. The latter statement might appear ridiculous to the reader, but a certain lady of unimpeachable patriotism once confided to me in a dread whisper that she believed her neighbor, Mrs. X, must be one of those Communist Reds because when she visited her she was offered some taffy wrapped in little red papers on hers were printed the words "Made in the USSR" What made the story amusing to me was the fact that I knew Mrs. X was a Seventh-Day Adventist and she just happened to like Russian taffy.

Here at this point, I am very unhappy to say, is the proper place to assure the reader that if ever there was a man who innocently got into trouble with the police as frequently and as easily as I, I have still to meet him. Fortunately, I am not superstitious and so I cannot regard my almost daily habit of getting arrested as the fulfillment of some predestined course.

What should happen at this time but that I blunder into an accident. I was riding with a Jewish grocer in a car which the Unemployment Council had hired to trail the Atlanta contingent of the BEF on its way to Washington. As we were crossing a certain square, an impatient motorist who tried to beat the traffic lights beat into our car instead and shattered his windshield. When our automobilist Paul Revere caught sight of the Jewish grocer, he thought it would be a fine opportunity to collect some easy money. Despite the fact that it was he who caused the accident, he decided to frame us. Perhaps it was because he had friends in the police department. As for the police, they were not too particular when it came to pinning down manufactured evidence against a "Jew" and a "nigger."

However, when the police discovered that the "nigger" was Angelo Herndon, they sent scurrying all their trained bloodhounds to apprehend me. I got wind of it in time and made myself scarce. It may sound laughable, but I was obliged to hide for more than two months on account of this absurd incident.

My education with regard to capitalist justice was already well on in its post-graduate state. Knowing the temper of the police and the judges and their special attitude toward me, I had not the slightest doubt that they were capable of presenting against me a case of a serious nature.

Unable to lay their hands on me, the police began to imitate the tactics of the Spanish Inquisition. They arrested a Negro worker who was a very dear friend of mine. Once in every twenty-four hours they took him out of his cell for "examination." The examining officer was a rubber hose.

"Talk, nigger—you know damn well where Angelo Herndon is."

My friend would rather die than tell them. So each time they questioned him they beat him to unrecognizability.

I was very much shaken when I heard how my friend was being tortured. My feeling of distress was so keen that I fell ill. The need of rescuing him from the danger in which he found himself forced me out of my despair. I began to use my wits and fell upon a stratagem. After all, wasn't I almost a detective once? I went into a telephone booth in a corner drug store and called the police station. I asked for the chief. The voice on the other end of the wire told me that he was sorry that the chief was not in, but perhaps he could help me. To this I replied with all the vocal authority I could muster:

"Maybe you can, captain. Now listen carefully, and get it straight. I am the superintendent of the Atlanta Plow Works. I understand you've locked up a nigger of mine by the name of Felton Wimbley."

"Yes, sir, boss, we have."

"Well, captain, he's my nigger and a good one too. Let me warn you that I am not going to stand for any monkey business. If you don't let him out of the coop by six o'clock this evening, I am coming down to the police station and give you wise guys all the hell you want."

My words had an astonishing effect upon the police official. He sounded all maple syrup.

"Yes sir, boss, we are terribly sorry to have given you trouble. I'll see what I can do about it right away."

"All right, don't forget," I muttered angrily into the receiver and hung up.

That evening I went to the house where my friend Felton lived. What was my astonishment to see him sitting at the dinner table shoveling food down with great scoops. Poor boy, they had starved him all the time he was in jail. My joy upon seeing him and my pride over the success of my "white man's" trick vanished when I looked at his bruised and swollen face and body. The savages had almost killed him!

CHAPTER SIXTEEN

The presidential campaign of 1932 was just getting under way. The Communist Party had chosen William Z. Foster and James W. Ford as its national standard bearers. That summer we were kept feverishly busy in Atlanta setting up numerous Foster and Ford for President Clubs in both Negro and white neighborhoods. I suppose it will come to many as a shock, but we had to carry on our work secretly. As for our rights as citizens, so far as the local authorities were concerned, the Constitution be damned! Who would have the temerity to stop them? Appeal to the United States Supreme Court? That costs thousands of dollars, and, besides, the Supreme Court is not inclined to interfere in the sovereignty of "states' rights." So the Southern industrialists and bankers rule without hindrance.

The designation of Ford for the Vice-Presidency created a great sensation. This was the first time in American history that any political party had selected a Negro to run for such high office, although there are more than fifteen million Negroes in America. The reaction of superior Nordics generally was that of amusement and disgust. Southern papers commented upon the choice with savage irony. They characterized it as "vulgar," and a "gross effrontery," and but the logical consequence of the agitation carried on by Jews and Russians that Negroes were the equals of whites. Did one need further proof that Moscow was invading America? Those damn Communists, editorial writers urged, ought either be deported to the country where they came from or better yet be made examples of with tar and feathers!

Different was the reaction of the Negro workers of Atlanta. They felt proud to see a Negro sharing honors with a white man—the highest honors a political party could bestow. While it is true that the lying press had succeeded in universally whipping up prejudice and hatred against Communists, these had penetrated in the Negro only skin deep. The Negro was sorely oppressed and he was made aware of it every moment of his life. So when the Communists came along and opened up their wounds and pointed out to them the reasons why they were oppressed and who their oppressors were, they thawed and broke down all their defenses against them.

The 1932 platform of the Communist Party was so simple and brief that even the most illiterate man could remember and understand it. There were only six planks and these were:

(1) Unemployment and Social Insurance to be paid at the expense of the state and employers.
(2) Against Hoover's wage-cutting policy.
(3) Emergency relief for the poor farmers without restriction by the government and banks; exemption of poor farmers from taxes and from forced collection of rents or debts.
(4) Equal rights for Negroes and self-determination for the Black Belt.
(5) Against capitalist terror; against all forms of suppression of the political rights of the workers.
(6) Against imperialist war; for the defense of the Chinese people and of the Soviet Union.

The Foster and Ford Clubs in Atlanta buzzed like bee hives despite the necessity of working underground. The color line passed unnoticed among our workers. Negro and white stood shoulder to shoulder, laboring together to the common goal. Of course we had no illusions about the outcome of our campaign. In the main, Communist sympathizers and adherents come from the working class and the poor tenant farmers. The state authorities found a cunning method to disqualify our voters. Negro and white poor alike were confronted by an unscalable obstacle: the high poll tax. We knew we would be deprived of many thousands of Communist votes in Atlanta alone by this un-American conspiracy against the rights of universal suffrage. But that did not diminish the energy of our campaigning. For Communists do not work for a day. We build an indestructible edifice, stone by stone and story by story, for all time and for all men—high poll tax or no high poll tax.

2

Absorbed as we were in the business of the campaign we did not allow ourselves to neglect our work among the unemployed. By June of that year the relief situation in Atlanta had reached the low water mark. The relief officials with farcical intent were giving the unemployed a free carousel ride. White unemployed recipients of relief were given less than sixty cents a week for each individual in the family. It goes without saying that Negroes got the leavings—and there was mighty little of that. As for those Negroes who got nothing, stars fall in Georgia even as they do in Alabama, and so they had the privilege of growing rapturous about the beautiful Southern nights, with fever-ridden eyes and bellies swollen with hunger.

As if this were not enough, the city and county authorities decided to drop twenty-three thousand families from the relief rolls. In consequence, those who had been driven by starvation from the farms were to be rounded up and shipped back again. This decision caused wild excitement among the unemployed. They read in it a sentence of death.

However, what still remained was the moral consolation of going down fighting.

The relief officials heard the low mutterings of a gathering storm, but pretended that they did not hear. The heart of Pharaoh was hard as stone, and his sense of authority was smug and overconfident. Just the same, the rulers of our lives were to meet with a surprise or two from us before long.

In explanation of their decision to drop twenty-three thousand families from the relief rolls, the city and county authorities declared that their treasuries were empty. They tried to blame it all on Washington, as usual preferring to pass the buck rather than to face realities. Then adding insult to injury, they made a pious grimace. What unemployment? The New Deal had done away with it already. Where? How? the unemployed asked in astonishment. The officials scorned to answer. However, in order that the myth of the democratic right to petition might be sustained, the Fulton County Commissioners made a grand gesture. They invited all those who were in actual need of relief to present their grievances in person. We accepted the invitation with little faith in obtaining any satisfaction from it.

The Unemployment Council lost no time and issued a call for a citywide emergency conference. All organizations of unemployed, regardless of their political tie-up, and all individuals abandoned to starvation by a government supposed to protect them, were invited to participate. The conference vibrated with militancy and bitterness against the high-handed and callous acts of the County Commissioners. It drew up a list of demands and one fine day, to the great amusement of the relief authorities, submitted them for their perusal. "Amusement" is a mild word to describe their reaction. Of all unmitigated nerve! We had the cheek to demand of them the following:

(1) The release of all workers arrested and framed up on charges of vagrancy.[57] For the repeal of the vagrancy law.
(2) That each unemployed worker with a family should get $4 weekly, no matter how small the family is. But in the case of a large family, the amount should be enough to provide for the whole family, e.g., if there are twelve in a family, the amount should be $12 per week, etc.
(3) There should not be any form of discrimination in the distribution of this relief, against Negro workers, mainly, and other workers who do not have families, etc.
(4) Half of the above amount to be paid in the form of cash and the other half in scrip, e.g., if a family were given $6, half of this amount should be paid in cash and the other half in scrip.
(5) That the city and county begin immediately to make arrangements to provide 1½ tons of coal for all unemployed workers for the winter, beginning with September first, and ending the latter part of April.
(6) That the city and county officials and their government provide shoes, clothing, free meals and carfare to schools for the children of the unemployed workers of Atlanta.

We ordered printed ten thousand leaflets calling for a demonstration at the court house. Because of the possible dangers that might be encountered during the day, we were obliged to work secretly, distributing them from house to house under cover of darkness. I could not sleep all night and waited impatiently for daybreak. All sorts of fears robbed me of my rest. Frankly, I was worried whether the demonstration would prove a success. If the workers failed to come in large numbers all our strenuous efforts in the past would be made negative. Workers generally would be discouraged from joining us and the relief authorities would refuse to have any dealings with us.

Early that morning before anybody stirred, I made my way to the court house. It was partly from anxiety and partly to collect my thoughts, for lack of sleep had made me groggy and restless. To my amazement and joy when nine o'clock arrived, which was just one hour before the meeting was scheduled to open, workers, both black and white, and small tradesmen began pouring into the square. At ten o'clock about one thousand workers, of whom more than half were white, formed ranks, and marching shoulder to shoulder, oblivious of color difference, filed into the courthouse building.

What a tragic lot of men and women these were! It was a great wonder that they had any strength left to protest. Listless, emaciated, with dragging feet and hollow eyes from which the light had been extinguished, they nevertheless seemed determined to do the last thing that their slowly expiring humanity dictated. What added pathos to the scene was the sight of many mothers walking into the building with their whimpering babies in their arms.

To one who has always lived up North a meeting attended by one thousand black and white workers would be regarded in a matter of fact way. Such things happen daily by the hundreds in Northern cities. But in the South such a spectacle caused alarm and consternation. It meant that the end of the world was at hand. This meeting in front of the court house was unprecedented in Atlanta. Never had such a huge gathering of black and white workers taken place in all the South. This was truly an historic occasion and the news reporters in the town went running around the court house with their eyes literally popping out of their heads.

But for all progressive workers this was a field day. It was a demonstration of the Southern worker's power. Like a giant that had been lying asleep for a long time, he now began to stir.

Despite the fervent hopes of the police and the yellow press, the demonstration was a model of order and peace. I have never seen a better-behaved audience even in the refined middle-class circles of Boston. In vain the police tried to provoke us, but we maintained an iron discipline. No one fell into the trap so deliberately laid for us by our enemies. It goes without saying that the meeting was a huge success. Nothing else was talked about the next few days in Atlanta and in other cities in the South with as much interest and excitement.

Our efforts succeeded beyond our wildest hopes. The following day the relief authorities announced that they had appropriated $6,000 for additional relief. Furthermore, the order about dropping the twenty-three thousand families from the relief rolls was rescinded. . . .

The reaction of Atlanta's unemployed to all this was most eloquently expressed in the following exclamation of a very old Negro worker who in his boyhood had been a slave in Georgia:

"Hot damn! Who would have thought it!"

'SOUTHERN TERROR'
LOUISE THOMPSON
FROM *THE CRISIS*
NOVEMBER 1934

"**B**irmingham is a good place for good niggers—but a damn bad place for bad niggers."

Thus spoke the officialdom of Birmingham, Ala., to me last May, and in the course of my experience there I learned what they meant. I was arrested as I went to enter the apartment of a woman whom I had known in the North. It so happened that the red squad was raiding her apartment at the time, and as I knocked at the door it was opened by a policeman who brusquely ordered me in. I did so, and was immediately placed under arrest. As they fired questions at me, one officer interrupted to ask:

"Gal, where you from? I know you ain't from around here 'cause you don't talk like it."

"My home is California," I answered.

"California, hell! You're one of those --- yankee ---, that's what you are!"

And with a few more remarks quite in keeping with the above, they loaded me into the "black wagon," along with the other persons in the apartment at the time, and off to the city jail we went. I was promptly locked up, with no chance given to me to communicate with friends or an attorney. My attempts to question the procedure met with laughter

---

*   Louise Thompson, "Southern Terror," *The Crisis,* November 1934.

or taunts from my jailers. "Held for investigation," I learned later from my cellmates.

I spend the night with fourteen other Negro women on charges ranging from drunkenness to pickpocketing to murder. One of the women was demented, and the two of us kept vigil that night, she, walking the floor and raving; I, wondering what was to happen to me on the morrow and what my friends would think when I did not return home that night.

The long night finally ended. Breakfast of huge soda biscuits, beans and a colored water which passed for coffee. Then I was called out, again taken for a ride in the patrol to the identification department for fingerprinting and "mugging" for the rogues' gallery. Though I was being accorded the treatment of a criminal I had yet to know what I was being held for, and when I would be permitted to communicate with the outside world.

During the cross examination which followed, my questioners were inclined at first to make a joke of the affair, taunting me about "my comrades," slyly alluding to some intimate relationship with the men arrested with me, and the like. But upon my refusal to answer any more questions until I had an opportunity to consult an attorney, their taunts turned to open threats which ran something like this:

"What about turning this gal over to the Ku Klux Klan? I reckon they know how to handle her kind."

"Yeah, or a little tar and feathering might help."

"How about talking to her through a rubber tube. She might be glad to talk then." (I later learned that "talking through the rubber tube" meant beating with a rubber hose in the third degree.)

Again, one officer turned to me, pointing his finger and said: "See here, gal, you're arrested now, see. And you say 'yes sir' and 'no sir'." I was told later by some of the women prisoners that I was lucky not to have been slapped when I refused to obey.

Eleven-Notch Gun

Later in the day my friends finally succeeded in getting an attorney in to see me, after reading in the papers of the raid. He immediately prepared a writ of habeas corpus to force the placing of a charge against me or my release. And again I rode from the city jail to Jefferson

'Southern Terror'

County courthouse where the Scottsboro boys are imprisoned. There I was turned over to the prize red baiter and "nigger" hater of the plainclothes squad, Moser, who boasts of eleven notches in his gun for helpless Negroes he has shot down. These were his words of welcome:

> So you're one of those ——— reds what thinks you are going to get social equality for niggers down here in the South. Well, we think Communists are lower than niggers, down here—fact is, we don't even allow them to 'sociate with white folks, let alone have white folks 'sociating with niggers. We know how to treat our niggers down here and we ain't going to stand for no interference from you ——— yankee reds. We ought to handle you reds like Mussolini does 'em in Italy—take you out and shoot you against the wall. And I sure would like to have the pleasure of doing it.

With which this "protector of law and order" escorted me to the courtroom where I was to meet my attorney for a hearing on the habeas corpus proceedings. When my attorney read the writ, Moser triumphantly stepped up to the judge with a warrant for my arrest as a "vagrant." Vagrancy is that convenient catchall which serves all purposes.

My bail was set for $300 cash, my trial for ten days hence. On the tenth day I entered the courtroom and took my seat on the side for Negroes to await the calling of my case. Surrounding the judge were a group of officers and others, whom I learned later to be members of the White Legion. From time to time they would suggest to the judge or prosecutor questions to be asked the Negro prisoners appearing before the bar of "justice." The word "nigger" rang out from lips of judge, solicitor, officers, White Legionnaires every second. Any attempt on the part of a Negro prisoner to dispute testimony against him was met by, "Nigger, do you dare to dispute the word of a white man?," or simply by loud bursts of laughter. Here was "southern justice" undisturbed by any militant interference!

My case was finally called and I stood before Judge Abernathy. The White Legion boys drew a little nearer, the police officers stepped up to testify. All eyes were focused upon me. The judge then listened to the testimony of the arresting officer, embellished with a few points to win the laughing approval of the crowd about the bench. Meanwhile the judge fingered the documents which disproved any charge of vagrancy against me, my status as a representative of the International Workers Order, the articles of incorporation which permit my organization to operate under state law, canceled checks for my weekly wages. He looked at me intently and then asked of the crowd about him:

"Wonder where this gal is from? Looks like she came from Mississippi—that's the way they mix up down there. Course it's got nothing to do with the case, but I'm going to ask her where she was born as I'm mighty interested in how these mixtures turn out." And to me, "Where were you born, gal?"

With no further questioning, the case was dismissed with the Judge declaring, "You can't arrest the gal for being an octoroon."

"No, she can't help that," was Moser's parting shot.

I was not yet entirely free for another warrant was produced to arrest me on the charge of concealing my identity. A few days later, however, this second case was thrown out of court without my having to appear again.

The Bourbon authorities learned that the workers throughout the country were ready to apply their weapon of mass pressure against my arrest—and their experience with the Scottsboro case, with the Herndon case, made them cautious. They wanted stronger grounds to prepare another frame-up against a Negro engaged in working-class activity.

The White Legion

Thus did I learn from first hand experience the kind of "justice" meted out to Negroes in the South, of the unswerving determination of the servants of the State and of vested interests to keep the Negro people in utter subjection. And more, of the treatment of those who would help the Negro people in their fight for emancipation from this oppression. All the others arrested with me were white, yet they fared no better than I did, for as Communist suspects they are bitterly hated and granted no more constitutional rights than are given Negroes in the South. Being a Communist in the South is synonymous with being a fighter for the rights of the Negro people, of being a "nigger lover," of trying to bring white and Negro workers and poor farmers, together— of fighting against lynching, of challenging of the southern ruling class' traditional manner of treating Negroes. John Howard Lawson, prominent Hollywood playwright, who came to Birmingham to write up the terror was arrested as he left Jefferson county courthouse, fingerprinted and "mugged" and ordered from town. When he returned later with a delegation of liberals he was arrested again and charged with libel for telling the truth about the terror of Birmingham's police and White Legion.

A word or two about the White Legion, this openly Fascist organization in Birmingham whose stated purpose is to fight communism and any move to lift oppression from the backs of the Negro people. Its membership fee is $5.00, which of course precludes any worker members. As a matter of fact it recruits its members from the officials of the city, merchants, and other middle-class elements. It maintains an office on one of the main streets of Birmingham and displays in the front window Communist leaflets and any material from the Negro or revolutionary press which advocates equal rights for Negroes. One week they displayed a picture of Langston Hughes with his poem "An Open Letter to the South," in which Hughes appeals to Negro and white labor to unite in struggle for a better world. The comment scrawled along the margin was: "If this bird thinks we are going to have social equality in the South, he's crazy!"

During the height of the terror against the Negro and militant white workers, the White Legion issued highly inflammatory leaflets seeking to provoke white against Negro workers. One such leaflet included this statement "How would you like to awaken one morning to find your wife or daughter attacked by a Negro or a Communist!" It wound up with an appeal to pay the membership fee so that the White Legion could handle such situations in the traditional manner. During the planning of action against the class-conscious workers of Birmingham, one wing of the Legion was for riding through the Negro neighborhood and shooting indiscriminately into the homes of innocent Negroes, but cooler heads in the gang realized that such an extreme form of terror was a bit premature.

'Social Equality'

The Southern press also played its part well during the reign of terror which did not end with our arrests, but went on in a series of raids upon the homes of workers over the entire city. The mining strike was at its height in Birmingham and for the first time Negro and white workers were militantly picketing together. The daily press came out with scare heads of "red violence" and "red plots" and references to "social equality." One paper carried a story of a raid upon a Negro home which produced a "highly inflammatory" document—it was the Bill of Civil Rights calling for full political, economic, and social equality for the Negro people. Yet those papers which went beyond the borders of the state carried not a line of the raids, the arrests, or the general terror.

That the press, the White Legion and the government officials always link the "reds" and Communism with the Negro question is not a mere coincidence. First of all, the International Labor Defense, through the Scottsboro case has aroused the Negro people and rallied to their defense workers over the whole world. And it is the Communist Party which has analyzed the Negro Question as that of an oppressed nation of people, defined the alignment of class forces for and against the Negro people's struggle for liberation, and begun the organization of white and Negro working masses together. Revolutionary leaders in the South are boldly defying all that the southern ruling class has striven to perpetuate, and terror and jail bars do not stop them. Down in the heart of Dixie, the Black Belt, some 8,000 sharecroppers have organized a militant Sharecroppers Union to fight the starvation program of the Agricultural Adjustment Administration, which deputy sheriffs' bullets have been unable to stop.

It is another matter, however, when organizations within the Negro group come forward as vehemently against any show of militancy on the part of the Negro masses and with as great enmity against a revolutionary program and revolutionary organizations as is expressed in the White Legion of Birmingham. Such organizations disregard the economic roots of the Negro's oppression, and through collaboration with the ruling class seek to restrain the masses of Negroes from militant struggle. Such organizations accept the present system of capitalism and are willing to be satisfied with what hollow reforms may come without any fundamental change.

Revolution Called Necessity

But it is impossible to take one step in the direction of winning for the Negro people their elementary rights that is not revolutionary. Capitalism developed in America upon the superexploitation of the

Negro people and through the division created between white and Negro labor. Any attempt to end this superexploitation, to destroy the enmity and to unite Negro and white labor is a blow at American capitalism. So it is that the Southern ruling class is not going to budge from its position of exploiting and oppressing the Negro people. And behind the southern Bourbons stand the amassed strength of American finance capital—US Steel, Wall Street investments in the plantations of the South, and the like. Any organizations among the Negro people which do not point out these class alignments must therefore become the voice of reaction in the midst of a people struggling for freedom. So it is that the leadership among the Negro people must pass into new hands—into the hands of working-class leaders, the Angelo Herndons, who will not be stopped by jail, by a desire to cling on to jobs, by death itself in leading the Negro people through the final conflict to complete emancipation.

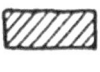 'SHARECROPPERS WITH GUNS: ORGANIZING THE BLACK BELT'
HARRY HAYWOOD
FROM *BLACK BOLSHEVIK*
1978

In the spring of 1933, Haywood Patterson of the Scottsboro Boys was declared guilty by a court in Decatur, Alabama. Following his conviction, a wave of indignation swept Black communities across the country. Mass protest rallies, demonstrations of all sorts, and parades culminated in the Free the Scottsboro Boys March on Washington on May 7–9, 1933.

The right danger took concrete form when the ILD leadership allowed themselves to be suckered into an agreement with the NAACP leadership. These leaders made overtures to the ILD, offering to help raise funds for the mounting legal defense expenses and particularly for those of the Patterson appeal.

This offer, however, was made with conditions which amounted to giving the NAACP veto power over all expenditures of defense funds, and thus over defense activities. It was a ploy which would allow NAACP leaders such as Joel Spingarn and Walter White to regain their position in the defense campaign and appear before the masses as leaders in this campaign.

---

* Harry Haywood, *Black Bolshevik: Autobiography of an Afro-American Communist* (University of Minnesota Press, 1978).

Since the beginning of the campaign two years before, the Spingarn-White crowd had used every possible means to wrest the defense from the ILD. Their efforts were in vain, but they continued to attack—not the lynchers—but the defense. For example, shortly after the Patterson verdict, the NAACP board of directors stated that the only hope for the boys was to "remove . . . the additional burden of communism."[58]

Now these leaders, largely discredited and isolated, attempted to get back into the defense. The sharp rise in the movement under the leadership of the ILD, which followed the Patterson verdict, forced them to make a tactical retreat. Realizing they had misjudged the temper of the masses they now attempted to regain a place within the defense in order to more effectively sabotage it. To this end they made overtures to the ILD, offering to help raise funds.

In an ILD staff meeting which I attended as head of the Party's Negro Department, the NAACP offer was discussed favorably by most of the staff. George Maurer, who played a leading role in organizing the Scottsboro defense, and myself were the only ones to object. William Patterson, national secretary, argued that there was no alternative if the organization were to gain the financial support we needed for the Haywood Patterson appeal and the future trials of the other boys.[59] As I recall, our objections were to no avail and the agreement was carried through.[60]

The deal was obviously set up by Samuel Leibowitz, one of America's leading criminal lawyers, who had become quite well known for his defense of certain gangster types. He had volunteered his services free of charge to the ILD and was accepted as the chief defense lawyer in the trial of Haywood Patterson. He won national acclaim by his brilliant conduct of the defense and emerged as a hero of that trial. On his return to New York from Decatur, Alabama, more than 3,000 people poured out of Harlem to greet him at Pennsylvania Station.

Leibowitz was a man of great personal ambition. (He later became a justice of the New York Supreme Court.) He was clearly uncomfortable in the company of revolutionaries and sought to avoid too close identification with the ILD. He brought the ILD and the NAACP together, ostensibly to achieve unity, but in reality to weaken the hold of the ILD on the defense and pave the way for an eventual takeover by the NAACP leadership.

The ILD went on to compound this original mistake. They not only accepted the deal but hailed the NAACP leaders for their "changed attitude." In fact, the agreement reflected no change of heart by NAACP leaders. They continued to draw a line between defense in the courts and the mass movement. They tried to confine their support to the courts and moved to sabotage the mass defense movement, both from within and from without. They refused to support the Free the Scottsboro Boys March on Washington, but this proved to be a serious blunder for the already crisis-ridden and isolated NAACP.

Shortly before the march on Washington, our right opportunist mistakes were continued in the Scottsboro Action Committee, a broad united front which was under the leadership of the ILD. The NAACP had become largely discredited and "left" reformists like William H. (Kid) Davis, publisher of the *Amsterdam News*, tried to step into the vacuum. Davis, along with Black politicians who served as fronts for New York's Tammany Hall, attempted to set up a new so-called nonpartisan defense committee for the purpose of the march. This was part of their effort to seize the leadership of the growing mass movement that was calling for a march on Washington. Davis attempted to divert it from a mass march into a committee of representative citizens who would present a petition to the president.

At the beginning of this move, the Scottsboro Action Committee tailed after the reformists. They failed at first to see through the left rhetoric of the group's criticisms of the NAACP. But within a short time, we corrected this mistake and regained leadership of the movement. We did the actual organization and formulation of the proposals for the march, which went over successfully.

I participated in the organization of the march on Washington along with Patterson, Ford and others—helping to prepare the program and working out technical details. The march involved people mainly from the cities of the eastern seaboard; there hadn't been time to organize a truly national demonstration. The demand of the march was "Freedom for the Scottsboro Boys," which was lied in with demands in the area of civil rights: an end to discrimination in voting, jury service, schools, housing, public accommodations, trade unions and the death penalty for lynching.[61]

These demands were summed up in the Bill of Rights put forward by the LSNR. The 3,000 marchers, led by Ruby Bates, Mrs. Jane Patterson (mother of Haywood Patterson) and William Patterson of the ILD, demanded to meet with President Roosevelt.[62] Roosevelt was in conference with Dr. Hajalmar Schacht, the special German envoy, and refused to meet the marchers.

We did visit various congressmen who all said it was a matter for the courts, they could do nothing. Oscar DePriest, a Black congressman from the Thompson machine in Chicago, showed his true colors—declaring that we weren't going to get him into this mess! We left the petitions with Louis Howe, the president's secretary; saw Vice-President Garner and the speaker of the house. We then paraded through the streets of Washington and headed home.

After the march, the Politburo of the Party reviewed the Scottsboro campaign since the Patterson verdict. The right mistakes before the march arose from a basic misconception of the united front. Behind this was the idea that a united front meant unity with everybody, under any conditions. Involved here was a definite underestimation of the class role of the Black reformist leaders as agents of the ruling class in the ranks of the Afro American people. Their influence could only be destroyed in the course of building a united front with the masses from below. It was the same as the situation in the labor movement with regard to the labor bureaucracy.

We decided that a resolution should be developed in the light of our discussions; the Negro Department was given the task of drafting such a resolution. We summed up these mistakes in a resolution which was adopted by the Politburo. In its criticism of the ILD's deal with the NAACP, the resolution stated that the ILD should have offered the NAACP a "straight forward and clear proposal of mass struggle and mobilization of the masses against the capitalist frame-up courts and Jim-Crow legal system."

If the NAACP had accepted this program, it would have clearly discredited their past policy of relying on the courts. "If they had refused such an offer, this also would have cleared the issues before the eyes of the masses."

The resolution went on further to state:

> In such a broad mass struggle as that of the Scottsboro conscious agents of the ruling bourgeoisie endeavor to

come into the united front for the purpose of smashing the mass movement and thus serving the bourgeoisie. . . . It is necessary . . . to warn the masses constantly of the class role of these elements. . . . Under all conditions it is necessary to maintain the independent role of the Party and of the revolutionary forces in such a united front both in regard to our agitation and our actions.[63]

Southern Tour

Our line, projecting the question of US Blacks as essentially that of an oppressed nation, called for making the South the "center of gravity" for work among them. Though I had spent a brief period in North Carolina, it was not the deep Black Belt South, the focus of the Party's concentration. I was eager to visit the area, to see how our theory regarding the national question and the role of the "Black peasantry" were being worked out in practice.

The opportunity came in the early part of 1933. In consultation with the Alabama district organizer, Nat Ross; Elizabeth Lawson, acting editor of the *Southern Worker* (the Party's Southern news paper); and Al Murphy, secretary of the Sharecroppers Union (all of whom were in New York at the time), it was decided that I should spend several weeks in the Alabama district.

Arriving in Birmingham, I had no difficulty in finding the hotel where the comrades had arranged for me to stop. It was on Fourth Avenue, downtown in a small Black business area, near the *Birmingham World*, the city's Black weekly.

When I registered, the owner and desk clerk said, "Oh, yes, Mr. Haywood. We've been expecting you. Your friends will be here shortly."

I was shown to my room and a few minutes later two young Black comrades, Hosea Hudson and Joe Howard, came to my room. Both were unemployed steel workers. They had been assigned as my liaisons to the local Party organization.

In Birmingham, the South's greatest industrial center, the ruling white supremacist oligarchy expressed the interest of local capitalist Black Belt planters of the adjacent counties, local representatives of northern based industrial and financial corporations. Most of these latter merged socially with their Southern counterparts. At the top of the corporate list was the gigantic United States Steel Corporation, sprawling over a section of the town itself. The Gentlemen's Agreement of 1877 remained in full force.

The principle enunciated by Judge Taney in the Dred Scott decision that the Black has no rights that the white man is bound to respect was still fully operative. Jim Crow laws in public places were strictly enforced. The purpose of it all was to preserve a cheap, subservient, divided and unorganized labor force of degraded, disenfranchised Blacks and poverty-ridden whites. The latter were psychologically compensated by being accepted as members of a superior race.

In Birmingham, racism was all-pervasive and blatant. One could feel it in the atmosphere. Birmingham was a mean town, a place where the police periodically shot down Black people to "keep them in line," the latter being mostly young and unemployed.

When we walked down the street, Hosea and Joe told me, "If you expect to work down here, you gotta look like the rest of us. You gotta cut out that fast walking with your head up in the air or these crackers'll spot you. Get that slouch in your walk. Look scared, as if you are about to run," he joked. These were big tough men talking now. Of course they were kidding—still, there was a grain of truth in these remarks.

Now a new element had entered the picture—the Communist Party. Formed in 1930 by organizers from the north, the Party in Birmingham took the first steps towards building a union of steel workers, laying the groundwork for building the CIO Steel Workers Union in 1935. It had initiated a movement of unemployed which organized a demonstration of 7,000 people on the steps of the Jefferson County Courthouse in November 1932.[64]

Though the numbers were not large, the Party grew rapidly during the 1932 election campaign. Three hundred Blacks and fifty whites gathered to greet William Z. Foster at an election rally. Foster, however, failed to appear because of illness. The following week, 400 Blacks and 300 whites attended a meeting to hear Hathaway; this meeting was broken up by vigilantes throwing stink bombs from galleries. There were also a number of mass meetings called on the Scottsboro issue, including one of 3,000 people at the Black Masonic Temple.

The Party had chosen Birmingham as the center for its drive into the deep South and as the logical jump-off place for the development of a movement among the small Black farm operators.

'Sharecroppers with Guns: Organizing the Black Belt'

The most dramatic struggle was the movement of tenants, sharecroppers and farm laborers centered in Tallapoosa County, southeast of Birmingham. The area bordered on the Black Belt plantation region and resembled the latter in respect to farm values, types of tenancy and racial composition. The first local of the Sharecroppers Union was organized there in 1931. That was before the Federal Relief Crop Reduction Program had been instituted. The small owners, tenants, croppers and farm laborers were hit the hardest by the crisis. Merchants and bankers had refused to "furnish" or provide them credit. Mortgages left them at the mercy of their creditors. Small operators lived under constant threat of foreclosure and eviction. The wages for farm laborers ran as low as fifty cents a day for men and twenty-five cents for women.[65]

The close proximity to the Party organization in Birmingham facilitated the organization of these poor farmers in the area. A number of them had worked in mines north of Birmingham and in steel plants and factories in the city itself, returning to the land to eke out a living during the Depression. There was a continuous movement to and from the city, and those who didn't make the move themselves had close relatives who did so. Thus the development of the sharecroppers' struggle in Alabama, in contrast to other regions of the Black Belt where oppression was equally intense (for example, South Carolina or Mississippi), took a more organized and consciously revolutionary form. This accounts for what struck me as the relatively high political development of union members.

Local farmers sent a letter to the *Southern Worker* in Chattanooga, asking that organizers be sent to help them build a union. The Party responded and sent several people, among them Mack Coad, a Black steelworker. Coad, arriving at the scene, met with the Gray brothers—Ralph and Tom—and other local leaders. It was decided that a meeting should be called for July 16, at Mary's Church near Camp Hill, to protest the Scottsboro convictions. Included in the agenda of the meeting would be plans for organizing a union around the minimum demands of the tenants. The most immediate aim was to force the landlords to increase the quantity of "furnishings" through the winter, and double the wages of the plantation laborers. A last minute arrangement committee of the leaders met the night before, on July 15.

The county sheriff and local gentry were aware of the defiant moods among the sharecroppers. The sheriff had been tipped off by a local stool pigeon that an outside agitator was in the area and that radical meetings were being held. The same stool pigeon informed them about the meeting of leaders on July 15. He and his deputies, seeking the "outsider," raided the meeting. They found that they were all from Tallapoosa County, and they convinced the sheriff that the meeting was just a harmless get together and that they knew nothing about an outside organizer.

The next night, July 16, the sheriff and his deputies approached the meeting, where they were confronted by Ralph Gray, who had been posted as a picket. Shots were exchanged in which both Gray and the sheriff were wounded. The sheriff and his deputies fled back to town, where a posse was formed amidst cries of "communist-instigated Negro rebellion," and a manhunt began.

In the ensuing battle, five Blacks were wounded in addition to Ralph Gray. A Black cropper helped carry him to his home, where Coad and several other armed Blacks had gathered. The posse approached Gray's home and a battle ensued. The croppers, faced with overwhelming odds, decided to disperse. Gray, however, refused to be removed to safety and insisted upon "dying in his own home." The croppers insisted that Coad must flee and helped him to escape to Atlanta. Gray's home was riddled with bullets by the posse and when they broke in, he was found dead.

In addition to the wounded, thirty more Blacks were finally rounded up and arrested in the manhunt that followed.

The brutal repression following Camp Hill did not crush the movement; the union regrouped underground and continued to grow. By spring 1932, the union claimed 500 members, mainly in Tallapoosa and Chambers Counties.

In December 1932, there were shoot-outs in Reeltown in Tallapoosa County involving Cliff James, a union leader in the area. The sheriff had tried to serve a writ of attachment on James's livestock as a result of his landlord's refusing him an extension on a year's rent.

The sharecroppers elected a committee to meet the sheriff and when the latter arrived to seize the property, he found union members armed and barricaded in the house. In the ensuing battles, the sheriff and two deputies were wounded, one sharecropper killed, and several wounded, including James and Milo Bentley. The sharecroppers scattered through the woods. James and Bentley made it to Tuskegee Institute, where according to several accounts, a Black doctor turned them over to the sheriff. They were then taken to Kilby Prison where both men with their wounds untreated were forced to sleep on the cold floor; both subsequently died from exposure.[66]

This shoot-out was followed by mob action and violence exceeding that of the previous year after the Camp Hill affair. A posse of more than 500 men went on a manhunt for Black farm operators and "communist agitators." Mobs raided homes of union members; several were reported to have been killed or beaten. Many union members fled to the woods for safety and the number of Blacks killed in the four-day rioting was not known.

I was told that some white farmers had hidden Blacks in their homes during the rampages of the sheriffs mobs. At the time, I was told by someone that the racists had trouble getting enough men for their posses from Tallapoosa County and had to go outside the county to recruit vigilantes.[67]

The bodies of the two men were laid out in Birmingham, draped in broad red ribbons decorated by the hammer and sickle. The *Daily Worker* reported:

> Day and night, a guard of honor, composed of Negro and white workers, stood at attention by the coffins. The funeral home was filled with flowers and wreaths. . . . Thousands of workers filed past the coffins to pay tribute to the martyred leaders of the sharecroppers.[68]

Some 3,000 people attended the funeral, 150 of whom were whites. Again terror failed to suppress the union. Despite the arrest of some of its most active members, union members and sympathizers poured into Dadeville (the county seat) before dawn on the day of the trial of those arrested. The courtroom was filled and the crowd overflowed into the square. On the second day of the trial, roadblocks were put up and whites filled the courthouse to prevent Blacks from attending. Nevertheless, Blacks came along the bypasses and across streams, demanding to be seated. The judge was put on the spot and requested the whites to clear half the courtroom. The trial resulted in the sentencing and conviction of those accused.[69]

The union nevertheless continued to grow and by 1933 had 3,000 members, including a few whites. Its membership and influence were extending to neighboring counties. The shoot-outs at Camp Hill and Reeltown brought into focus the explosive character of the struggle of the region's Black soil tillers. It revealed that the fight for even the smallest demands by the sharecroppers and tenants could lead to armed conflict. In fact, any demand that would give Blacks a voice in renting and determining wages was regarded as insurrectionary by the local gentry.

It was this explosive feature which distinguished the movement of Black soil tillers from that of the white farmers in the rest of the country or even the South itself. The demands of the Blacks were more revolutionary than those of the whites for they represented the demands of the agrarian and democratic revolutions, left unfinished by the betrayal of Reconstruction.

Following all this in New York, I was eager to visit Alabama and the sharecroppers. I was curious to know how the union had grown in the face of all that terror. What were the methods of organization they used? Al Murphy told me to go down to the area itself.

Murphy was a tall, jet-hued Black, an ex-steelworker and the most important organizer of the sharecroppers. Soft-spoken and modest to the point of self-effacement, he had given me a rundown on the Sharecroppers Union, playing down his own role and disclaiming credit for its achievements. Murphy was a self-educated Marxist, a genuine worker-intellectual.

He praised the local leaders and their high level of political development. He said the people built the organization from their own experience and that the croppers had a tradition of underground organization. Any people who had experienced that kind of oppression, he said, would have done the same thing.

Discussing the matter with local comrades in Birmingham, it was agreed that I should go to Tallapoosa County, but I had to wait for them to arrange security. The opportunity came when Lem Harris and Hal Ware, leaders of the Party's national farm work, passed through Birmingham on their way to an executive board meeting of the Sharecroppers Union. They were heading for Dadeville.

We left Birmingham at dusk, driving at night so as not to attract attention. The car was a Chevrolet coupe—the two-door model with a fold-down rumble seat in the back. I sat in the rumble seat. When we got to Dadeville it was dark. Hal turned to me saying, "You'd better

'Sharecroppers with Guns: Organizing the Black Belt'

pull down the top of the rumble seat over you." I hastily complied as we were in enemy territory and didn't want to attract attention.

We soon passed the lights of Dadeville. A short distance out, we came to a farmhouse and stopped. This was Tommy Gray's place. He was a small independent farm operator and like most of his fellow operators in the area, he was deeply in debt. Greeted by Gray who had expected us, we went into the house. He had met Hal and Lem at the Farmers' National Relief Conference the year before. He took our coats and put them in the bedroom which looked like a small arsenal.

There were guns of all kinds—shotguns, rifles and pistols. Sharecroppers were coming to the meeting armed and left their guns with their coats when they came in. Everyone came and left at night; the meeting lasted, as I remember, two days. There were fifteen or twenty people there, members of the executive board. I was impressed by the efficient manner in which Gray conducted the meeting; they were an impressive group overall.

I was introduced as a member of the Party's Central Committee. As I recall, I spoke about the international situation and the Scottsboro and Herndon cases. Hal and Lem said a few words about the farmers' movement in other parts of the country and the follow up of the National Farmers Conference.

I was most impressed by the reports of the leaders of locals about their areas. They described conditions, how they were preparing for a strike, and gave reports on different landlords. I was also impressed that they could spread a leaflet over four counties inside of fifteen minutes. They had a tight underground organization.

I learned there of an attempt to assassinate Tommy Gray. It seemed that Tommy was fishing at the creek, when he heard a shot and a bullet whizzed past his ear. He turned quickly and saw a man running whom he recognized as Charles Harris, a cropper and union member. The union had set up a committee to investigate the incident and they brought a report back at the meeting I attended. One of the reporters told the group that they had visited the accused man and uncovered other information. He had evidently been hired by somebody from the town, a sheriff or landlord, to kill Tommy Gray. They had bribed the man with a promise not to call his loan in if he would do their work.

A discussion followed the report, as people wondered what to do with the turncoat. Some argued he should be permanently got rid of.

But other, cooler heads, argued that this would only play right into the hands of the sheriff. He would use it as an excuse to come down on the whole group. The sober point of view prevailed. It was decided a committee would visit the man and tell him to get out of the area; if he didn't, then they would deal with him. I heard later that this tactic was successful, and the man and his family left after the delegation's visit.

I left Dadeville in high spirits, more than ever convinced of the correctness of our line; that the Black Belt peasantry under the leadership of the working class and the Communist Party was the motor of Black rebellion in the deep South. I felt that the Sharecroppers Union was definitely a prototype for the future organization of the Black, landless, debt-ridden and racially persecuted farmers of the area.

The union continued to grow after I left. By the fall of 1935, it claimed 12,000 members, including some poor whites; 2,500 of these were scattered in Louisiana, Mississippi, Georgia, and North Carolina. In 1936 it was liquidated—a victim of Browderism.

On my return trip to the national office in New York from Birmingham, I decided to stop over in Atlanta for a few days. This would be a chance for me to check on the Party's activities in this important city and to see Ben Davis Jr. Ben was the young Black attorney who had courageously and dramatically defended Angelo Herndon in the famous "insurrection" case. It was this case which brought young Davis national attention. Along with Scottsboro, it had become a symbol of the fight for Black rights.

As I neared Atlanta, I tried to recall what I knew of Ben. Although we had never met, I had learned about his background from friends who were active with him in the Herndon defense. Ben's father was a self-made man from a poor Georgia family. He had worked his way into prominence and some wealth in Atlanta, and was high in the councils of the Republican Party, once having served as a national committeeman. An old-style Republican in the tradition of Frederick Douglass, he was a determined fighter for civil rights, voting, education, and opportunity for Black business.

He had become owner and publisher of the *Atlanta Independent*, an influential Black newspaper. He was also the district grand secretary of the Negro Odd Fellows, the largest fraternal order in the state. From this position, he was able to build the Imposing Odd Fellows business block on Auburn Avenue. Ben Senior had had ambitious plans for his only son. He had sent him to exclusive New England schools—Amherst and Harvard Law School. But the Depression had interrupted these plans.

The Depression had an especially devastating effect on the Black community. Not only were poor and working-class Blacks driven into deeper poverty, but the small and growing Black middle class, which was already on marginal foundations, was almost completely wiped out. Ben Davis Sr., became a victim of the Depression. He lost the newspaper and the business block passed into the hands of an insurance company.

Coupled with economic decline was the inauguration of Hoover's "Southern Strategy" of replacing Black Republicans with a lily-white faction. Ben Senior was removed from his post as Republican national committeeman, with a corresponding loss of his powers of patronage.

Young Davis returned from his Ivy League education to find this devastated situation. A young Black attorney in the South was forced to work in a very narrow field. It was unheard of for a Black to argue a case against a white attorney. This left Ben Junior with drafting deeds, wills, contracts, divorces and other such matters relating only to Blacks—a severely restricted arena for his Harvard Law School training. Ben hung up his shingle in the old Odd Fellows building, and soon formed a partnership with another Black attorney, John Geer.

He was soon dissatisfied and angry; however, as his frustration grew, he found himself "challenged by the thought of what could be done if one put up a really tough fight for the constitutional rights of Negroes in a Georgia court."[70]

The Herndon case provided Ben with just such an opportunity. Effectively employing a working-class policy in the trials, Ben conducted a militant and aggressive defense. He appeared before the court as a tribune for Blacks and poor whites against Georgia's white supremacist oligarchy. The trial had been a high point of class militancy.

Arriving in Atlanta by car on a Sunday morning, I went directly to the Davis home. Ben, his father and sister (his mother had died the year before) lived in a large house on Boulevard off Auburn Avenue in a Black middle-class neighborhood. The family's past affluence was evident by the five-car garage in the rear of the house. I was warmly greeted by Ben, who had been expecting me. He was a huge, dark-skinned young man. Six feet two inches tall with the bull shoulders of a football lineman, a position he had played at Amherst.

Ben showed me into their large living room. We had a long talk before his father and sister joined us. He filled me in on what was happening in Atlanta. By this time he had joined the Party and a considerable movement had developed around the Herndon case. An ILD office and organization had been established. The Party was still quite small, though there were a number of white members.

The next day Ben took me down to his office on the fifth floor of the Odd Fellows building. He spoke about the threats against him by the authorities and the Ku Klux Klan, which was virtually an arm of the state. Men took off their police uniforms to put on the robes of the Klan. He talked of the hounding and the threats as a result of his fight in the court.

He showed me a hole in the door between his office and an adjoining room. Just a few weeks after the trial, he was sitting at his desk and noticed a kind of tube sticking out of the hole in the door. Ben went up to examine it and discovered it was the barrel of an empty revolver which was set up against the door. He pulled a paper out of the barrel and read the message: "The Ku Klux Klan rides again. Georgia is no place for bad niggers and red communists. Next time we'll shoot."

He also told me about what had happened downtown, at the ILD office on Peachtree Street. A white comrade, the wife of ILD attorney Irving Schwab, was in charge of the office. Ben came into the office, which was in a white neighborhood downtown, fairly often. Once, as he was coming out of the door, a whole gang was waiting for him. He thought they were from the neighboring offices in the building. He was backed up against the wall, into a corner. No one touched him, but they shouted at him, calling him a nigger son-of-a-bitch, threatening to get him or run him out of town.

With the jailing of Angelo Herndon, the authorities assumed they had disposed of one enemy. They now found themselves faced with another one—Ben Davis. In addition, the Atlanta movement had begun to grow. There were mass meetings around the Scottsboro and Herndon cases which had drawn many Blacks. The ILD was militant and growing along with a small but active Communist Party. While I was in Atlanta, I visited a meeting or two of the ILD and the Party. I recall a Party meeting that was held in the home of the Leathers, an old white Southern working-class family, long active in radical politics.

'Sharecroppers with Guns: Organizing the Black Belt'

There seemed to be about three generations of the Leathers living in that house. This included Nannie Washburn who was then a young mother. Otto had recruited her into the Party and she played a leading role in the Herndon and Scottsboro defense. She was to remain active in the struggle long after the Party's desertion of the South. Jailed in the civil rights and anti-war movements, Mrs. Washburn remains today a staunch fighter in the cause of proletarian revolution.

I was worried about Ben Davis, about his safety. I didn't think the threats were idle—they could be carried out—especially after the trial, when there was a lull in the movement. Worries I had had in New York about the situation in the South were borne out by what I now heard in Atlanta. The more I thought about the matter, the more I felt Ben should be pulled out of there—for a time, anyway.

I had sized him up as an up-and-coming young communist, with great leadership potential. He would be a good addition to our growing body of cadres—we didn't need another martyr, we needed living activists. He was such a dynamic aggressive person; if we got him to the center and national work, he would develop more fully as a communist.

So upon my return to New York, I presented my opinions to the Politburo—we should draw him out of Atlanta. He agreed to come to New York, where he was first made editor of the *Liberator*, relieving Maude White; he later worked on the *Daily Worker*. He became a city councilman in the forties and a member of the Politburo of the Party after Browder's demise.

He grew into an important Party leader with whom I was to have strong political differences in later years.

In March 1934, I was back in Birmingham, Alabama. On my previous visit Nat Ross, the district organizer, had talked about building the revolutionary movement in Memphis, along with New Orleans, the great financial and commercial center of the lower Mississippi Valley. I had agreed on the necessity of such a step.

Memphis, however, would be a hard nut to crack. Twice the Party had tried to build an organization there. Twice our organizers had been run out of the town by the Memphis police. First it was Tom Johnson, then I believe, Mack Coad.

In those days Memphis had the reputation of being the murder capital of the nation. It boasted the country's highest homicide rate and had attained the distinction by police murders of Blacks.[71] In this respect, it was worse than in Birmingham where the growth of the communist movement had resulted in curbing police killings, to some extent.

In Memphis, the police were unrestrained; it was open season on Blacks, especially on weekends. Victims were usually among the lowest strata, unemployed, friendless and homeless migrants from the countryside seeking employment in the city. They fell into the catchall category of vagrants, persons with no visible means of support.

Clearly a breakthrough in Memphis required careful planning and most of all, capable organizers. Now, according to Nat, these requisites were present. He had received word from members of a Jewish branch of the International Workers Order (IWO) in Memphis that they were willing to subsidize an International Labor Defense organizer. The IWO was a left-wing insurance organization among whose members were a number of communist and Party sympathizers. I knew the organization, but did not know it had a branch in Memphis.

Nat also informed me that there were two young comrades from New York available for the project—Forshay, an ILD organizer, and Boris Israel, a young communist journalist who was writing a series of articles on the South for the *New Masses*. Israel offered to accompany Forshay.

"Now," Nat said, "if we could only find a good Negro comrade."
"When do we leave?" I asked.

He looked at me with feigned surprise and said, "You really think you should go, Harry? And that it would be alright with the Central Committee?"

"Of course," I replied. I was anxious to undertake this assignment, my first organizing job in the South. I could stay there a little while to help get things started and help make contacts with the Black population.

I was then introduced to the young comrades and at midnight we were on our way to Memphis.

My two young friends, who shared the driving, were in the front seat. When I woke up it was dawn with the Mississippi countryside all around.

It was Saturday morning and we passed a number of trucks loaded with Black sharecroppers and their families, apparently on their way to buy "stores" in Oxford. Some of the trucks were driven by white

'Sharecroppers with Guns: Organizing the Black Belt'

Simon Legree-looking characters, whom I assumed to be plantation riding bosses or planters.

We drew up to the gas station to fill our tank, just outside of Oxford. The attendant, a native cracker type, peered in at me with an expression of curiosity on his face. Then, as if he had figured it all out, he drawled, "What're yo-all doin' with that boy—taking him home?"

"Yeah," said Boris, with a mock Mississippi drawl, "takin' him on home."

Then turning to me the guy said, "Yo glad to be home, boy?"

Falling into my "field-nigger" drawl, I replied "Yahza, cap'n, I shore am."

We pulled away and drove through the town of Oxford, passing the old state capitol and courthouse, dating from antebellum times. (Oxford's only claim to fame was that it was the home of William Faulkner and the University of Mississippi, "Ole Miss.")

A short distance out of town, we pulled up at the home of a comrade named Ufe, whose address had been given us by Ross. Ufe's wife and sister-in-law were the owners of a small plantation.

As a young man, he had emigrated from his native Denmark and settled in the South, where he married into a former slaveholding family. By this time, the plantation had been hard hit by the crisis and mortgaged up to the hilt. There were, I believe, five sharecroppers on the place. I was to learn that they considered Ufe a fair-minded man. Their contracts included the right to sell their own crop and the right to plant gardens. The homes were equipped with electricity and running water. Recruited by Ufe himself, they were all members of the Sharecroppers Union.

Despite his wife, Ufe had never imbibed the white supremacist doctrine and he insisted that he was not a planter but a farm manager. A member of the Socialist Party of Denmark, he had begun to read socialist papers in the US, then the *Daily Worker*, and was finally recruited into the Party by the Birmingham comrades.

I pondered this unusual story which I had heard from Ross and others as we entered the driveway to his home. It was an old run down antebellum structure with columns and all. Ufe, a small wiry man, had been expecting us, and led us into the big living room where a dozen or so sharecroppers and field bands were sitting before a large open fireplace. It was March cold and a huge log was burning. Ufe introduced us to the sharecroppers.

As we talked, I told them about my visit to Dadeville and other things in the outside world. They all listened attentively. We had supper and stayed overnight. His wife was strangely absent, although I'd seen her puttering around in the kitchen.

We left the next morning for Memphis. Arriving there in the afternoon, we drove directly to the house of a Jewish friend, where the IWO was meeting. Our hostess interrupted the meeting, introduced us, and suggested that the matter concerning our visit be discussed presently, under "good and welfare."

Israel, Forshay and I sat in an adjoining room to wait. I picked up a newspaper lying on the table, I believe it was the *Commercial Appeal*, one of the city's big dailies. A front-page article—no more than three or four paragraphs long—caught my attention. It was a story about a young Black man named Levon Carlock who had been killed by police the night before, after allegedly attempting to rape a white woman.

According to the story he had been shot while attempting to escape the scene of the crime. The article listed prominently the names of the officers involved and also the name and address of the alleged rape victim. The murder of Blacks by the police had apparently become such a routine matter that the latter didn't bother to present even a plausible story.

I passed the paper over to Israel and Forshay, exclaiming, "Here's our issue! Let's get to work."

After reading it, they simultaneously declared, "Jesus Christ! That's made to order."

By this time, the meeting in the adjoining room had come to our point on the agenda. I looked over the group. They were middle class people, storekeepers and the like, several professionals, and, as I later learned, one wealthy jeweler. I was surprised that the majority of the group were young couples, some of them born in the South and speaking with Southern drawls. They were very definitely revolutionary in sentiment.

Some were readers of the *Freiheit* (the Yiddish language communist daily) and the *Daily Worker*. Several of them, I was to learn, had participated in the two previous attempts to form a revolutionary organization in Memphis. They represented the left wing of the Jewish

'Sharecroppers with Guns: Organizing the Black Belt'

community in Memphis and reflected the hatred of an entire community for Boss Crump's reigning political machine in Memphis. Crump was not only a rabid racist, but a Jew-hater as well.

As regarded our mission, there was nothing much to be said. We had come there at their invitation. So they proceeded to the immediate question of the subsidy for Forshay, as the ILD organizer. They had agreed on a salary of sixteen dollars a week, with room and board. He was to stay with the jeweler, who had a large house.

Boris also was to stay with Forshay at the jeweler's and I with a young couple—storekeepers who lived close to the Black neighborhood. That settled, I informed the group about the news article concerning the alleged rape.

Their response was "this happens every day"—it was a common thing. They described the beating and killing of Blacks in the station house, of young Black boys disappearing after they were taken to the station by police, about Blacks being beaten unconscious right out on the street.

We were anxious to pick up on the issue while it was hot. We sent Boris Israel to check on the story while Forshay and I remained at the house, where we set up temporary headquarters. We were quite fortunate to have on our team a man like Boris, with his experience and training as an investigative reporter.

Several hours later he returned, having uncovered a shocking story of racism, murder and police brutality. He had gone directly to the address of the "rape victim," whom he had found to be a prostitute living in the red light district that adjoined the Black neighborhood. Interviewing her, he had found gaping irregularities in her obviously rehearsed story. At first she had talked openly, unrestrainedly about her "horrendous experience." Then suddenly she clammed up, blurting out, "The police cap'n said I was not to talk to anybody." Then she closed the door on Boris.

Boris then interviewed the widow of the murdered man. She lived in a rooming house not far from the scene. She was just a slip of a girl—sixteen she said—but looked even younger. The incident had left her in a state of shock. She was being consoled by an older woman, who turned out to be a maid who lived in the whorehouse.

She began to tell her story. She and her seventeen-year-old husband, Levon Carlock, were newly married and had just come up from Mississippi, where both their families were ruined sharecroppers. She had gotten a job as a maid in one of the white whorehouses. Levon, who was still unemployed, would come to pick her up every night at about 2:00 a.m. and escort her home.

On the night of the tragedy, he had been waiting out in the street for her as usual, when the police officers shot him down. Overcome by grief, Mrs. Carlock then burst into tears and could no longer continue. At this point, the older woman led Boris into another room and continued the story. She had seen the whole incident from a second-story window above the alley.

She said four policemen had taken Levon around into the alley. She had heard noises and cursing, cries of "you Black son-of-a bitch." "You're the nigger that raped that white woman." They were beating the poor youth unmercifully with their clubs and fists, she said.

Levon kept protesting that he had come to take his wife home.

Then, one of the officers appeared escorting a white woman. She said, "I recognized her as one of the prostitutes that lives across the street."

Then the officers asked the woman if Levon was the one that had tried to rape her, and she said "Yeah, he's the one." Then she went back to her house.

They started beating Levon again, knocking him to the ground and pulling out their revolvers. Levon begged for his life, but it did no good. "They shot him down in cold blood, right there in the alley," she said. As they turned and walked away, one of the cops said, "You know that nigger son-of-a-bitch is still alive?" I guess they heard moaning. They stopped, and one of the officers went over and pointed his pistol at Levon's head and blew his brains out right there in the alley. Then a short time later, a Black undertaker came and took his body. The police must have had him laying in wait.

Mrs. Carlock had heard some of this, but hadn't seen it. She had fainted and after she had come to, was hysterical. We kept her in the house overnight; the landlady gave her some pills. In the morning, I went with her to the undertaker to identify Levon's body. Later we got the maid to put her story in an affidavit.

Well, there it was. A perfect issue!

Hoping through such a mass campaign that we could build a Party organization in Memphis, we immediately began our campaign to stir up Memphis. We knew that the issue would take hold of the Black population and we hoped to take advantage of the anti-Crump sentiment among whites to win some of them to our side.

We set out to build a broad united front, under the auspices of the LSNR, which I represented, and the ILD. Then and there we worked out a leaflet, slogans and plan of action. Our slogans were: "Stop Police Murder of Negroes in Memphis!" "Levon Carlock Must Be the Last!"

We called for immediate expulsion of the officers involved, their arrest and prosecution on charges of first degree murder and indemnity to the widow. Our program of action called for the establishment of block and neighborhood committees and mass protest meetings.

The slogans caught fire. Within two or three weeks we had a considerable movement going. Outside of our Jewish friends, we knew no one in Memphis, but they introduced us to their few acquaintances among Blacks. Our most important contact was the editor of the *Memphis World*, Memphis's Black newspaper, and his staff. They were sympathetic and wanted something to be done about the murders. Then we met with a number of lower echelon leaders—ministers, educators, lodge leaders and a few business men. We soon had an ad hoc committee going, while we stayed in the background. A number of meetings were called at which Mrs. Carlock appeared, and some neighborhood or block committees were set up as a result.

At the beginning, we had contacted the national office of the ILD and informed Patterson of our plans. We called for a nation wide support campaign, linked up with the Scottsboro and Herndon campaigns. The national office gave us a green light to go ahead with our plans and get a local (white) lawyer to prosecute our case against the police.

A rain of telegrams from across the country poured into the Memphis mayor's office and the *Memphis World* carried news of the campaign. Our Jewish friends succeeded in getting a local lawyer, a white anti-Crump man. "He didn't care so much about Negroes, but he sure hated Crump!" they said.

The campaign spread. Its effectiveness was confirmed by two incidents. Our friends on the *World* kept us informed about everything going on in the community. They told us that a delegation of Uncle Tom leaders had gone to see the mayor. They were alarmed by the threat our campaign posed to their leadership—they were unable to keep the Blacks in line. They pleaded for at least some token concession on the part of the police. For example, a statement from the mayor to the effect that an investigation would be held. Something they could use to counter the "red invasion" of the Black community.

The mayor not only refused to budge, but told the delegation that the police were doing their duty—and they had better do theirs! The city and police, he asserted, would brook no rebellion from the niggers—and you'd better tell your folk that, too! As regards the "red invasion," the mayor said that he was aware that there were a dozen or so reds in the city and that they would be taken care of when the time came. They were apparently waiting for a lull in the movement to move in.

It was also through the *World* people that we met Robert E. Lee, a lieutenant of Bob Church, the Black Republican National Committeeman from Memphis. Lee himself was a prominent man in the community. He sought us out to inform us (in private) that Bob Church liked what we were doing and wanted us to keep it up. He evidently felt that our campaign strengthened his position vis-a-vis Boss Crump.

Daisy Lampkin, national field secretary of the NAACP, came to Memphis in the midst of our campaign. She came there to help the local branch in its annual membership drive and was unaware of the growing movement initiated by the ILD. The whole thing was quite an unpleasant surprise for the woman. The Party and the ILD had had run-ins with her regarding Scottsboro, and she became frantic when she found out about our work in Memphis. Her campaign was low key; conducted under the abstract slogans of "Equal justice and opportunity," which carefully avoided the burning issue of police murders right under our noses.

The NAACP was in an embarrassing spot. They called a mass meeting in one of the largest churches in connection with their membership drive campaign. We invaded it, with Mrs. Carlock dressed in mourning black, and demanded a place on the platform for her. As I remember, she was given the platform and she spoke of the murder, asking for help from the NAACP to prevent anything of this sort from happening again. She proposed a united front of the NAACP, ILD and LSNR against police brutality. The chairman passed it off by referring it to the local board. But after the meeting, Lee told us later, the proposal failed to pass the board by only one vote—he personally had voted for it.

This was to be the beginning of a downturn in our fortunes. Next was the disappearance of our star witness, the maid who worked at the whorehouse. The local attorney asked us to bring her up to his office, but when we went to get her, she had gone. She didn't work there anymore. We speculated that the police had frightened her into leaving town after we sent the affidavit she had given us to the national office and they had published it—either in the *Daily Worker* or the *Labor Defender*. We had a weak reed in the first place, since she was vulnerable herself to a frame-up.

The legal side of the case was important, but now our attorney was helpless without a witness. Without the legal case, we couldn't keep up with the public campaign and it began to lose momentum.

The situation was becoming threatening. The cops were getting ready to move in. We discussed this with our friends and they said we'd made a hell of a good fight, but it would be better to send someone else in, now that we were known. So the three of us went in to the office of the *Memphis World* and the editor said we were lucky, we had just missed the four cops who were looking for us.

We decided it was time to leave town. We first decided to go by the telegraph station to pickup some money Patterson had wired us. Forshay and Israel went in to get the money. I stood outside waiting for them. Two cops came up and looked at the Alabama license plate on the car.

Then Forshay and Israel came out of the office—Boris took in the scene in a glance. He jumped into the car and shouted at me, "Come on, Sam! Let's get out of heah."

"Yassuh," I drawled, and climbed in the back. We kept driving until we got to Mississippi!

It wasn't a total defeat. Forshay stayed behind and continued to organize for the ILD. Our work put the cops on notice that they couldn't get away with the kind of crap they had been dishing out. The raw stuff had to stop; otherwise they would have trouble. The flood of telegrams had an impact. It also helped lay the base for future activity there.

'REPLY TO MISLED WORKER'
FROM *SOUTHERN WORKER*
NOVEMBER 15, 1930

A letter, expressing the white supremacy ideas of the boss class and showing how even some white workers who call themselves revolutionary are victims of these false ideas, has been received by a communist worker in Winston-Salem, N.C. So important is it to combat these wrong ideas in the minds of workers that we are printing this letter and our reply. We want both white and Negro workers to enter into this discussion, and write in their opinions for publication in the *Southern Worker*. The letter from the worker follows:

Dear Comrade:

I am writing to you in relative to your letter of the 16 in regard to the *Southern Worker*. I went out last Sunday a week ago, got one subscriber, and last Sunday he came back and got his money back. He said it was nothing but a Negro paper. I can't get subs for a paper that devotes 90 percent of its news to Negroes and 10 percent to the whites.

Personally it does not affect me. But when you approach white workers who still have the race hatred in them, they simply won't take it.

---

* "Reply to Misled Worker," *Southern Worker*, November 15, 1930, Marxists Internet Archive.

I shall vote the Communist ticket straight and get all the votes I can. I wish the Party well. I am not turned against it at all, but I am disgusted with some of the tactics. You know that both the whites and blacks are taught to hate each other, so why not work with them separately until you get them class-conscious, then put them together.

If the Communists had never taken a Negro into the union, I mean here in the South, they would today carry the whole South on Nov. 4. My plan is to get in power, then use legal means to put thru the program.

Now, don't take this personally, as it is not meant that way, but see, if something can't be planned out to win the white workers. They are the ones the capitalists use to do all the dirty work, their thugs, strikebreakers, police and national guard. The Negroes are not used very much in this way because the bosses cannot trust them, either can the workers organizations under a Proletarian dictatorship. They will have to be disciplined for 50 years, since the Negro has just emerged from serfdom and is now tasting the fruits of capitalism or thinks he is, thru schools, churches and all the other social orders. He is 50 years behind and cannot make a jump from serfdom to socialism on his own initiative. It will have to be forced on him, so why retard the movement by using them in the limelight, in all the papers and magazines?

Hoping you will consider these few remarks. I am yours very comradely,

C. R. S.

A Revolutionary?

First we should tell our readers what we know about this white worker who writes in this letter. Like all other workers he has suffered in this crisis, being unemployed for about six months. He was a member of the Socialist Party State Committee of North Carolina for years. He repudiated the Socialist Party and joined the Communist Party last February, but was later dropped for reasons that are evident in his letter.

It is evident to any class-conscious worker, that although the writer of this letter may call himself "revolutionary," he represents a point of view that is distinctly anti-labor and is against the interests of both white and Negro workers. In spite of the fact that this worker has left the Socialist Party he still retains the same point of view as that party, as shown by the letter received by a Texas Communist from A. F. Van Blon, who was Socialist candidate for lieutenant governor of Texas, in which he says "You know the South well enough to know that it will not be class conscious enough for at least 50 years to tolerate voting for a colored man."

'White Supremacy'

This worker has allowed himself to be taken in entirely by the boss talk of "white supremacy." The white ruling class wishes to make the Negroes appear as "low down," not quite human, never to be given the same . . . [illegible] as a white—in order to be better able to exploit the Negro workers and farmers after separating them from the entire class. In order to prevent an effective fight against this exploitation and the extreme lynch law practice, the ruling class uses the system of segregation and Jim-Crowism to keep the white and Negro workers divided. Any worker who accepts these ideas of the bosses helps to tie the chains of exploitation around him the harder—for it is very clear that no fight can be made against unemployment, low wages, . . . [illegible] working conditions, unless that fight is waged by Negro and white workers together. If it is not the bosses . . . [illegible] will use either the Negro workers against the white, or the white against the Negro in order to suppress that fight.

'Negro Paper—White Paper'

The worker tells about the subscriber to the *Southern Worker* who later came back and got his money returned, because it was a "Negro paper" and although the writer of the letter says that he personally don't care "about 90 percent of the news" being devoted to Negroes, it is clear the letter that he does. The *Southern Worker* is no more a Negro paper than it is a white paper. It is a revolutionary working class paper. Just because of the fact that the Negro worker and farmer in the

South are the most exploited in the country and the most persecuted because of the fact that the "white supremacy" ideas of the bosses, the AFL and the socialists have crippled and prevented the organization of the Southern workers—that is why the *Southern Worker* devotes so much space to the Negro question. You see, news about Negro workers is not just for Negroes, nor is news about white workers just for whites—both are for all workers. And in order to make possible a real united struggle against the brutal Southern ruling class, it is necessary to educate the white workers especially and expose to them how they are being fooled by the bosses' race prejudice.

This worker's talk about "discipline for 50 years" and "just out of serfdom" is all the same sort of rot that the bosses want to make us believe. Doesn't this white worker, who has been unemployed for six months, think that he and the other white workers of the South, begging for a bite to eat, are not also kept in serfdom? During slavery the Negroes in the South were chattel slaves, today both the Negroes and the white workers are wage slaves, or virtual peons to white landowners. Shall we then wait until the white ruling class chooses to free us from wage slavery? Not by a long shot! We will fight Negro and white together, to free ourselves.

Carrying The South

The white worker also says that if the Communist had not admitted a single Negro to a union or to the Party in the South we would have carried the whole South on election day. If we had done as this worker suggests, we could no longer call ourselves Communists, but instead we would be just as great traitors and contemptible curs as the AFL officials. The Communist Party is not a "white" party as this worker infers, with the power to exclude Negro workers form membership in it. The Communist Party consists of both Negro and white workers from the membership to the leadership. If we were willing to give up all the principles for which our Party stands, we will agree that we may even be elected to the White House, but then we would no longer be a workers' party, but just another boss outfit, and there would be a real worker's party to take our place. But there is no fear of that, fellow workers. The vote obtained by the Communist Party in the South in the election is worth everything for it stands for the uncompromising principles of revolutionary working class solidarity. We are not out merely to obtain votes—the Communist Party uses the election campaign to explain and rally the workers to its entire program.

This worker would also have us organize white and Negro Workers in Jim-Crow organizations, like the AFL. We all know what that means—crippling the whole working class. The only method by which we obtain our final aim, the overthrow of the present system and the erection of a workers and farmers government, is by the united fight of workers of all races. We cannot first "get in power and then organize" as this worker says. We must first organize—yes, white and Negro together—and then get in power as a workers and farmers government of all races, not by voting, but by struggle.

'SAVE THE SCOTTSBORO BLACK YOUTHS'
CLARA ZETKIN
MOPR PERIODICAL FOR THE STRUGGLE AND THE LABOR OF THE INTERNATIONAL RED HELP
1932

C omrades and friends of the MOPR and all those who still possess a humane mind and heart, unite in order to prevent a particularly incredible and heinous judicial crime which, without your decisive and quick action, will enter the annals of judicial crimes in the United States which are already redundant with horrible outrages!

The protest and revulsion over Sacco and Vanzetti (two innocent individuals who after a correct trial of bourgeois class justice were burned upon the modern pyre of the electric chair) have not yet totally ebbed, when the executioners want to use this means of torture and murder once again in order to kill, at one strike, eight more innocent victims.

In the State of Alabama, of nine young Blacks who have hardly emerged from adolescence (the oldest is 20 years old!), one received "only" lifelong imprisonment whereas the eight others have been condemned to death.

This judgment was made even though it has been clearly determined that they did not commit the crime of which they stand accused, namely, the rape of two white prostitutes. The accusation is a conscious lie which was designed for sinister purposes by landowners and manu-

---
* Clara Zetkin, "Save the Scottsboro Black Youths," *MOPR Periodical for the Struggle and the Labor of the International Red Help*, 1932.

facturers. These forces want to incinerate these Black youths in order to terrorize the Black masses which are rising up against their exploitation and are beginning to form a common front with their white brothers and sisters against hunger, imperialist wars and bloody white terror.

From the very beginning, the serious indictment lacked any basis and could not withstand any serious investigation. One of the prostitutes finally admitted that her initial accusation had been false. The judges, however, totally ignored this fact. The most despicable race hatred of white against Black, this lowest expression of arrogance and low human and cultural values, has awakened the beast of lynching. This beast is traversing the State of Alabama and is demanding victims. For its gratification, eight Black youths are supposed to be incinerated on the modern pyre.

The Supreme Court of Alabama has not yet spoken. That is why there has not yet been an appeal to the Supreme Court of the United States concerning this despicable verdict of lowest racial hatred. Yet the atmosphere of racial hatred and lynching brutality, which marked the trial and the judge's verdict, raise the fear that the confirmation of the bloody verdict by the Supreme Court of Alabama will come so late and the execution so rapidly, that there will not be any time to take the matter to the Supreme Court of the United States of America.

In the face of this horrendous possibility, you must act immediately and with all of your energy.

No time must be wasted and every minute must be used so that eight young lives will be spared the possibility of being burned in the electric chair.

Comrades and Friends of the MOPR of all countries! It is clear that you will continue with all of your power and devotion to support the demand: "Let us get the eight Black youths off the electric chair and out of prison. Let us also free the brave and innocently convicted labor leaders Tom Mooney and Warren Billings along with the Harlan miners and all other political prisoners." Yes, you will accomplish the seemingly impossible and increase your unselfish and energetic effort to save the eight Black youths. Thus you remain the firm, unshakable vanguard in the fight against the threatening crime of racial hatred, lynch justice and exploitative greed. In order to prevent the judicial murder of eight Black youths, the strong and invincible forces of the masses must be employed.

'Save the Scottsboro Black Youths'

All those of you who still possess a humane mind and heart! Let us save these eight young men from the executioner and the pyre of the electric chair. Their only crime has been that they were born with Black skins. Speak and act! In your front ranks there will be innumerable, unbiased and humane individuals from the United States of America. They have not forgotten that there existed in the United States, men and women with highly developed spirits and characters who, risking their reputation, their social positions, their health and not uncommonly their lives, fought for the end of Black slavery and for the liberation and equality of their Black brothers and sisters. The wonderful example which was set by these great deceased people must not only remain enshrined in the paper of scholarly works, but in the living deeds of people. The history of the United States contains forever the deeds of heroic men and women who, fearlessly lifting high the banner of liberation and equality for all the downtrodden and despised people, have fought in the mass battle for human rights against deep-rooted hatred and bias. It must not happen that alongside these luminous pages of history appears an augmentation of the dark, blood-stained chronicles of lynchings and judicial crimes by the murder of eight Black youths. Think of the indescribable suffering and horror which must be caused by their long investigatory confinement. Every day and every hour they are confronted by the burning question whether tomorrow or the day after tomorrow, the executioner will cross the threshold of their cell in order to sacrifice the eight selected victims upon the altar of race hatred.

MOPR Comrades, MOPR Friends, all of you who still maintain a humane mind and heart. Raise your voices! Act! The strong, irresistible shout of the gigantic, innumerable masses must overcome the verdict of race hatred of the judge. It must drown out the scream of the lynching beast. The hands of the gigantic, innumerable masses must be clenched into one gigantic fist which will tear up this judgment and topple the electric chair. Every person that remains silent in this battle for the salvation of the eight Blacks, and perhaps even steps aside in a resigned, nonchalant manner, must share the guilt of a heinous crime which would become an indelible mark of shame in the history of the United States and humankind.

The battle for the rescue of these eight young lives from the torture and murder of the electric chair, is part of the worldwide historical struggle between unbiased, cultured humanity and narrow-minded, brutal and bloody race hatred whose uncivilized, barbaric roots, reach into the past. In this struggle, humaneness must emerge victoriously. Its victory is certain if everybody, consistently and courageously, will do his best. Let us work and fight with devotion! Let us work and fight, therefore, also for a strong MOPR, which is steeled in the fight against the White terror. Long live the international solidarity of the workers of all races and nations!

SECTION 03

THEORY

About Section Three: Theory

The texts in this section bring forth the theoretical debates and considerations being made in the United States and internationally about the Black Belt Thesis.

The section begins with two selections from Tom Johnson, a Communist Party organizer sent to Birmingham, Alabama in the 1930s. The first piece, "The National Revolutionary Struggle of the Negroes," is a series of three articles written for the *Southern Worker* in 1931. These articles explore the basis and consequences of the "special oppression" of Black workers, the role of revolutionary white workers, and debates over the self-determination of the Black Belt. The second piece, an excerpt from *The Reds in Dixie*, provides a particularly salient argument: Johnson argues that the Black Belt Thesis was not being imposed from the Communist Party, but was a theory already being acted upon on the ground by workers, organizers, and leaders in the region.

Several chapters from James S. Allen's *The Negro Question in the United States* detail the agricultural, industrial, financial, and governmental conditions that characterize the Black Belt. Allen ultimately argues that "only in the realization of the right of self-determination for the Negro people in the Black Belt" can liberation of the US South be achieved.

A 1946 article by Claudia Jones, "On the Right to Self-Determination for the Negro People in the Black Belt," tackles the distinction between opposing strains of thinking on the thesis, such as that between the CPUSA's Black nationalist position and Earl Browder's "revisionist" position. Jones argues that "any 'internationalism' that denies the right of self-determination to the subject peoples is false, a mere cover for imperialist chauvinism."

Lastly, in a chapter from his 1948 book *Negro Liberation*, Harry Haywood explores the question of land in the Black Belt—its ownership, distribution, and use—and its connection to the entire system of white supremacy.

'THE NATIONAL REVOLUTIONARY STRUGGLE OF THE NEGROES'
TOM JOHNSON
FROM *SOUTHERN WORKER*
1931

FROM VOL 1, NO. 28 (FEBRUARY 28, 1931)

(This is the first of a series of three articles. The other two will appear in successive issues of the *Southern Worker*.)

It is only within the past year that our Communist Party has succeeded, with the help of the Communist International, in developing a truly Bolshevik program of action for our work among the 13 million American Negroes. Moreover it is doubtful if there is another portion of our program so little understood not only by the masses of workers but by our own party members as well. Yet the winning of the millions of Negro workers and poor farmers for Communism is a task of the greatest importance. To talk of a workers' revolution in this country without the active support of the Negro toilers is to give up all thought of a successful revolution. Particularly here in the South this

---

* Tom Johnson, "The National Revolutionary Struggle of the Negroes," *Southern Worker*, February 28, 1931, Marxists Internet Archive; Tom Johnson, "The National Revolutionary Struggle of the Negroes," *Southern Worker*, March 7, 1931, Marxists Internet Archive; Tom Johnson, "The National Revolutionary Struggle of the Negroes," *Southern Worker*, March 14, 1931, Marxists Internet Archive.

task is of decisive importance to the development of the revolutionary movement. It will be, therefore, the purpose of this article to set forth the program of the Communist Party on the so-called Negro question, as clearly and as simply as may be possible.

Most Oppressed Group

In the first place it is clear to every worker in the South that the Negroes form a group which is *especially oppressed*, oppressed even more than the white workers and farmers. Every worker knows that in the shops and mines the Negroes can get only the hardest and heaviest work; that the Negro workers are forbidden in many cases from following skilled trades; that as a rule on the same job Negroes are paid less than white workers. It is common knowledge that on the farms in the Black Belt the Negro croppers are little if any better than slaves. They have no voice whatever in determining what crops they shall plant, how the crop shall be cultivated and how and for what price it shall be sold. All this is taken care of by the white landlord, who, at the end of a season takes over the whole of the crop and then gives to the Negro cropper whatever he chooses. In many sections it is not uncommon for Negro croppers to be sold and traded with the land by the white landlords.

Secondly, every worker knows that the oppression of the Negro is not confined to the job. The Negro in the Black Belt has no political rights whatsoever. He cannot vote or run for office. He is forbidden to serve on juries. No pretense is made of giving the Negroes any voice at all in the state, county, or city governments. Further, in his daily life outside the shop the Negro worker and Negro farmer, no less than the worker, is Jim-Crowed and segregated, forbidden to associate on terms of equality with the whites.

Its Basis—Profit

What is the basis for this oppression? Why do the white boss men and big farmers oppress the Negro more than the white worker? Why does the white ruling class carry on a constant campaign in the schools, the press on every side, to keep the white worker convinced that he is "superior" to the Negro, that the Negro "must be kept in his place"? Is it because the Negro happens to belong to another race? Is it because the Negro's skin is black and the white bosses' skin is white?? Not at all! The Negro is *oppressed more than the white for one reason and for one reason only—because it means more profits for the white bosses and landlords.* This works out in two ways.

First, by means of this extraordinary oppression the white ruling class is able to beat down the wages to even below the minimum needed for existence. This is true of both the Negro farm workers and croppers. It must be clear to everyone that if the Negro had even the few rights of the white workers it would be much more difficult for the bosses and the landlords to keep wages so low and to cheat the cropper out of most of his crop. Thus, we can see that by this whole system of oppression of the Negroes, the white ruling class is able to force wages and conditions on the Negro workers and farmers than would otherwise be possible, and this means extra profits for the white bosses and landlords, of course.

Keep Wages Low

Second, by keeping the wages and conditions of the Negro workers down below that of the working class as a whole the ruling class is able to use this as a club to beat down the wages of the white workers as well. Every worker knows that the standard excuse in cutting wages of white workers is that "Negroes will do the work cheaper." Every worker knows that in any strike in the South, the bosses always try (and often succeed) in breaking the strike by deliberately playing up the racial hatred they have created. When Negro workers strike it is white workers who are brought in to scab on them, and when white workers strike it is Negro workers who are used to break the strike. Thus we see that through the special oppression of the Negroes the bosses are able to keep down wages of all workers, and of course make more profits for themselves.

FROM VOL 1, NO. 29 (MARCH 7, 1931)

The fact that the Negroes are black-skinned and the whites are lighter in color is not the reason for the special oppression of the Negroes, as we have seen. This fact merely makes this oppression easier and is used to incite the white workers against the Negroes.

This intolerable oppression and discrimination against the Negroes; the fact that they are deprived of all so-called "democratic" rights which the whites have; the added fact that this special oppression and discrimination is practiced against all sections and classes of the Negro population, particularly in the South, has the effect of binding the Negro people more firmly together as an oppressed nation, struggling against the oppressor nation, ruled by the white master class. Further, there exists in the South the economic basis for this national struggle of the Negro people. In a whole section of the South—the Black Belt, which starts up in North Carolina and runs down through South Carolina, across Central Georgia and southern Alabama and over into Mississippi—the Negroes outnumber the whites. In this wide belt in which there are 264 counties where the Negroes are in a majority, the oppression of the Negro masses takes its sharpest and most brutal form. Here all of the "democratic" rights granted the white population are denied the Negro. Here lynching and mob violence rule supreme. Here the millions of Negroes are carefully segregated from the whites by Jim Crow laws. Here actual slave conditions exist on the farms.

Struggle against White Bosses

In the struggle against such conditions the Negro people are bound to see that this struggle is a hopeless one as long as the state power remains in the hands of the white ruling class. Here the Negro people are bound to see that the only way they can throw off this intolerable system of oppression and can win and keep for themselves even those few rights granted the white population, is by a struggle against the white ruling class and against the powerful white ruling class government which is the instrument used to oppress the Negro people and deprive them of all rights. Here they are bound to see that the only guarantee to end lynch law and this existing oppression of a whole nation, that their only guarantee for full equality with the whites, is the transfer of the government power from the hands of the white ruling class into the hands of the oppressed Negro nation.

This developing struggle of the Negro people against national oppression in the Black Belt is certain to be expressed in the demand by the Negro nation for the right, in the Black Belt where they are in the majority, to separate from the rest of the United States and to set up their own government, controlled by the Negro people and not by the white ruling class. This means a demand that the Negro nation shall have the right to self-determination, whether or not it shall separate from the rest of the United States. It means a demand that the Negro people shall have the right to determine their own national existence. It means a demand for the right of self-determination. Around this demand for the right of self-determination, there can be rallied the whole oppressed masses of the Negro toilers.

Same Enemies as White Workers

But this struggle of the Negro people for the right to a separate national existence is taking place at a time when the revolutionary struggle of all workers, both Negro and white, against the white ruling class and against capitalism is growing and developing. Therefore this special national struggle of the Negro people becomes bound in with and a part of the general working-class struggle against capitalism. This is true because both the national struggle of the Negroes and the revolutionary working-class struggle are directed against the same common enemy—the white ruling class. Therefore, these two revolutionary movements supplement and support each other. In other words a blow against the white ruling class struck in the struggle for self-determination is a blow in defense of the working-class revolution against capitalism, and the struggle against capitalism is at the same time a struggle for the right of the Negro people to self-determination.

Furthermore, as we have seen above, one of the main sources of extra profits and hence of power of the ruling class in the United States is exactly the extraordinary oppression of the Negro people. Therefore fighting any movement which is directed against this special oppression of the Negroes tends to weaken the power of the ruling class, and to the extent which it does this, aids the working-class revolution.

For those reasons it is clear that the revolutionary white workers must give every possible support to the struggle of the Negro people against oppression and for the right of self-determination.

FROM VOL 1, NO. 30 (MARCH 14, 1931)

To fail to support this struggle of the Negroes against the common enemy of all those who toil means in effect to give support to the enemy—to the capitalist class.

The ruling class realizes very clearly that the best guarantee they have against a successful struggle of the working class against capitalism is the present division in the ranks of the workers. Therefore they do all possible through discrimination against the Negro, through segregation of the Negro from the white worker, through a whole elaborate system of Jim Crow laws, to keep the white and Negro toilers from uniting in common struggle against the common enemy. Therefore they deliberately stir up racial hatred and incite mob violence against the Negroes.

Smash the Barrier!

It is one of the most important tasks of the Communists in the South to smash through this barrier the bosses have set up between the white and Negro toilers. Through careful and consistent propaganda, through pointing out the lessons of all strikes and labor struggles, the Communists must win the masses of white workers away from their ideas of "white supremacy" etc., pumped into them by the boss. And at the same time the Communists must do all possible to break down the justified distrust of the Negro masses toward even the white workers. On every hand and in every struggle the Communists must constantly struggle to unite the white and Negro farmers and workers on a common platform of struggle against the ruling class.

Struggle against Misleaders

It is the duty of the Communists to give every support to, and to fight in the front ranks of, the battles of the Negro people for the right of self-determination. But at the same time the Negro and white Communists must carry on a consistent struggle against those misleaders of the Negroes, such as Marcus Garvey, who are trying or will try to lead the national struggle into incorrect channels or to use it for their own selfish benefit. The Communists must systematically expose such misleaders to the masses of Negroes and must point out continually that although at certain stages of the struggle even the small Negro bosses, store keepers and professional people, and plantation owners may give some little support to the national struggle, these people will in the end betray it. It is the duty of the Communists to struggle always to the end that the leadership of the national revolutionary struggle shall be taken over by the Negro workers in the shops and mines, as the Negro workers alone are capable of giving correct revolutionary leadership to the whole movement.

This great revolutionary national struggle of the Negro people, which is destined to become the most important ally of the working-class revolution in the South, will not develop overnight. It is the task of the Communists to develop this struggle for the immediate partial demands of the Negro masses.

The manner in which this struggle must be developed, the demands which must be raised in the struggle, will be dealt with in another series of articles to appear in the *Southern Worker* at an early date.

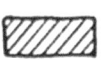 # SELECTIONS FROM THE REDS IN DIXIE: WHO ARE THE COMMUNISTS AND WHAT DO THEY FIGHT FOR IN THE SOUTH?

TOM JOHNSON
1935

From Maine to the Gulf and from the Atlantic to the Pacific, the country has been rocked this year by the greatest series of strikes and labor disputes in all its history. In every last one of these strikes the issue of Communism was raised. In the textile strike, in the Birmingham coal and ore mine strikes, in the General Strike in San Francisco, and in countless others, the strikers saw the Communists on the picket lines, saw them fighting back the scabs and facing the bayonets of the National Guard. Likewise in the struggles of the unemployed the workers saw the Communists organizing and leading demonstrations for more relief, strikes for higher wages on relief jobs—saw them active in the workers' struggles everywhere. Yet in spite of this, few people really know who the Communists are and just what they are trying to do. The bosses and the landlords in their newspapers, over the radio and in the movies, tell the workers that the Communists are all foreigners—mostly Jews—who in some way are "against America" and

---

* Tom Johnson, *The Reds in Dixie: Who Are the Communists and What Do They Fight for in the South?* (New York: Workers Library Publishers, 1935).

are always stirring up trouble. Here in the South they say we want to tear down the churches, incite race riots, force whites to marry Negroes and eventually turn America over to some foreign country—probably Russia. Even some of the highly paid trade union leaders link Francis J. Gorman of the United Textile Workers Union, Robert Moore of the Alabama State Federation of Labor, William Mitch of the United Mine Workers and others, repeat these stories and try to stir up the workers against the "Reds." A worker hardly knows what to believe when he sees Communists leading picket lines, working day and night to build powerful unions, and then is told that they are trying to wreck the unions and the country, that they are "un-American."

To put an end to this confusion we propose to tell in this booklet just who the Communists are, what they want and how they expect to get it. We Communists have nothing to conceal; we state our aims openly and honestly. Then every worker must decide for himself whether in his opinion it is good or bad; whether he is with us or against us. We are confident of the result.

Who Are the Communists?

First of all, they are working people. The great majority of the members of the Communist Party are men and women who work in textile mills, coal and ore mines, steel mills, on the railroads, in laundries, etc. Of course the Communist Party also takes in sharecroppers, cash renters and even small farm owners, but it does not take in any bosses, or landlords, or rich farmers who work their land with hired labor. In other words the Communist Party is an organization of the poor people of this country.

But the bosses say that we are all foreigners; that we are "un-American." How about that? The fact is, as every schoolboy knows, that every single person in America, outside of the Indians, either came here from a foreign country or is descended from people who did. Some came later than others, that is all. For instance, the Negroes first reached America 300 years ago, but shall we say they are more "American" than most Southern white workers, whose people came to America 150 years ago, or even later? Of course not! The important thing is that no matter when these people of different nationalities arrived in America, today most of them are working in American shops and mines or are farming American land. Native-born white, native-born Negro, foreign-born white, Jew or Gentile, Protestant or Catholic, all work for the same bosses, get the same wage cuts, stand in the same soup lines when they are unemployed. Some may be worse off than others but all suffer alike under the rule of the bosses. Our Party membership represents every section of the American working class.

Now we can see who the Communists really are: They are workers, black and white, native and foreign-born, who work in American industries or starve in American soup lines. Who has a better right to call themselves Americans than those who do America's work?

What Do the Communists Want?

We said the Communists are workers. To understand just what they want let us first of all see what the workers and sharecroppers of the South want and need.

If you are out of a job (and with millions unemployed in the South, the chances are pretty good that you are) you want most of all enough relief to provide your family with sufficient wholesome food, with a home to live in and with clothes to keep them warm. Most workers want their relief in cash so that they can spend it where they want to and on the things they need most. If you have a relief job you want decent wages and union conditions on the job.... Now what about the Communists? They are fighting for these very things for every unemployed worker in the country—and, what is more, they are winning them.

It is clear that no unemployed worker can obtain better relief simply by asking for it, with no organization to back him up. Therefore the Communist Party does its best to help the unemployed organize into Unemployment Councils which will look out for their interests, just as a trade union protects the interests of its members, and will lead the fight for more relief. In the same way Communists everywhere take the lead in organizing the workers on relief jobs in order to carry on a struggle for better wages and conditions.

Way back in March 1930, long before the American Federation of Labor, the Socialist Party or any other working-class organization had even discussed the question of unemployment, the Communists organized the first big gatherings of the unemployed throughout the country to demand unemployment relief. In New York City alone, over 150,000 workers met in a great mass meeting on March 6, to demand that the city immediately appropriate money for unemployment relief. The meeting was attacked by police and after a hard fight they finally broke it up, but that same week New York City provided its first funds for unemployment relief. In Memphis, in July 1933, the Communists led 5,000 white and Negro relief workers on strike and in one day won an increase of 25 cents a day for every relief worker in the city. In New Orleans, in the latter part of 1934, a militant demonstration of unemployed forced the city to continue relief payments. These few examples (and we could give hundreds more) show that the Communists not only say they are in favor of more relief, but that they also organize the fight for it and win it.

What Do the Sharecroppers Need?

Now, let us say that you are a sharecropper, or a cash renter, or even a farmer who owns a bit of land he works himself, what do you need most of all today? The first thing the poverty-stricken croppers and small farmers in the South need is enough to eat. Nowhere in the whole country is there as much hunger, suffering and actual starvation as on Southern farms. Second, the cropper and cash renter want the absolute right to gin and sell their share of the crop themselves without interference from the landlord. They want, if they are to live, they must have lower rent. They want the checks mailed farmers by the government, for land left out of cultivation, sent direct to them and not to the landlord. And they don't want the landlord's, or the storekeeper's, or the banker's name on the check either. That check must be theirs to do with as they see fit.

They want the repeal of the insane Bankhead Bill, which forces farmers to restrict the planting of food and other staple crops, while the farmers themselves and millions of others go hungry. They want a stop put to the foreclosure of mortgages on small farms, to the eviction of any cropper, renter or poor owner from the land he works, and an end to the practice of seizing tools and stock for debts. They want the wiping out (cancellation) of all debts and obligations which the cropper and poor owner cannot pay back because the prices he receives for cotton, corn and tobacco are so low. They want full school terms for their children, free school books and free buses to carry the children to and from school. And finally the Negro croppers want freedom from the chains of semi-slavery which bind them to the landlord.

The farm workers, the cotton pickers, choppers, etc., want higher wages, an eight-hour day and the right to organize and strike.

The Communists Fight for These Demands

Isn't this just about what the croppers and poor farmers of the South want and need? Well, these points were copied almost word for word from the program of the Communist Party in the South. The Communist Party is leading the fight for every last one of these demands. Moreover, the Communist Party saw to it that in the 73rd and 74th sessions of Congress bills were introduced containing these demands and providing in addition for the appropriation by the government of two billion dollars for immediate cash relief for the starving croppers and poor farmers.

As a vital part of this struggle for the needs of the croppers, the Communists in the South have aided greatly in the organization of the Sharecroppers Union, which today has over 8,000 members in the heart of the Black Belt. This year, through its militant struggle, the Sharecroppers Union has won the right to gin and sell their own cotton for large numbers of croppers and renters. It has forced the county relief stations to give groceries and clothes to hundreds of farm families. As this is written, it is in the thick of a fight in Lee and Tallapoosa Counties in Alabama, to force the planters to pay a minimum of $1 a hundred and $15 a month food allowance to the cotton pickers. Already these demands have been won on some plantations. All over the country the Communist Party is helping to organize the renters and poverty-stricken owners for similar struggles.

Can any cropper or small owner afford to reject this program and say he is opposed to it? Will it hurt the farmers of the South or will it help them? Of course it will help every poor farmer in the South—and that is why the Communist Party fights for such a program.

Why Wages Are Lower and Conditions Worse in the South

The truly terrible position of the Southern cropper—always underfed, ragged and often barefoot even in winter, denied the right to sell his own crop, chained by debt to a landlord who usually treats him little better than a slave—is typical of the conditions of life and work of the whole working population of the South. Here wages are lower, hours longer and relief scarcer and harder to get than in any other section of the country.

Nor is it just confined to wages and hours. The whole level of life is lower and more backward south of the Mason and Dixon line. School terms are shorter and there are fewer schools (particularly for Negroes). Nowhere in the country are there so many grown men and women who have never had a chance to learn to read and write. Methods of torture such as the chain gang, the dog house and the lash, long ago outlawed in most countries, are still in common use in our jails and prisons. And it is no accident that Memphis and Birmingham have more murders and shootings in proportion to their population than any other city in the world. Here, too, pellagra, the bloody flux, and a half dozen other starvation diseases flourish as they do nowhere else.

And here the oppression of the working people by the bosses and great landlords know no limit. Half the population is denied even the fundamental right to vote by means of Jim Crow regulations and the poll tax. Traditional American liberties, supposedly guaranteed by the Constitution, such as the right to gather in mass meetings to protest grievances, the right to publish working-class newspapers, etc., are trampled underfoot. Union organizers are murdered and strikers shot down with machine guns, while protest against this bloody rule is followed by KKK raids and often a lynching.

How does all this happen? Why is the South more backward than the North? Why is it that Southern workers must suffer more than those in the North or the West? It isn't hard to figure out. There are two main causes:

First, the fact that before the Civil War the slave system prevented the South from developing industry and kept it poorer than the North, where big shops and factories were springing up all over the land. The real industrial development in the South began only since the World War and especially during the postwar period. This development came about as a result of heavy investments by Northern capitalists. That is why so many mines, mills and factories that have opened in the South, like those of the Tennessee Coal and Iron Corporation, are owned by Northern bankers and bosses. That is why since that time the South has been more or less under the control of the greatest bankers and bosses in this country with headquarters in Wall Street. Even those Southern bosses who do own mills and mines are tied up with the Wall

Street finance magnates who dominate the Southern industries. The Northern capitalists saw fit to invade the South because they faced more and more resistance in the North on the part of the workers who were organizing into unions and striking for better conditions. The Northern bosses and bankers saw a fertile field in the South, where they could take advantage of the fact that the workers had a lower standard of living and knew almost nothing of trade unions. And they hoped to perpetuate this condition, and low wages, by taking advantage of the division among the workers due to circumstances shown below. The second reason why wages are lower and conditions worse in the South, is the fact that slavery in the South has never been completely abolished. It is true that a Negro worker cannot be bought and sold like an animal any more (although there are cases where this has been done lately in the Black Belt), but no one who thinks the question over would say that the Negroes are free today. Negroes are a part of the working class, in some industries they are in the majority, and yet they can't vote, and are liable to be lynched if they try to organize. In the Black Belt the Negro croppers are in even worse shape—with few more rights than a slave had in the old days. Now, how can the working class put up a real fight against wage cuts, long hours and starvation, as long as almost one-half the workers are not really FREE but are practically slaves? It is clear that the white workers cannot do much to improve things as long as the Negroes are in chains.

Just as important is the fact that the old traditions of slavery are used—and used successfully—to divide the white and Negro workers. We have seen in the Alabama coal and ore strikes and in the textile strike what happens when the ranks of the workers are divided and they fail to act together. This very division between black and white in the South is largely responsible for forcing lower wages and worse conditions on every Southern worker—be he white or black. Let us see just how it works.

What Happens When White and Negro Are Divided

Any worker who has been through a strike in the South knows something about it. Let us take a foundry, for example, where 50 white and 50 Negro moulders are employed. Let us say that all the whites belong to the Moulders Union and that their local refuses to admit Negroes to membership (and many Southern Locals of the Moulders Union do bar

Negroes) on the usual ground that colored moulders are just "niggers" and should not be allowed to join an organization of the "superior" whites. Moreover, let us suppose that the white moulders and their Union are continually trying to get the boss to fire the Negroes and hire whites in their place (and this is going on in almost every foundry in the South that employs both white and colored moulders). And last, let us say that the Negro moulders are getting less pay for the same work than the whites (and this is the usual thing in the South.)

Then there is a wage cut and the whites are cut to the same pay as the Negroes. They decide to strike. They ask the Negroes to come out with them, for they realize that unless the Negro moulders also strike, they cannot hope to win. As soon as the boss gets wind of the strike plans he rushes to the Negroes and tells them the old story, "Why should you strike together with that white trash? They refused to accept you in their union, they abused you in the shop and then even tried to get me to fire all of you and hire white men in your place. If you boys go out and help them win they'll start the same thing all over again when they get back in the shop. Better stick with me and get some of your colored friends to come in and break the strike of this white trash. I'll see that you colored boys get a square deal."

Now those Negro moulders may strike or they may fall for the fine promises of the boss and refuse to go out—and considering the treatment they have received from the white workers, who could blame them if they refused to strike? And if they don't strike the chances are 100 to 1 that the white moulders will lose their strike. Whose fault will it be if they do lose through lack of support from the Negroes? Their own, of course!

If the Negro moulders go on strike, the boss merely works the same trick in reverse. He brings in white moulders as strikebreakers and he sings them a different tune: "Those strikers are just a bunch of dirty 'niggers' anyway. It isn't like scabbing on white men. And besides, if you'll help me break the strike I will agree to do what you have always wanted—kick all the 'niggers' out and hire only white moulders. Come on in and take the jobs; we whites have got to stick together against those black apes." And so the strike is broken.

This is the way the boss-inspired idea of "white superiority" always works out in practice. Wherever it is accepted it results in broken strikes, smashed unions and the lowest wage scales in the country. It has done far more than any other one thing to keep wages at starvation levels throughout the South.

The Question of Social Equality

Many white workers will agree so far, and say, "Yes, it is true that white and colored have to stick together in strikes and on the job, if they want to win anything. I am in favor of that. And it may even be necessary to give the Negro the vote in order that we working people can elect some of our own kind to office—men who will stick with us and not the bosses. But when it comes to letting down the Jim Crow bars altogether and giving the colored man social equality, I say nothing doing."

This white worker forgets just one thing: That if you want a man to fight your battles shoulder to shoulder with you, you have to treat him like a human being and a brother long before the fight starts and all along the line. It's a pretty poor sort of man who will treat another like a hound dog all his life and then when he needs his help come running to that same man for assistance. That is exactly what white workers do when they treat Negroes like inferior people, often barring them from their unions or discriminating against them within the union, and then ask these same Negroes to come out with them in case of a strike. It must be said, to the everlasting credit of the Negroes, that in spite of such shabby treatment, they are usually the first to strike and the best fighters once they have struck.

Is It True That Whites Are 'Superior' to Negroes?

We have seen how the bosses work the old "white superiority" trick to break strikes and lower wages. Now what about the idea itself; is there any truth in it? The answer is, none whatever. In the World War American Negro troops proved themselves to be among the best fighting men in the whole world. In the fields of science, literature, music and art—in fact, wherever a good brain counts—Negro men and women have shown themselves to be the equal of any race, once they have an equal opportunity. The findings of the greatest scientists and students of racial characteristics all prove that under similar conditions the Negro is in no sense the inferior of the white man. Finally, any white worker who went through the recent mine, textile or longshoremen's strikes (to mention only a few) knows that no more loyal and courageous union man exists than the Southern Negro.

Will 'White Superiority' Bring Better Conditions to the White Worker?

This fairy tale of "white superiority" is false from top to bottom—a lie carefully cultivated and drilled into the minds of the white workers for just one purpose—to split the ranks of the working class and weaken the fighting power of the workers. Does it fill the stomach of the white worker when he is starving to believe that he is superior to the Negro? Does it get him higher wages and better conditions? Of course not! It serves the interest of but one class and one alone—the bosses, the capitalist class.

Just as the Communist Party fights any other anti-working class policy of the bosses, so too it fights the idea of "white superiority." And it fights it in the only practical way it can be fought: by organizing and leading the daily struggles of the Negro people for full equality in every field of life, and above all by drawing the white workers into the forefront of these battles.

By means of demonstrations and joint protests of white and Negro workers the Communist Party leads the struggle to end discrimination against Negroes in the distribution of relief and jobs, and on the job. It gives expression to its demand for equal political rights by running Negro candidates for office in the heart of the South, as it did in the last elections, and by organizing a national campaign for the right of Negroes to vote in the South. In the Scottsboro case of legal lynching the Communists have roused the whole world of Labor to protest against the death verdict passed on these innocent Negro boys by a Southern boss-controlled court, and have saved the boys from the electric chair for three long years.

Only the Communist Party has called for the organization of defense groups of white and Negro workers to protect the Negro people from the lynch mobs of the bosses and landlords by all possible means, and demands the death penalty for all lynchers. Only the Communist Party openly defies the Jim Crow laws and regulations of the Southern ruling class and smashes these bars between black and white wherever possible.

Does all this mean that the Communist Party demands that white men must marry Negro girls or that Negro men must marry or sleep with white women? Of course not! This is simply another lie of the bosses—and a pretty stupid one at that. The Communist Party does not attempt to order the personal lives of its members or any worker. Whom a worker shall marry is up to the man and woman involved and no one else.

On the other hand every Southerner knows that nothing is more common than for white men to sleep with Negro women—frequently in spite of the violent objection of the woman. Nor is it unknown for white women to sleep with Negro men. It's done under cover, that's all. These are facts which no one can deny. The Communist Party proposes to put an end to this damnable sneaking, around-the-corner, and in-the-back-door stuff. While forcing no white person to marry a Negro and no Negro to marry a white person it demands the absolute right of white to marry Negro and Negro to marry white where both parties desire this. In other words it demands and fights for complete and unrestricted social equality for the Negro people in every field of human relations.

The Negro People in the Black Belt

A large part of the Negro people live in what is commonly known as the Black Belt. This territory, including over 200 counties, stretches thousands of square miles in a continuous line, although crossing into several states. In this territory the Negro people are a majority of the population, especially of the laboring population. Here it is the Negroes who do the work, raise the cotton and corn and work in the turpentine and lumber camps. The whites, outside of a comparatively small number of croppers and renters, are mostly landlords and bosses of one kind or another.

Practically since the beginning of its settlement the Negroes outnumbered the white by far. It is with their toil, with their sweat and blood, that the cotton plantations and all the other wealth of the Black Belt were developed. For generations this has been and it still is the homeland of the Negro people. And yet, right in this territory, where they are a majority of the population and produce all the wealth, the Negroes are even more oppressed and exploited than elsewhere.

Here, in the homeland of the Negro people, the Negroes, although supposed to be free men under the law, have no rights at all and are hardly better off than slaves. They are bound to their plantations by a heavy burden of debts to the landlords. Should a Negro attempt to escape this slavery and leave the plantation, he runs the risk of being arrested and sent to the chain gang.

In this territory the Negro can be beaten, shot, lynched by the first white landlord who may or may not have some grudge against him. And the Negro can have no protection from the landlord-made and landlord-enforced law. Here the land which they have tilled for generations is owned by the white landlords. The government, and all its agencies, is in the hands of the worst enemies of the Negroes, a handful of white bosses and landlords. In this homeland of the Negro people, they are in the same condition, if not worse, as are the native peoples in the colonies who are held in subjection by armed force by foreign rulers. As, for instance, the native peoples in India under British rule.

The Question of Negro Rule in the Black Belt

The Communist Party believes that the Negro people in the Black Belt, if they are to be really free, should have the right to control and govern this territory and to develop their life and their culture in their own way. It believes that the Negro people in the Black Belt should be secure from interference either by the white bosses and landlords in this territory or by the Wall Street gang and the Federal Government which they control.

This does not mean that we want to establish some sort of Jim Crow State. On the contrary, the white croppers and workers in the Black Belt would be welcome to stay. They would have equal rights, would have a voice in the government, and their rights would be fully protected. It simply means that the Negro people, as the majority in this territory, would have the right to self-government, the right to determine what kind of government it is to have, and what connection, if any, this nation is to have with the US Government.

The Negro people may not want to set up a separate nation from the US, and the Communist Party would never think of forcing it on them. Moreover, if the Negro people in the Black Belt should get the opportunity of self-government at a time when the working class would be in power in the US, the Negro Communists would undoubtedly advocate that this nation should remain a federated part of the Soviet US. But the Communist Party will support and fight for, and calls upon the white workers to fight for, the right of the Negro people in the Black Belt to full self-government, their right even to establish a separate nation, if they should wish to do so. This is what we mean by the demand for the right of the Negro people in the Black Belt to self-determination.

For a United Working Class

Most important of all, in the course of the struggles for our day-to-day demands we must and will succeed in achieving for the first time in our country a truly united working class. As long as our class is split into warring groups, with the white arrayed against the Negro, Methodist against Catholic, Democrat or Republican against Communist, just so long will the capitalist class be able to slash our wages and starve us in the soup lines, without serious or successful resistance by us. The situation in the South today and the whole experience of the class struggle proves this inescapable fact beyond all doubt.

Not every worker may, as yet, agree with the Communists that a revolutionary change, which will put the workers in power, is both necessary and unavoidable in this country, but every honest worker, who has his own interests and the interests of the working class at heart, must agree that it is both possible and vitally necessary for all workers to unite on a common program of struggle against wage cuts and for higher wages, for unemployment insurance, for the right to freely organize and strike, for full equality for the Negro people. The Communist Party calls on the workers and poor farmers of the South, without distinction, to join hands with us, in common struggle for these immediate demands.

To those Negro and white workers and poor farmers who agree fully with the Communist program: The Communist Party declares that it is both your duty and your right to join now, today, the Communist Party of the United States, and fight shoulder to shoulder with the tens of thousands of your revolutionary American fellow workers for a Soviet America.

How the Bosses Use Religion to Divide the Workers

There is one other issue which, although it is not so dangerous for the workers as the issue of white superiority, is frequently used by the bosses to divide the workers. That is the question of religion. The Ku Klux Klan, for example, does its best not only to stir up white against Negro, but also Protestant against Catholic. This is just one more fake issue which the bosses use to divide the workers and prevent them from united struggle against wage cuts. It ought to be clear to Protestant workers by now that the main enemy is not the Pope in Rome, but the boss, right here at home. The Pope may not be much good, he may even be harmful (and frankly, we Communists think he is), but it is against the boss right here in America, who cuts the wages of both Methodist and Catholic, that we must direct the main fight. And the only way to do it successfully is for Catholic and Methodist to forget their religious differences and unite to fight their common enemy—the capitalist class. As usual, the bosses try to use the religious question also against the Communists. They say the "Reds" want to tear down all the churches and force everyone to stop worshiping God. Just another lie, of course. The Communist Party, as a Party, is not a religious organization, nor does it subscribe to a belief in any God. It believes we workers have to make a better world right here and not wait for it until we get to any heaven. At the same time the Communist Party points out that the preachers (especially the best paid ones) and the churches are often used by the bosses to discourage union organization and to break strikes. Every miner in Birmingham knows how the steel and coal companies got many local preachers to try their best to convince the workers not to strike. Every Negro knows that many of the biggest preachers fought the defense of the Scottsboro boys from start to finish. But the Communist Party does not and will not tear down the churches where workers wish to worship, nor does it force anyone to renounce their religion. The Communist Party welcomes into its ranks workers of any and every creed, so long as they agree with our program and honestly wish to fight for a better life for all workers. All such lies about the Communists are simply attempts of the bosses to split the ranks of the workers. Intelligent workers will treat them with the contempt they deserve.

What about the Question of 'Revolution'?

Finally, the bosses try to frighten the workers away from the Communists by shouting that the Communists want a "revolution," that they are "against the government," etc. They talk as if the Communists had invented the idea of revolution and had some kind of a patent on it, when every child knows that the United States was born and became a separate country, as the result of a revolution—and a mighty bloody one at that. Of course that revolution, while it was a step forward in the development of the country, was a revolution of one set of bosses (American bosses) against another set (the British bosses). Although it was the workers and farmers who fought and bled and died in 1776 to free this country from the British, it is the bosses who have reaped its benefits and have taken over the country we won for them for themselves.

When the bosses find they can't scare the workers away from the Communists by shouting that we want a revolution, they add the word "violent" to it, and try to convince the workers that we believe in bombing, murder, rape and what have you. What are the facts? In the first place it is the bosses and their police and National Guards that are guilty of violence. Who murdered 16 workers in the textile strike? Not the Communists or the non-Communist workers but the police and sheriffs. Who bombed the house of John Davis, the Communist candidate for Governor of Alabama in the last elections? Surely not the Communists, but certainly some labor-hating outfit like the White Legion. Who is responsible for the lynching of 64 Negroes since January, 1933? Certainly not the Communists, who lead the fight against lynching, but exactly the bosses and big landlords of the South. Who is it that tries to stir up trouble, incite riots and murder workers in every strike? Again we say, not the Communists but the bitterest enemies of Communism—the bosses and their thugs and police.

The Communist Party always has and always will condemn and fight against the use of bombs, murder and individual terror in the labor movement or outside of it. We know that such methods can't win—they can only hurt the cause of the workers. But the Communist Party will never advise the Negro people to submit meekly while they are cheated, beaten, and lynched by the landlords. Nor will it ever advise workers to make no defense when they are attacked and murdered by the White Legion thugs or the police and National Guard. On the contrary, the Communist Party strives to organize the workers to protect themselves from the violence of the bosses and their thugs by all possible means. The same thing will be true of the revolution when it comes. If a majority of the poor people of the country have decided that a revolution is necessary and start to carry it out, and a handful of bosses, backed up by their police and army, try to prevent it and attack the workers, then we workers will defend ourselves and our revolutionary program from their violence with arms in hand—just as our forefathers did in 1776. Now for the facts concerning this question of revolution.

We are living in a country where a very small group of men (the biggest bosses, bankers, etc., that is, the capitalist class) either own or control all the shops and mills and mines and most of the best land. In other words this small group just about owns the country and runs it to suit themselves. None of these people do much work themselves (if any) and yet they have by far the biggest share of the nation's income. On the other hand, the great majority of the population are working people of one kind or another. In order to live we have to get a job from one of the bosses and go to work in his factory or mine or on his land. We do the work and at most we get just a bare living out of it.

The Capitalist Class Makes a Mess of Things

This is bad enough at any time, but it is much worse if it turns out that the capitalist class which owns and runs the industries and the country, is unable to run it efficiently enough to even give work to the rest of us who must work in order to live. That is what has happened now. The factories for producing clothes, shoes, autos, everything one needs, are standing idle. The workers who were employed in them are tramping the streets looking for jobs they can't find. And meanwhile we all suffer from the lack of the same clothes, shoes, and so on, that those idle factories should be producing.

Things are even worse on the farms. The government had us plow up every third row of cotton one year, and now they are paying farmers to plant less cotton. Meanwhile, the very farmer who is paid not to raise cotton, hasn't got a whole pair of cotton jeans on his legs or a whole shirt on his back. In the Middle West the government is buying up hogs, butchering them and throwing the carcasses in the rivers. Wheat farmers are paid not to produce wheat, while at the same time half the country goes without meat and has no wheat for bread. It all sounds kind of insane, doesn't it?

Well, it is insane, but the capitalist class can't very well help it, as we shall show. Take your own boss, for example. If you are a textile worker, your boss established the mill where you work (or more likely, used to work), and runs it for just one reason—to make money. And it stands to reason that the less he has to pay you in wages the more money he will make. Therefore every boss—that is, capitalist—is interested in cutting wages just as low as possible. And why does your boss use the stretch-out and force you to do more work? Also because it means more money, higher profits, for him. Of course this stretch-out, and the continual installation of machinery to do the work of men, mean that fewer and fewer men are needed to run the mill. As a result, when you go to work one fine morning you find that you "are no longer needed"—you're laid off.

When you were working, even at low wages, you were able to buy things for yourself and your family. If you are a skilled worker you probably bought not only food and clothes but also a radio or a washing machine for the wife, maybe even a cheap car. Then, when your wages were cut, you could buy less and less of these things; it was all you could do to buy food and clothing and pay the rent. Now you have lost your job and as a result you can buy nothing.

What Causes Unemployment?

This is mighty tough on you, and although he probably doesn't realize it, it is going to do your boss some harm also. In the first place you have to realize that there are some 17,000,000 workers in this country who have lost their jobs the same as you. Second, that the 20-odd million who still have jobs have had one wage cut after another and have barely enough money in the pay envelope every week to keep alive on. Third, that in the long run, it is the workers and poor farmers who buy most of the goods produced by the factories of America. Now, if 17,000,000 of us are unemployed and can buy hardly anything, and those working are getting such low wages that they can buy no more radios, autos, etc., and have to cut down even on the money they spend on clothes and food, it is clear that the capitalists won't be able to sell the goods their factories produce.

Your boss, for instance, finds that he can no longer sell at a profit the cotton cloth his mill was making. Why? Because you, and 17,000,000 like you, are no longer able to buy cotton shirts and underwear. As we said before, your boss is interested in just one thing, making money. When he sees that he can no longer make money by running his factory he promptly shuts it down, and throws a few thousand more workers out on the street. And remember, this same thing is happening all over America.

Now, ask yourself another question. Who built that mill, who built the machines in it, who spun the yarn you use in your loom, who mined the coal that runs the power in the mill? The answer is:

workers, men and women just like yourself, produced all these things. And what did your boss, the owner of the mill, produce? Absolutely nothing. He may never even have seen the mill. He may live in New York, or in Germany for that matter, and may have bought your mill with the money his father left him, or that he stole, or that he made out of other workers like yourself. And yet, simply because he can no longer make money with this mill which the workers built, he shuts it down and throws the men and women who depend on it for a living out on the street to starve.

We Communists do not think that your boss, or any other capitalist, should be allowed to close down your mill and doom thousands of workers to continual hunger and perhaps starvation, merely because he is not making money. In fact, we don't think the capitalists should exercise any control whatsoever over the mills and shops of this country. In the first place these things belong to the working class by the best possible of all rights—because the workers built them with their sweat and labor. In the second place, the capitalists have shown themselves incapable of running the industries of the country in a manner which will give every worker a job and every poor farmer land of his own, and will give all those who work enough food, shelter, clothing and the other necessities of life. The capitalist class has made such a mess of the whole business that it is fast becoming absolutely necessary for the workers to take over the mills and mines and run them themselves if the whole country is not to run into a complete smash up.

The Workers Can Prevent Unemployment and Starvation

And the workers can do the job! If the working class, led by the Communist Party, was in power tomorrow, we would open the warehouses where the food and clothing the capitalists cannot sell at a profit, and therefore will not sell at all, is stored. We would distribute these goods to the unemployed who are hungry and in rags today. Then we would open the closed factories, which the capitalists will not open because they cannot run them at a profit. The millions of the unemployed would go back to their jobs and together we would produce an abundance of everything the people need. We could do it because we workers are not interested in profits—we are interested only in producing the goods the people need.

Russian Workers Show the Way

Don't think all this is an idle dream. Way back in 1917 the Russian workers succeeded in throwing their bosses off their backs and in taking over their country for the workers and poor farmers. As a result in the Soviet[72] Union (Russia) there is no crisis or depression today and no unemployment. Wages have increased steadily every year—last year by 10 percent. In December 1934, another increase of 10 percent was announced, which took effect in January 1935, while the seven-hour day has been established by law. There is no blacklisting and jailing of union men and women in the Soviet Union. On the contrary, the Soviet workers are organized 100 percent and the trade unions take a leading part in directing the affairs of the country. There workers and toiling farmers, people like yourself, are in control of the whole country. The oppression of the scores of minority nationalities which prevailed under the tsarist government has been absolutely stopped under the workers' rule. Every nationality or racial group within the Soviet Union is given the fullest opportunity to develop its own life in its own way, up to and including the right of self-determination for every large national group within its borders. Negro workers from the USA who are working in the Soviet Union have full rights. They are treated as equals by the native workers, who have shown this in many cases by electing Negroes as their representatives to the Soviets.

If the Russians can do all this why can't we American workers do the same thing? The Communist Party believes that we can, but it is not going to be an easy job. A handful of people cannot make a revolution. The Communist Party will never lead the workers in an attempt to seize power in America until the majority of the working class and poor farmers believe firmly that a revolution is the only solution for their problems, and are ready to fight to the end for victory. And who has a better right to demand and carry through a revolutionary change than the majority of the poor people of the country? Therefore the big task of the Communists today is to convince the workers that their present misery and poverty, brought on by the capitalist greed for profits, can only be permanently overcome by ending the rule of Wall Street bankers and the big bosses, and setting up in its place the rule of the working class.

Capitalists Will Fight to Bitter End

But even after a majority of the city and country poor are convinced that a revolutionary change is necessary, and even though the majority of the middle class (small businessmen, lawyers, doctors, engineers, etc.) agree with the working class, will the capitalist class surrender their power without a struggle? We hardly think so.

Our country is supposed to have a democratic form of government, where the majority rules. But somehow the handful of the very rich, the bosses and bankers, have always managed to have their way against the majority. They own and control the newspapers and radio broadcasting stations, they dominate the schools and the churches. They are thus enabled to miseducate, misinform and mislead large sections of the population. They have powerful lobbies in Washington and in every state capitol to exert their corrupt influence on Congress and the state legislatures. If need be, they can resort to, and many a time they have resorted to, intimidation, bribery, vote stealing, and ballot-box stuffing.

They have done these things even in cases when it was only a question of giving up a tiny mite of their wealth, squeezed out of the laboring majority of the population. The capitalists today insist on forcing lower wages and worse conditions on the workers. As every worker knows they always stubbornly resist every demand of the workers for slightly higher wages, or shorter hours, or an easing of the unbearable stretch-out. Surely when the whole profit system of exploitation and robbery will be threatened, when it will come to the question of who shall rule the country, this handful of greedy and unscrupulous men can be counted on to resort to every means to fight the majority and to insist on retaining power in their own hands at all costs.

The Government Is Controlled by the Capitalists

Above all, it must be remembered, they will have behind them the government itself. Every worker who has been through a strike knows only too well that the local police forces are always controlled by the bosses and always act against the strikers. The textile strikers know that the state governments, which sent the National Guard to shoot them down, are also under the thumb of the capitalist class. The same thing is true of the federal government at Washington. As we have shown, the National Recovery Administration codes were drawn up to suit the bosses and not the workers. As we saw in the textile strike, President Roosevelt, in spite of all his promises, was ready to send in the regular Army to break the strike—and it would not be the first time the Army has been used to murder strikers and break strikes. This year the country is controlled by the Democratic Party, led by Roosevelt. A few years ago it was ruled by the Republicans, but strikes were broken, strikers murdered and Negroes lynched in the same brutal manner that the Democrats employ today. Both parties are the loyal servants of the capitalists. Besides these the capitalist class will count on its hired thugs and murderers, organized in the KKK, the White Legion, etc., to fight their battles. Then, if the capitalist class continues to resist the will of the majority of the poor people—and this means the overwhelming majority of the population—the working class will have to use other means and defend themselves and their interests with force, if necessary, against the capitalists. Only when the workers are prepared to go to any lengths to satisfy the burning demands of the majority of the city and country poor, will a successful revolution be possible.

For a Soviet America

This, then, is the final goal of Communist activity—a working-class revolution and the establishment of Soviet Power (that is, the power of the organized working class in alliance with the poor farmers and the Negro people) in America. It is not an easy road, but there is no other that will lead to the final solution of the problems facing the workers and poor farmers today. Every strike, every struggle of the unemployed for more relief, every struggle of the sharecroppers for the right to sell their crops themselves, is a step forward along this road to freedom. In the course of these struggles we will learn how to fight, we will test our leaders in the heat of the battle and we will hasten the day when we, the workers of America, will win our country for our class.

SELECTIONS FROM THE NEGRO QUESTION IN THE UNITED STATES
JAMES ALLEN
1936

FROM CHAPTER 1, 'THE BLACK BELT: AREA OF NEGRO MAJORITY'

Historical Continuity of the Black Belt

The Black Belt is not a recent phenomenon. It has been maintained over a long period and its history is intimately linked with the rise of the slave plantation. A portion of the Black Belt had already taken form in the South Atlantic seaboard regions during the colonial period. Its creator and its jailer was the plantation.

Chattel slavery was the only means of assuring a labor supply on the plantations. Early colonists could take with them a working force of indentured servants, but they could not transport the capitalist relations of production with which to force workers to remain wage slaves or starve. There were no peasants to be expropriated from the land and transformed into an army of wage workers; instead there was a tremendous extent of free public property which could be transformed into private property and individual means of production by these very indentured servants. These forced laborers soon turned settlers on

---

*   James Allen, *The Negro Question in the United States* (New York: International Publishers, 1936).

their own account and together with the free colonists were creating in the North the basis for the development of the capitalist relations of production. But the plantation system which had been established along feudal European lines in the Virginia colony, and which served as a model for the later plantations in the South, could not flourish as long as its labor supply remained uncertain. The slave trade, which in time assured the major portion of the wealth accumulated by the northern merchant capitalists, found at hand in the insipid southern plantation, the form of exploitation best adapted to slave labor.

The products grown on the early plantations in Virginia, Maryland, and along the southern Atlantic coast—tobacco, indigo, and rice—and the topography of the Coastal Plain, lent themselves to large-scale cultivation by gangs of laborers under close supervision. Transported from a decimated homeland, the African Negro found himself thrust immediately into a discipline of the most primitive and direct form of forced labor, in a social environment which was entirely strange to him. His ties with his own social base had been completely and irrevocably sundered. Out of the background of his fellow slaves he could not even piece together common bonds which could serve as the starting point for creating the solidarity of a uniform social class. His fellow slaves came from diverse peoples of Africa, in varying stages of social development, and spoke different languages. It was only within the completely new conditions of the slave economy, with the past practically a total vacuum, that the slaves could develop mutual bonds and a common language, and create a new social consciousness. Clearly designated from the rest of the population by marked physical characteristics, the Negro slave could not, like the indentured servant, find refuge in the expanse of unsettled land, although some of them did make common cause with Indian tribes.

The concentration of large numbers of slaves on the plantations was an unavoidable weakness of the slave regime. Living in daily contact with each other, subject to uniform conditions of exploitation and of life, the slaves soon developed that class solidarity which, in the form of numerous slave revolts, presented a constant danger to the Bourbon power.

Even in the early period, when the plantation system was taking form and before cotton became the stimulus for its rapid expansion, the Negroes were a significant part of the population in the southern colonies. From some early census enumerations supervised by the British Board of Trade, from estimates of colonial officers and references in contemporary diaries and letters, it is possible to piece together a record of southern population before the first federal census of 1790.[73] From this data it would seem that South Carolina had a Negro majority as early as 1699, when, it was estimated, there were four Negroes to each white man; at any rate it seems to be fairly established that between 1715 and the Revolutionary War, when a large number of slaves were deported by the British, the Negroes were in the majority in the colony, although the 1790 census reported that the proportion of Negroes was only 44%. A census of Virginia in 1755 reported 103,407 "tithables," of whom 60,078 were Negroes. In 1790 the Negroes were 34.7% of the total population of Maryland, 26.8% in North Carolina, 41% in Virginia. Georgia, a late comer among the colonies, in 1790 already counted 35.9% of its total population Negro.

The Negro slaves were concentrated, however, in those areas where a staple crop made possible cultivation of large fields under the plantation system. Thus, before it was discovered that rice could be grown along the South Carolina coast, the settlers were getting on as best as they could in small-scale and individual farming units. But in 1694, rice was introduced from Madagascar, and when its cultivation proved successful, a large number of slaves were imported. By 1708, an official count of the population along the seaboard of what is now South Carolina revealed 3,500 whites (of whom 120 were indentured servants), 4,100 Negro slaves and 1,400 Indians held in captivity. The slave population increased with the growth of rice production:

> ... In 1724 the whites were estimated at 14,000, the slaves at 32,000 and the rice export was about 4,000 tons; in 1749 the whites were said to be nearly 25,000, the slaves at least 39,000, and the rice export some 14,000 tons, valued at nearly 100,000 pounds sterling; and in 1765 the whites were about 40,000, the slaves about 90,000, and the rice export about 32,000 tons, worth some 225,000 pounds.[74]

A similar development took place on the tobacco plantations of Virginia, which in 1619 received the first group of slaves to be landed on the North American mainland. By the end of the century the Negroes formed the bulk of the plantation gangs.[75]

The manor system was already well established in Maryland by the latter part of the 17th century, but the planters could not afford to buy many slaves because of the poor quality of the tobacco, and there were more indentured servants on the plantations than Negroes. In the tobacco-producing colony of North Carolina the first comers arrived in 1660, but these and those who followed continued as small farmers. Only above Albemarle Sound, in the northeastern section of the State, did the plantation system attain full development, and to this day the Negroes still outnumber the whites in this region. Towards the south, however, the land was too barren and the system of agriculture developed on the basis of small proprietorship. Negroes never formed a large part of the population. North Carolina, with the exception of the northeast where the early plantations were located, does not today have an agrarian economy fully typical of the Black Belt and has a correspondingly lower proportion of Negroes.

The forms of exploitation developed even during the early colonial period left an indelible mark on the future history of the South. Wherever the plantation system was deeply rooted, no matter how much it deteriorated later, it left powerful remnants which persist to the present time. A state census of certain Virginia counties was taken in 1782–83. In eight of these counties the average slaveholding ranged from 8.5–13 slaves, 15 planters had more than 100 slaves, and 45 planters between 50 and 100 slaves.[76] Although the plantation has deteriorated in these regions the same eight counties are today situated in the Virginia section of the Black Belt.[77] The three chief plantation counties of Maryland (Ann Arundel, Charles, and Prince George), according to the 1790 census, had about the same scale of slaveholding as the eight Virginia counties. Yet, despite the close proximity of these counties to areas of high industrial development, which exert a powerful attraction upon their populations, they still have a high proportion of Negroes.

The South Carolina colony offers an even more striking comparison. By 1790, indigo which had gradually replaced rice, was in turn giving way to cotton in the area around Charleston. The change in product did not necessitate a change in the system of exploitation. According to the federal census of that year, among the 1,643 heads of families in the Charleston District there were 1,318 slaveholders owning 42,949 slaves. The rest of the South Carolina coast, comprising the Georgetown district to the north of Charleston and Beaufort to the south, had a similar scale of slaveholdings.[78] Today in the counties of Georgetown, Charleston, and Beaufort the percentages of Negroes in the population are 64.4, 54.2, and 71.4 respectively. Even before the cotton gin was invented (1793), the plantation system was already well developed in Virginia, Maryland, northern North Carolina, and along the South Carolina coast into Georgia. In the plantation regions of these colonies, the Negroes already constituted the majority of the population. Within a decade after its invention, the cotton gin was in widespread use and driving cotton cultivation westward at a tremendous pace. When the slave trade was formally closed by an Act of Congress in 1808, there were already 1,000,000 Negro slaves in the country. Their numbers multiplied by forced breeding on the old plantations and supplemented by additional slaves smuggled into the country, they supplied the labor for the new plantations. By 1809 cotton was already a staple in the settlement around Vicksburg in the Mississippi territory; but prior to the War of 1812 the cotton plantation developed principally into the Carolina-Georgia Piedmont and tended southwestward into Alabama.[79] This section, the oldest large scale cotton growing region in the South, forms the Carolina-Georgia region of the Black Belt today.

In the meantime, sugar plantations were being founded in the delta lands of southeastern Louisiana. The labor supply from the Atlantic Coast was supplemented by slaves brought over from San Domingo by landowners fleeing the slave revolution. By 1830 there were 691 sugar plantations with 36,000 working slaves in this area and by 1850 the number of slaves in the sugar parishes had doubled.[80] This region is to be found within the present Black Belt.

While the westward movements in the North and into Tennessee, Kentucky, and Missouri carried with them the seed of capitalist development in the form of self-sufficing free pioneer farming, the westward movement in the South extended the slave regime. When the capture of Mobile from Spain during the War of 1812 and the defeat of the Indians assured an outlet for the products of the interior cotton plantations, the movement into Alabama and Mississippi developed rapidly. Between 1810 and 1860 the population of Alabama and Mississippi grew from

200,000 to 1,660,000 and the proportion of slaves from 40% to 47%. During the same period the slave regime expanded through Louisiana and into Arkansas and Texas. Its barren soil saved Florida from the plantation, and with the exception of a small region in the northwestern part of the state, it remains outside the Black Belt today.

The black soil prairies across central Alabama, which is today an area of great density of Negro population, was first opened to cotton culture in 1814 and within 20 years the slave plantation system was extending throughout its whole length. The Mississippi River valley, reaching from Tennessee and Arkansas to the mouth of the Red River, today the largest plantation area in the Black Belt, had already been rather well settled by 1840.

By 1860, on the eve of the revolution which would destroy it, the slave regime had reached its zenith. The capitalist power of the North had already become strong enough to hinder further expansion westward. The limits of the slave plantation area in 1860 also mark the limits of the area of continuous Negro majority. The 1930 Black Belt remains essentially the same area on which the mass of Negroes were enslaved by King Cotton, waving the scepter of chattel slavery. Impose the outlines of the area of continuous Negro majority in 1930 upon an economic map of the South of 1860, and see that they are almost identical with the plantation area of over 75 years ago!

FROM CHAPTER 2, 'THE ECONOMIC SURVIVALS OF SLAVERY'

Rise of Southern Tenancy

The real content of the economic slave survivals is to be found in an examination of southern tenancy, particularly of sharecropping and share-tenancy. Large-scale landownership in itself is not a symptom of feudal survivals; it is to be found in highly developed capitalist farming as well as under feudal or slave regimes. The relations of production, i.e., the relations between the actual tillers of the soil and the landlord, differ in the various systems of social production, and it is in the distinction between tenancy in the North and tenancy in the South that the distinction between capitalist and semi-slave relations of production is to be found.

Tenancy as it exists in the North and in the South are the culmination of altogether two different historical processes and have arisen on different economic bases. In the South, tenancy, with the exception sometimes of cash and standing renting, grew out of chattel slavery; it is the distinctive mark of the incompletion of the bourgeois-democratic revolution. To prevent the possession of the land by the landless Negro peasantry, whether by outright seizure or even by purchase, became the pivotal point of the land policy of the large-scale landowning Class.

One of the prerequisites for large-scale cotton farming is the assurance of an abundance of "cheap" labor. Once the question of the land was settled in favor of the big landlords, the settlement of the labor "problem" could only follow in its train. If the former slaves had been given land from the large estates, then large-scale farming could only develop as in the North on the basis of a seizure of the public domain by capitalists and the expropriation of the petty producers. But large scale farming in the cotton belt developed on the basis of the slave plantations and on the basis of labor which had never really been free. Here it was not necessary to free the tiller of the soil from the means of production—the land and farm implements—for he never had any; at most, Abolition had only destroyed a portion of the means of production, the slave, but had not taken the trouble to attach the potential free workers it had just created to their own means of production. The whole strategy of the Bourbon land policy now became to prevent just such attachment and to substitute for it a forced attachment to the soil. The tenant system as it evolved in the years immediately following the Civil War served this function.

The transformation of the plantation during the Reconstruction period was marked by a struggle on the part of the planters against the use of wage labor. Towards the end of the war and for a brief period after the principal emphasis was upon wage labor as the form of labor to supersede slavery. The Freedmen's Bureau, created by the federal government towards the close of the Civil War and whose main function was to supervise the labor relations of the former slaves, envisioned at the beginning a system of free wage labor, at a level, of course, far below that of the North. During the brief period in 1864, when the Treasury Department had control over freedmen's affairs, its plan was to hire out all over 12 years old on the basis of fixed money wages.

The department published the following schedule of minimum wages: $7 per month for males over 15 years old; $5 for females over 15; for children between 12 and 15 half of the above amount.[81] The verbal emphasis continued to rest upon the free aspect of labor, as far as the Freedmen's Bureau was concerned. One of its assistant commissioners in 1865 substituted for the wage schedule three general directions: (1) labor was to be free to compete in the open market; (2) the contracts between the employer and the employee were to be "equitable" and enforced by the Bureau "upon both parties," and (3) the unity of families was to be preserved.[82] Almost simultaneously with this order, General Howard, head of the Bureau, instructed the assistant commissioners and other officers to "never forget that no substitute for slavery, like apprenticeship without proper consent, or peonage . . . will be tolerated"—but, he made it distinctly understood, that it was not his purpose to change the existing laws in the South. "In fact," he declared, "it is the easiest and best way to solve every troublesome problem . . . relating to Negroes, by the time-honored rules established by wise legislation for other people."[83]

The former slaves had obtained their first taste of free wage labor on the confiscated plantations supervised by agents of the Treasury Department and the Union Command or contracted out to operators. Wages here were supposed to range from $7 to $10 a month. But these wages rarely materialized. When the crops failed the workers received nothing and even when good crops were made the lessees swindled them out of their wages. When the Freedmen's Bureau was organized in 1865 it continued to administer these plantations until the end of that year when most of them were returned to their former owners.[84] The government plantations often served as a source of labor for planters unable to force the Negroes to enter into a yearly labor contract. We find one newspaper advising the planters that "from these plantations planters can draw the hands they wish to employ and they are not only permitted but are required to accept the offer of employment, on penalty of treatment as vagrants."[85]

It seems, from the fragmentary reports available, that wage labor was more in use during 1866–67 than in the following years. Thus, the *Jackson Clarion*, from the heart of the Mississippi Valley, reported that in 1866 the planters had furnished laborers with provisions and in addition paid them from $10 to $15 and sometimes $18 a month (a rate much above that paid farm hands in many sections of the South today). The same method was used in 1867.[86] But in the face of a great shortage of labor, occasioned by the withdrawal of large numbers of women and children from field work and the movement of other Negro laborers to the cities and to the newer lands of the West, where higher wages prevailed, the planters turned their chief attention to binding the Negroes to the plantations.

If wage labor was able to persist even for such a short time it was because of the rebellious state of the former slaves. They were adamant in their demand for land and refused to take on the yearly contracts offered by the planters through the services of the Freedmen's Bureau. Chaos in labor conditions prevailed and the labor supply was completely disorganized. Spontaneous possessions of land by Negro squatters occurred here and there; there was constant fear of further land seizures and insurrection if Congress did not supply the "forty acres and a mule" as had been promised by the Radical Republicans. Occasional confiscation of large landed estates for the benefit of the former slaves as well as actual squatting by Negroes occurred in the early days of Reconstruction. A notable example of the first, was the confiscation of the 10,000-acre plantation of Jefferson Davis, which was turned over to the former slaves and was run as a colony under the protection of Negro troops. Forty thousand Negroes squatted on the plantations of the Sea Islands (off Charleston, S. C.) and along the Georgia and South Carolina coast, where they established self-government and refused to abandon their rights to the land.[87] In southeast Virginia, freedmen settled on abandoned plantations until forcibly ejected.[88] All accounts testify to the fact that the Negroes demanded land, expected to receive it, and, in a number of instances, armed clashes ensued when they attempted to seize land.[89]

Under such circumstances, wage labor, even with the powerful forced labor ingredients prevalent in the South, did not give the planter any assurance of retaining labor for the whole growing year. The struggle against wage labor, as a form of labor, was in effect a struggle by the planters against capitalist forms of labor and against the higher degree of freedom inherent in such forms. The first steps taken in this direction were the vagrancy and apprenticeship laws, known as the Black Codes, which were passed in the first new state legislatures in 1865–1866, which were completely under the control of the planters. These laws were intended to assure a steadfast, thinly-veiled slave supply for the plantations.

The apprenticeship law empowered the county authorities to apprentice to employers all children under 18 years of age who were "without visible means of support" or whose parents "refused to provide for such minors," with the provision that former masters have the preference. The would-be master usually petitioned the court to bind minors to him. It often happened that the planter would thus obtain the children of freedmen working on his plantation, by declaring that such children had no means of support.[90] The vagrancy laws permitted the courts to try any one, as the Alabama Act had it, who was "stubborn, refractory, or loitered away his time" for vagrancy, and if found guilty and unable to pay the fine the "vagrant" could be hired out to work it off. The Mississippi vagrancy law declared that:

> All freedmen, free Negroes and mulattoes in the state over the age of 18 years, found ... with no lawful employment or business, or found unlawfully assembling themselves together; either in the day or night time, together with all white persons so assembling with them on terms of equality, or living in adultery or fornication with Negro women, should be deemed vagrants.

The law further provided that any Negro, between the ages of 18 and 60, who could not pay a tax of $1.00 (curiously enough called "poll tax"), was to be considered a vagrant whom the sheriff could seize and hire out for the amount of the tax and the costs.[91] Cash was so scarce among the Negroes, that this law practically condemned all the former slaves to servitude. It was in such manner that the planters attempted to guarantee themselves a labor supply which was not too far removed from the status of chattel slavery. When Congressional Reconstruction became effective towards the end of 1867 and a military dictatorship was established in the South, these laws were inoperative for a time.

All efforts were made to enforce the yearly labor contracts which were negotiated through the offices of the Freedmen's Bureau. The Bureau commissioners as well as the southern press generally complained bitterly that the Negroes refused to take on these contracts because they smacked too much of slavery and because the freedmen expected a division of the land. One writer points out that this system, which he has the audacity to call "free hired labor," had little to differentiate it from slavery.

> If the Negro expected to receive a daily or weekly wage—he writes—he had to work every day and work as directed. From daylight to dark was the universal rule on cotton plantations. Where no alternative of renting or hiring for a share presented itself, the freedmen attempted to reserve his liberty of movement by refusing to hire for a year. He greatly preferred to hire for a week or for a month, and in many cases would not contract for more than two days in the week. The presence of the overseer became extremely irksome to the Negroes, even where the control was very liberal.[92]

The vagrancy laws were called into service to enforce the yearly labor contract. Thus, in Alabama an "Act to Regulate Contracts and Enforce the Same" was in operation in 1865, providing that any freedman who abandoned labor was subject to the vagrancy law, and that any one who attempted to entice him away from his place of employment or help him in any way to desert it was subject to imprisonment and fine.[93] During the same year General Swayne, head of the Freedmen's Bureau in Alabama, issued an order under which the "Negro laborer is required to keep his part of the contract and to work faithfully, in penalty of being declared a vagrant and put to labor on some public work."[94] Thus the whole pressure, not only of his former master but also of his new friend, the representatives of the northern bourgeoisie, was brought to bear upon the former slave to bind him to the land.

With the cooperation of the Freedmen's Bureau, the planters in 1865 began to form county associations through which they could establish a uniform system of regulating labor. One of these, for instance, called the Labor Regulating Association of Clarke County (Alabama), open to any white inhabitant of the county who employed Negroes, controlled labor contracts and was to act as a sort of "arbitration board" to "settle" disputes between laborer and planter. Among its tasks were: to see to it that the Negro complies with the contract, establish provisions of the contract, prescribe labor rules, prevent Negroes from breaking contract to sign with another planter.[95] An Alabama editor cautioned the planters that they must do all possible to hold their labor supply, which was being threatened by the lure of higher wages in the Mississippi Valley. "Every kind of inducement should be held out by the Southerners to their former slaves to stay here. . . ."[96]

From such forms of forced labor and veiled slavery which first appeared on the southern post-Bellum plantation it was but a short step to sharecropping. In fact, sharecropping was also taking form simultaneously on the plantations. In a letter to General Howard, Commissioner of the Freedmen's Bureau in Washington, a large landowner reports that he had already engaged about 400 freedmen for his plantations in Arkansas and Tennessee on a sharecrop basis, and reported others doing the same. He thanks General Howard for his help.[97]

But only towards the end of 1867 was there a marked turn towards sharecropping, revealing the defeat of the revolutionary course in the settlement of the land question. Planters of Tuscaloosa County, Alabama, meeting in December 1867, for instance, decided that the "general failure" of the planters was to be attributed to the "unfaithful work of the Negro, and in many instances, to the large wages paid for labor." The meeting planned a uniform wage and was in favor of payment by share of the crop. It set one-fourth of the crop plus rations the uniform plan for farm laborers. Only "when the freedman is better instructed as to economy and the profit of field labor" is money wages to be paid, which should not exceed $6 per month for first class hands, and $4 and $5 for second- and third-class hands. It was also resolved that no "unfaithful hands" should be permitted to remain on the plantations.[98]

FROM CHAPTER 5, 'FINANCING THE PLANTATION'

Role of the Banks

The whole credit structure in the South is maintained by finance capital. Banks have played the pivotal role in financing, bolstering and prolonging the semi-feudal structure of Black Belt economy. This is how Vance described the role of the local banks before the federal government practically took over their function under the Roosevelt administration:

Selections from The Negro Question in the United States

The merchant and the planter must also be financed.... It is safe to say that most plantation owners preparing to plant a crop now go to see their bankers. After a conference covering details of amount of acreage, number of plows, cost and production, the planter is given a line of credit secured by personal note. The loans are to be issued according to seasonal needs; so much for furnishing, planting, chopping and picking. The supply stores are granted credit by wholesale houses. This, however, is considered precarious business since the failures of 1914, 1921, and 1926. Accordingly, many supply merchants now borrow from banks to pay off their thirty day bills with the wholesaler.[99]

Hubbard, member of a leading firm of cotton brokers, who is certainly in a position to know, describes the role of the country banks as follows:

> ... They provide a link between the farmer and small merchant and the larger financial centers. These banks all have correspondents in the large cities, not alone in the South, but in the North as well. Through these channels filter down one way the financial opinions of the large cities and large banks, and up the other way, the views of the interior upon the state of trade and the conditions of the crop. To the country bank come all classes of farmers and merchants, from the small renter to the large planter, and from the small county merchant to the interior shipper, engaged in moving the cotton to the mills either at home or abroad. The small farmer and the smaller country merchant will do all their business with the country bank. The larger men, of course, do business elsewhere also, since the resources of the interior banks will not suffice for their needs. The crop notes, originally discounted by the country bank, will be found in the loan portfolios of the larger institutions of the cities, as the money to make and move the crop is sent out through the usual banking channels.

The country banker has great influence on the farming communities for it is to him the farmer goes in the spring for funds and for advice. Even if the farmer is being financed by the country merchant, the result is the same, for the latter is doing business with the bank. It may be surmised that the country banks can exercise much influence upon the acreage in the spring and upon the marketing in the fall. It is the refusal of the country bank to advance additional funds with unpaid paper still on their books which has much to do with the curtailment of acreage in a year of stress, such as the spring of 1921.... Similarly in the fall they can exercise considerable influence upon the marketing of the crop.[100]

The small country banks, of course, do not play an independent role. They simply act as local agents for the larger financial institutions, and are the arms of finance capital reaching into the hinterland of the country. It is through the country banks that finance capital has fastened its control over cotton production and marketing, and it is through them that it has maintained the plantations and the whole tenant structure of southern agrarian economy. Just as finance capital in its exploitation of the colonies has sought support from and granted support in return to the reactionary, retrogressive, backward classes, and the social institutions which maintain them, it has entered upon the same kind of alliance in the South with the large plantation owners and the overlords of the tenantry. It is the chief beneficiary of the surplus profits obtained from the semi-slave labor on the cotton plantations, which produces a crop second in value among all crops in the United States, and first in value of all exported agricultural products. Finance capital, through its control of credit, appropriates to itself the great bulk of the returns from the vast semi-feudal domain in the South. It has accepted as its basis in southern agriculture, nourished and thrived upon the economic survivals of slavery.

Government as Financier

In the South, more than in any other section of the country, the Federal government has participated directly in the economic functions of finance capital. Even before the Roosevelt administration became a large-scale farm mortgagee, the Federal land banks[101] were the largest holder of farm mortgages in the South. On January 1, 1928, 21.7% of the farm mortgages in the South Atlantic states, 34.5% in the East South Central states and 23.7% in the West South Central states were held by the Federal land banks as compared with 12.1% for the United States as a whole. The next largest holders of farm mortgages in the South were the insurance companies who held 12.5% in the South Atlantic states, 28.0% in the East South Atlantic states, and 25% in the West South Atlantic states as compared with 22.9% for the country as a whole, where they were the largest holders of farm mortgages.[102]

The crisis rapidly increased the direct financial stake of the Federal government in southern agriculture. The chief consideration of the government during the crisis was to prevent the collapse of large financial institutions. The policy of the Hoover administration was to advance large sums of public funds to the large concerns in difficulty, chiefly through the Reconstruction Finance Corporation. Only when the failure of many local banks in the farm area, combined with the presence of large surplus stocks of farm produce and low commodity prices for farm products, threatened seriously to deplete the resources of the insurance companies and the large banks holding farm mortgages, did the government allocate funds for direct loans to farmers. The Regional Agricultural Credit Corporation, organized by the Reconstruction Finance Corporation, was the result of pressure brought to bear upon the Federal government chiefly by the large stockbreeders and the large cotton growers of the plantation area. Credit in the South was practically dried up by the failure of the banks and credit merchants, and the remaining banks refused to extend further credit with large debts still outstanding and no prospects for a higher price of cotton which would assure them collection of interest and principal on further loans. The Regional Agricultural Credit Corporation to a large degree replaced the banks in advancing credit and, like them, served the larger-scale producers, which in the South means principally the plantation owners. Credit from this source was closed to the small tenant farmers in advance by the provision that a waiver of the landlord's lien must be obtained before a loan is even considered. The average loan was $1,000 and its collateral requirements so heavy that they could not possibly be met by the small farmers.

FROM CHAPTER 6, 'SOUTHERN INDUSTRIALIZATION AND THE BLACK BELT'

The New Negro Proletariat

Despite the peculiarities of the development of the textile industry, capitalist development in the South itself was bound to, and did, create a Negro industrial proletariat, although its extent and its relative strength has generally been overestimated. The 1930 census reports two and one-half million Negroes ten years of age and over as gainfully employed (excluding farmers and tenants, but including a small number in the professions) in the twelve states where the Black Belt is located. But of the total number of these workers 20% are agricultural wageworkers and 36% are engaged in domestic and personal service. More than half the Negro wageworkers in the South, therefore, are still closely bound either by the semi-slave forms of labor which pertain in southern agriculture or by the isolated and servile circumstances of domestic and personal service, with their corresponding low wage and cultural level. Of the other groups listed by the census, 590,000 or 24% of the Negro wage earners, are reported in the manufacturing and mechanical industries of the South, and 240,000, or about 10% in transportation and communication.

But it would be highly misleading to consider even the wage earners listed in the manufacturing and mechanical industries as modern, "free" industrial proletarians, as wageworkers in the usual sense of the word. Fully one-fifth of those listed by the census as in the manufacturing and mechanical industries are in the saw and planing mills, where in the close supervision of workers in camps, in the method of payment by scrip and in the utilization of company commissaries—all of which result in debt slavery and peonage—conditions are not far removed from the semi-feudal exploitation of the plantations. On the other hand, no more than half of those reported in the manufacturing and mechanical industries are factory workers, the unskilled laborers of the various factories, most of them small, scattered throughout the South. With the exception of the heavy industrial center of Birmingham and the large units of the highly monopolized chemical and tobacco industries, these factory workers do not constitute a closely knit and integrated industrial proletariat such as has been created by the textile industry in the South and large-scale industry in other parts of the country. This weakness in the composition of the Negro proletariat in the South is common to the proletariats of all backward regions where modern industry has not transformed the agrarian economy found at hand, and reflects the retarding forces operating specifically against the Negro people living in the South.

Half of those listed in transportation and communication are employed on the steam railroads, for the most part on the track repair gangs, and one-fifth as laborers in the maintenance of streets, roads and sewers. Thus, while industrialization in its general effects could not help but create a Negro industrial proletariat, the Negro has been practically entirely excluded from the principal branch of industry, has been chiefly employed in those industries in which the forms of labor are determined by the South's agrarian economy, and has been restricted to the most unskilled, the lowest wage jobs in other industries. The entry of the Negro into industry in the South did not necessarily mean an appreciable improvement over his conditions of life on the plantation, and in this, the plantation master was to a certain measure protected against too powerful an attraction upon his own labor supply which would be offered by higher wage levels so close at hand.

Industrialization in the South has not accomplished those feats with respect to the Negro which were hoped for by liberals, namely, the serious weakening of the role played by the plantation in southern economy and the consequent easing of the semi-feudal restrictions upon capitalist development in agriculture. Nor has it brought about the social changes corresponding to these economic transformations—the lightening of the oppression of the Negro people, a swift and thoroughgoing development of a large Negro proletariat and middle class. But in two respects industrialization has changed the dynamics of the Negro question in the South. In the first place, in the creation of a southern Negro proletariat (despite its lack of compactness) and, secondly, in the creation of a white industrial proletariat, whether isolated as in the textile industry, or side by side with the Negroes as in the Birmingham area, industrialization has lent new forces to the liberation struggle of the Negro people which were not, and could not have been, present during the bourgeois revolution of the Civil War period.

Considering retarding influences which have been at work and those limitations which we have pointed out, the Negroes constitute an important part of the southern proletariat. Of the total number of persons listed as gainfully employed by the 1930 census in the 12 southern states, the Negroes constitute:

> 74% of the workers in domestic and personal service
> 48% of the agricultural wageworkers
> 33% of the forestry and fishing workers
> 31% of the workers in transportation and communication
> 24% of the workers in manufacturing and mechanical in industries
> 23% of the workers engaged in the extraction of minerals
> 12% of those in trade, public service and professional service
> 2% of those in clerical occupations

Industrialization has not only produced that class among the Negroes in the South capable of decisive revolutionary action, but has made the Negro an integral and important part of the southern proletariat as a whole. The most important objective condition is present, on the one hand, for the creation of working-class solidarity between white and black labor; on the other hand, the development of the white and Negro proletariat gives living embodiment to the essential connection between the struggle of the peasantry as a whole against the remnants of slavery and the revolutionary movement of the proletariat. It is a living guarantee of the link between the two phases of the revolution which is developing in the South. Industrialization has not directly weakened the survivals of slavery, but it has supplied the best force for their destruction.

The only heavy industrial area of the South, in and around Birmingham, is of special significance because of the development there, in close proximity to the Black Belt, of a concentrated body of Negro and white industrial proletarians. In this region there are about 25,000 coal and 7,000 iron miners, and about 28,000 workers engaged in all branches of iron and steel production. About one-half of the miners and one-third of the iron and steel workers are Negroes. The proletariat here is older and has had more experience in the class struggle than any other body of Southern workers. The development of the class struggle in the Birmingham region cannot but produce salutary effects upon the white agrarian population, especially in those sections where the Negro croppers and farmers are already organizing and struggling (as in the Black Belt counties to the southeast of Birmingham where the Sharecroppers Union is strongly entrenched). Birmingham has become the key to unlocking the barriers which have prevented working-class solidarity in the deep South and it can be a powerful generating center of the proletarian revolutionary movement. One of the elements of industrialization feared most by the landlord-capitalist rulers of the South, and which they succeeded in avoiding in the textile industry—the creation of a compact white and Negro working class—is asserting itself strenuously in the Birmingham area.

Although isolated from the Negroes, the textile proletariat constitutes a powerful anti-capitalist and anti-feudal force. Fifty-nine percent of the country's textile workers are in the South; in South Carolina two-thirds of the industrial workers are in textiles, one-half in North Carolina and over one-third in Georgia. A backward mass of mountain and upland farmers, formerly totally isolated from contemporary currents, have been drawn into the modern class struggle. The textile workers of the South come from historically anti-Bourbon sections, and although they have been instilled with race prejudice, still the very conditions under which many of them have been forced off their meager holdings on the land and the severe exploitation in the mills turn these workers into a powerful force making for eventual unity with the Negroes against a common enemy. In proportion as their class consciousness and political education mature—which today is no longer a matter of an extended period: the 1934 general textile strike was an indication of the rapidity with which the Southern workers are beginning to develop these qualities—and under the influence of the rising movement among the Negroes in the South, these workers will learn to appreciate the effectiveness of an alliance with the Negro masses in the struggle for the overthrow of capitalism.

Despite the advance of industry in the South, Southern economy is still essentially bound by the remnants of chattel slavery which constitute that peculiar, distinctive factor characterizing the South and distinguishing it from other sections of the country. Industry in the South did not develop on the ruins of the slave system or its remnants; it developed side by side with them and on the grounds of mutual support. The semi-slavery economy, it might be said, determined the nature and extent of industrialization, determined its location, limits and the nature of its labor supply. Only as regards the "poor whites" was there a corresponding transformation in the agrarian economy, although this transformation was by no means thoroughgoing, but left rather the agrarian economy of the uplands as a ruin, with its self-sufficing nature and its domestic handicrafts destroyed and with nothing but a small peasant economy of the most impoverished kind to take its place.

FROM CHAPTER 7, 'NORTHERN INDUSTRY AND BLACK BELT'

The New Negro Proletariat

Although the migration failed to meet the hopeful expectations of reformists, it has had profound results in the subsequent development of the Negro people. The migration itself was, of course, merely a phenomenon evoked by a more fundamental process. The Negro people have experienced the most intensive and important social transformation since the Civil War period. Previously, only very gradually and on an isolated scale, were Negroes involved in the fundamental processes of the capitalist development. But now, during the course of a few years, over a million Negroes found themselves transported from a semi-feudal region into the very heart of highly developed capitalist industry. In 1860 only 13.6% of the Negro population lived in the North. During the course of the next fifty years this proportion had been increased to only 15%, a measure of the painfully slow, practically inoperative, process of involving the Negroes into the orbit of capitalist development. But at the end of the next twenty years, in 1930, over one-fourth (26.1%) of the Negro people was in the North.[103] No matter that this redistribution of the Negro population had reached its limits even before 1930, that now a reverse redistribution is even taking place. This shift in population, as temporary and as limited as it was, was accompanied by permanent changes.

The most important of these changes was the creation of a relatively large Negro industrial proletariat in the North. Negro migrants appeared in practically every branch of decisive industry. Over 75% of the Negro population of the North is located in the principal industrial areas; almost 40% lives in the four cities of New York, Chicago, Philadelphia and Detroit.

Selections from *The Negro Question in the United States*

The migration has resulted in situating the largest and most basic Negro proletariat in the North. According to the 1930 census, there are over 1,000,000 Negro industrial workers in the northern states, almost double the number in the 12 states in which the Black Belt is situated, although these states contain about 70% of the Negro population of the country. The composition of the Negro working class in the North is also better suited for the more rapid development of a proletarian revolutionary movement. Of the 1,599,912 Negroes listed by the 1930 census as gainfully employed in the North, 69% are in the manufacturing, mechanical and mining industries, as compared with 25% of the 2,500,000 Negro workers in the South. Only 3% of the Negro workers in the North are agricultural laborers, as compared with 20% in the South.

The Negro workers were located in northern industry to much better advantage than in the South with respect to large-scale and basic industry and were therefore in the more decisive and strategic sections of the proletariat. In the iron and steel industries of the Pittsburgh district (including Youngstown, Ohio) 16,000 Negroes were employed in 1923, and the number of Negro coal miners in this area in 1925 was estimated at 8,000.

The size of the Negro industrial proletariat connected with these industries was therefore greater in the Pittsburgh district than in the Birmingham area, the only heavy industrial center of the South. In addition, a number of new centers of the Negro proletariat appeared in the North, where compact units of Negro industrial workers arose in closest contact with the most strategic sections of the proletariat as a whole. In Chicago there were about 15,000 Negro workers employed in the Pullman shops, over 5,000 in the stockyards, and 6,000 or 7,000 in the food packing plants. In Detroit, about 24,000 Negro workers were employed in the industrial plants of the city up to 1929, most of whom were in the auto industry (the Ford Company alone had 15,000 Negroes in its Detroit plants). In St. Louis and East St. Louis, there were 3,335 Negro workers in 22 iron and steel mills, about half of the workers in the plants of the American Car & Foundry Co. were Negroes, three meatpacking plants alone employed over 2,000 Negro workers. There were about 24,000 Negro coal miners in the West Virginia fields in 1925. Forty percent of the Negro workers on the railroads before the crisis were in the North.[104]

In addition to these principal and basic centers of the Negro proletariat in the North, large numbers of Negro workers were also employed in the lighter industries and in construction. About one-fifth of the workers in the steam laundries are Negro women. In the garment trades of New York up to 1929 about 6,000 Negro women were employed and there were as many Negro longshoremen in the city.

While northern employers welcomed Negro workers for a time, it must be remembered that they were welcomed as unskilled and underpaid workers only. If they had appeared in Northern centers merely as unskilled, raw peasants in search of industrial employment, their situation would have been equivalent to that of the immigrant worker. But the shadow of the modern plantation followed them North and served as a basis for all the social, as well as economic, relationships which have developed around the Negro in the North: segregation, social ostracism and discrimination, prejudice. They were received by the employers as members of a people oppressed by American imperialism, suffering from the restrictions of semi-feudalism. Capitalism has given a new base and new life to these survivals of the past, prolonged them in the North as well, by utilizing them to even greater advantage than the national differences among the immigrant workers. Color offered a convenient peg on which to hang lower wages, the worst jobs, prejudice as a weapon with which to prevent working-class solidarity.

By bringing Negroes, untutored in the principles of working-class solidarity and organization, into jobs which had been struck, by undermining the wage and working standards of the white workers by submitting the Negroes to a lower wage-scale, capitalism provided the spark for such fratricidal warfare as the East St. Louis and Chicago race riots. To this must be added the activities of the National Urban League and similar groups among the Negroes and the attitude of the American Federation of Labor, an outgrowth of the opportunism which infested its policies. It does not fall within the scope of this book to discuss the labor movement as such. But we must point out here that the chauvinism and opportunism in the AFL arose primarily from the fact that it was based organizationally upon the skilled section of the working class and was almost entirely oblivious to the needs of the overwhelming mass of workers, the unorganized and the unskilled. This attitude on the part of the leaders of the main body of organized labor encouraged and, in part, caused the upsurge of

Negro petty bourgeois nationalism, exemplified in the Garvey movement and in the early strikebreaking activities of a number of Negro organizations.

So effective were the barriers erected by capitalism to the economic progress of the Negro, that a decade after the migration into industry, no more than five or ten percent of the Negro workers can be classed as skilled or semi-skilled labor. On the eve of the economic crisis there was even a decline in the number of Negro mechanics and artisans as compared with 1910.[105] The swift pace at which the Negro worker during the present crisis is losing whatever hold he had obtained in industry, reflects the marginal status to which he was forced.

But despite all these forces operating against the growth and organization of the Negro proletariat, the fact that a sizable proletariat did develop under the more favorable conditions of northern capitalism is of great progressive significance from the point of view of the working class as a whole as well as for the final solution of the Negro question.

The most decisive strata of the Negro proletariat are today situated in the North, in close association with the more advanced working class. This is a prerequisite for overcoming white chauvinism in the ranks of the working class and creating class solidarity on the basis of the modern class struggle. It is making possible the beginning of a complete reorientation with regard to the Negro on the part of the workers situated in the main centers of industry. A change in ideology is being hastened by the crisis which is undermining the economic status of the "aristocrats of labor" upon which the old-line AFL leadership has based its policy of class collaboration. The growth of the Negro working class in the North has also provided the basis for overcoming in the ranks of the advanced, revolutionary section of the workers the bourgeois theories which have hampered a correct revolutionary program for Negro liberation.

These developments have also stimulated the development of the labor and revolutionary movement in the South. The presence of the Negro proletariat in the North brought home sharply the need of carrying on organization in the South and emphasized the close connection between the aims of the proletariat and the liberation struggle of the Negroes. One of the first results of this clearer conception of the nature of the Negro question on the part of the Communists was the organization of the Party in the South, especially in Birmingham, in the textile regions and in some sections of the rural Black Belt. This proceeded hand in hand with an energetic drive for equal rights in the North and a sharp struggle against white chauvinism in the ranks of the labor movement.

Of special significance is the work that has been done in organizing both white and Negro croppers and tenants. For the first time in the history of the South such Unions have been grounded and have maintained themselves against typical Southern terror. The Sharecroppers Union, with its principal strength in the Alabama Black Belt, and the Arkansas Tenant Farmers Union, have been able to lead successful strikes and spread their organizations. These developments, coupled with the growth of trade unionism in the South, are opening up a new reservoir of power for the labor and revolutionary movements. The migration made possible the growth of working-class solidarity and enriched the proletarian content of the struggle for Negro freedom. The southern situation has been brought out of its isolation, especially through such a mass movement which rose to the defense of the Scottsboro boys. The struggle for the rights of Negroes and for their demands has become a central point in the militant sections of the labor movement.

FROM CHAPTER 9, 'THE RIGHT OF SELF DETERMINATION'

An Oppressed Nation

What, then, is the nature of the Negro question? It must be correctly analyzed before an effective program can be evolved for its solution. Historical, economic, and social data substantiate the Communist view that the problem of the Negro is the problem of an oppressed nation. The Negro question in the United States is essentially of the same nature as that of retarded and oppressed peoples in Europe or in the colonies. Like these peoples the American Negroes have been retarded in their social development by American imperialism. Like them, the Negro people has been repressed by a more powerful nation and has been prevented from emerging as a free and independent nation on an equal footing with the other peoples of the earth. Like many of these peoples, the American Negro is retarded by pre-capitalist forms of exploitation; a large sector of the Negro people is still bound by

Selections from *The Negro Question in the United States*

semi-feudalism in the South. Like other oppressed nations and colonial peoples, the Negroes—not as a class nor as a caste, but as a whole people suffer from social and political oppression and from inequalities of all kinds. In addition to the problems of the various classes among the Negro people—problems which are shared with corresponding classes among other nations—the Negro people as a whole still face the problem of national liberation, of independence and freedom.

While the Negro question exhibits all the fundamental features of a national question it has its own special characteristics arising from the specific conditions in the United States. The powerful anti-imperialist, anti-capitalist potentialities of the liberation struggle of the Negro people have already been pointed out. But it is not sufficient to recognize this in general. It is necessary to gauge the class relationships involved, to see clearly the relationship of the Negro question to the development of the class struggle as a whole. We must therefore view the Negro question in its larger perspective, from the vantage point of ultimate program and ultimate solution if we are to know how best to grapple with the immediate problems of the day.

The fundamental task in the struggle for the liberation of the Negro people, around which all phases of the battle for equality hinges, is to uproot the economic and social remnants of chattel slavery. The proper tasks, historically speaking, of the bourgeois-democratic revolution of 1861–1877 have never been completed. The Civil War decade was in reality the historical prologue to the struggle for Negro liberation in the present period. The demands voiced by the representatives of the former slaves and by bourgeois democrats during that period can be raised just as pertinently today. The continual agitation for land in the Union Leagues, the Negro conventions and the Reconstruction state legislatures touched the key point not only of that period but of the present South. The same is true in the domain of civil rights. The Colored People's Convention of South Carolina, held in Charleston in November 1865, sent a memorial to Congress which bore the stamp of the bourgeois democratic revolution more legibly than any other document produced by it. Above all it demanded that "a fair and impartial construction be given to the pledges of the government to us concerning the land question." (Radical Republican leaders had promised "forty acres and a mule.") All the democratic rights were demanded in this document—equal suffrage, a free public school system, the security of the press and the church, the right of jury service and office-holding, "the right to assemble in peaceful convention, to discuss the political questions of the day; the right to enter upon all avenues of agriculture, commerce, trade; to amass wealth by thrift and industry." The Memorial also asked Congress to permit the Negroes to retain their arms. The demands cover the whole gamut of bourgeois rights, from suffrage and the right to bear arms to private property.[106] This document remains as pertinent today as when it was presented to Congress. The prime issues which were on the order of the day in the South in the Civil War period have been handed down to the present era for solution, on a higher plane of social development, in a changed social milieu.

The completion of the bourgeois-democratic revolution in the South—which at the same time provides the basis for the solution of the Negro question—is in fact the outstanding peculiarity and most prominent native feature of the proletarian revolution in the United States. To fail to grasp the importance of this fact is to miss the whole perspective of the socialist revolution in this country, is to lack the slightest appreciation of all the class forces and social strata involved in the revolution.

Any one seriously concerned with the perspectives of proletarian revolution—not as a chimera, but as a reality—must recognize the oppressed Negro people as a powerful supplementary and even initiating force. This is true in the North as well as in the South. But the plantation South has all the prerequisites for providing a "Peasant War" as ally of the proletarian revolution. The plantation economy, its byproducts and its social superstructure, existing in the midst of a highly developed capitalist country, has engendered in the South contradictions, social antagonisms, class conflicts more violent and sharper than in any other section of the country. The contradictions inherent in capitalism are here sharpened by antagonisms left as a heritage from a previous historical period. How such a combination of forces has the possibilities of quick maturity into conscious social upheaval was shown in the Russian Revolution of 1905 and even more conclusively in the Russian Revolution of 1917.

To complete the Civil War revolution is the key to the solution of the Negro question. But it would be ridiculous to envision a new "Civil War" in terms of 1860–1865. The tasks remain essentially the same; the destruction of the plantation and tenant system, the confiscation of the landed estates for the benefit of the tenants and poor farmers, and the achievement of the fullest democracy for the masses. But conditions are no longer similar. The slave survivals exist in the midst of a highly developed capitalist country. Tasks which, historically speaking, were within the proper domain of the bourgeois revolution of the 19th century have been passed as a heritage to the proletarian revolution. This revolution cannot develop and succeed without at the same time destroying all pre-capitalist forms of exploitation. In the United States the uprooting of the slave survivals and the solution of the Negro question are the most important of these.

Since the Civil War, class alignments have changed. In the first place, the present plantation masters, instead of finding their chief opponents in the industrial capitalists as during the Civil War, now find themselves fully at one with the capitalist class as a whole and especially with the financial oligarchy. Secondly, the plantation and tenant peasantry find at their side a large proletariat whose class interests propel them towards a final struggle against capitalism. In the sixties there was but one principal question—the struggle against the slave power.

Today the struggle against the plantation system develops in the midst of a general struggle against capitalism. Thirdly, during the Civil War decade the chief ally of the Negro was the northern bourgeoisie, which because of its own class interests was bound to and did desert the Negro masses to the power of the former slaveowners. Under present circumstances, a revolutionary proletariat finds its most important ally in the Negro people, who in their struggle against the relics of chattel slavery must at the same time strike a heavy blow at capitalism. And the Negro people find their only dependable and their most powerful ally in the proletariat, whose class interests encompass the solution of the Negro question.

The Communist solution of the Negro question is premised primarily on the analysis of the Negro question as a national question and upon that perspective of the proletarian revolution in this country which includes the solution of the bourgeois democratic revolution in the South.

The abstract, formalized slogan about "equality" in general has for the first time been given real content and application.

The slogan of equal rights for Negroes has for so long been, at least verbally, in the program of petty-bourgeois democrats that its "justice" is generally conceded. It has been written upon the banner of northern liberalism by the Abolition movement, the Civil War and the consequent struggle for civil rights. Today they understand it only in a formalistic, juridical sense, although in the past revolutionary means were employed by their class to make civil rights for Negroes a reality. The Communists have broadened the concept of equal rights, in the first place, by extending it beyond the social and political field to the economic sphere as well, as expressed in the demand for "equal pay for equal work," "the right to all jobs," etc. Secondly, the Communists maintain that the struggle for equal rights and against all forms of discrimination and persecution should be organized and led, not in a reformist or opportunist fashion, but in such a way as to involve the broadest masses of whites and Negroes in a militant movement for Negro liberation. Thirdly, the Communists hold that the working class must become the chief protagonist and leader in the current, everyday struggle for equal rights in all spheres.

The Solution of the Negro Question

But the most basic programmatic difference between the liberals (as well as Socialists) and the Communists hinges around the application of the program of equal rights to the South, and therefore to the fundamental source of Negro oppression throughout the country, a difference based upon diametrically opposed concepts of the nature of the question. The slogan of equal rights applied to its fullest extent to the specific conditions pertaining in the South can culminate only in the realization of the right of self-determination for the Negro people of the Black Belt. This is a fully realizable and historically necessary solution. The right of self-determination is the necessary concomitant of the struggle against plantation slavery and for equal rights and is, in fact, the key democratic demand arising from the historical task of wiping out all the remnants of chattel slavery. It alone can guarantee the final solution of the Negro question.

To realize the right of self-determination in the Black Belt is to realize democracy in the South. But this is connected with a change in the basic structure of southern society.

Any real, basic, complete transformation of the plantation economy can come about only as the result of an agrarian revolution in the South. We have already discussed the factors which are maturing this revolution, which are propelling the farming masses toward rebellion

Selections from *The Negro Question in the United States*

against plantation overlords. The plantation is situated precisely in the area where the Negroes are the majority of the population. The confiscation of the landed estates and the realization of the primary agrarian aims of the revolution would give rise to new political institutions carrying with them the fullest democracy for the masses of the people. A really democratic transformation in the Black Belt, in the plantation area, would mean, first of all, that the Negroes, hitherto excluded from democracy, would now in fact be the very carriers of the widest democracy. There is no better assurance of such complete democracy than that the Negroes are today the most oppressed of all in the South and that they constitute the chief revolutionary sector of the plantation populace.

During the Reconstruction period those who had been just freed from chattel slavery were the most vigorous proponents of bourgeois democracy, demanding and fighting for the whole range of democratic rights. With the tremendous social power released by an agrarian revolution and directed into conscious channels by a proletariat there can be no doubt of the tremendous role that will be played by the Negro peasant masses in uprooting the semi-feudal institutions of the South completely, basically and irrevocably.

The revolutionary governmental power which is created in the Black Belt as the result of a democratic-agrarian overturn will represent those classes participating in and making the revolution. While the immediate tasks performed by the agrarian revolution will be bourgeois-democratic—first on its order of business will be to secure the destruction of the semi-slave economy and the distribution of the land to the landless—it is out of the question that the revolution will be limited by its bourgeois-democratic aims, or that it will develop under the leadership of the bourgeoisie. Such a course of development was possible only in the earlier stage of capitalism, when bourgeois revolutions could have no other aim but the overthrow of the feudal ruling class and the establishment in power of the bourgeoisie, when the chief contending classes were the landed aristocracy and the rising middle class. But today the bourgeoisie has long been in power and the prime question of the day is the socialist revolution. The historical course of development has given the proletariat the task as well of securing the bourgeois democratic revolution in the South. In 1860–1877 this was not yet the case: the working class was still too immature, too undeveloped to play a leading independent role in the Civil War revolution. That lot fell to the rapidly growing industrial bourgeoisie of the North. Today, due to the high stage of the development of capitalism at which the agrarian masses of the semi-feudal South are being swept into motion, the leading role would be played by the working class.

The role played by the proletariat in the fundamental Negro liberation struggle cannot and will not be sectional, i.e., restricted to the proletariat of the South. The presence of a large Negro proletariat in the North, in the area of the most highly developed capitalism, provides the intimate link between the proletariat as a whole and the agrarian-emancipatory struggle in the South. The participation of the working class throughout the country in the struggle for Negro rights incorporates the aims of the democratic liberation movement in the program of the proletariat as a class. But the development of capitalism in the South itself has created on the spot a white and black proletariat which must play a decisive role in the democratic Revolution.

The role of the working class in the democratic revolution in the South can be compared with that of the Russian proletariat in the Revolution of 1905. Lenin estimated the character of the 1905 Revolution as follows:

> The peculiar feature of the Russian Revolution is that in its social content it was a bourgeois-democratic revolution, but in its method of struggle it was a proletarian revolution. It was a bourgeois-democratic revolution, since the aim towards which it strove directly and which it could reach directly, with the aid of its own forces was a democratic republic, an eight-hour day and the confiscation of the immense estates of the nobility—all measures achieved almost completely in the French bourgeois revolution in 1792 and 1793.
>
> At the same time the Russian Revolution was also a proletarian revolution, not only in the sense that the proletariat was the leading force, the vanguard of the movement, but also in the sense that the specifically proletarian means of struggle—namely the strike—was the principal instrument

employed for rousing the masses and the most characteristic phenomenon in the wave-like rise of decisive events.[107]

The situation in the South is different in that it takes place in the milieu of a much more highly developed capitalism and in the same sense that the Revolution of 1917 differed from the Revolution of 1905. In other words, the proletariat is now most directly concerned with the revolution for the overthrow of capitalism and the solution of the bourgeois-democratic tasks in the South are linked up with and are a part of its ripe class aim. The Negro people and the agrarian masses play the role of allies of the proletariat in the socialist revolution. But in the democratic movement itself the proletariat will play a role similar to that of the Russian working class in the Revolution of 1905. Due to the maturity of capitalism today for the socialist revolution, the bourgeois-democratic phase in the South, whether it precedes or follows the proletarian revolution in the United States as a whole, will very rapidly grow over into a socialist revolution.

As a result of these peculiarities of the revolution in the South, the governmental power which is created in the Black Belt as a result of the democratic revolution would be a dictatorship of the workers and the peasantry. It would be a democratic peoples' government, i.e., power would be not only in the hands of the workers (a dictatorship of the proletariat) but in the hands of the workers and peasantry (the sharecroppers, poor tenants and farmers), in the hands of the overwhelming majority of the people. The character of the governmental power, therefore, reflects the essential democratic nature of the revolution in the plantation area, as distinguished from the essential proletarian nature of the revolution in the rest of the United States, where remnants of feudalism transported from Europe had been wiped out in the course of capitalist development at a very early period, where, therefore, there never was and cannot be today any question of completing a bourgeois-democratic revolution.

The highest political expression of the fulfillment of the democratic revolution in the South is the creation of the Negro Republic in the area approximating the present Black Belt. The demand for a democratic people's republic in the plantation area, therefore, is likely to be the prime slogan of the revolutionary democratic movement in this area, the summation of all the bourgeois-democratic aims of the revolution there. We use the term "Negro Republic" not in the sense of "Negro domination" or a "dictatorship of Negroes." The class composition of such a governmental power, as we have already explained, is working class and peasant, both white and Negro. In such a government, from the local administrative units to the top bodies, the Negroes would be greatly predominant, because they form the overwhelming majority of these classes in the area where such a transformation would take place, and because the completion of the bourgeois-democratic revolution is intimately bound up with, is in fact the achievement of, the liberation of the Negro people from the yoke of imperialism. The term "Negro Republic" signifies that as a result of the fullest democracy, won for the first time in the South, the Negro necessarily plays the leading and most important role in the new Republic.

We can cite a comparable situation from our own history. The Reconstruction state governments of the South from 1868 to about 1875 included representatives of the northern bourgeoisie, the southern middle class and small landowning whites, and the ex-slaves. In the Black Belt counties the local offices were held almost exclusively by Negroes. The lower houses of three southern state legislatures (South Carolina, Mississippi and Louisiana) had a majority of Negro representatives, while a number of Negroes were sent to both the House and Senate of the United States. If fuller democracy had been won, there would have been a much higher proportion of Negroes in the state bodies and in Congress, and they would have held most of the governmental positions in a number of southern states. And if the Black Belt had not been dissected by the existing borders of the states in such a way that the upland white sections of each state cut down on the representation of the Negroes in each state body, there would have been a much more complete expression of democracy. In the course of a modern "Civil War," when an entirely new Republic would arise out of the Black Belt territory, created by really democratic classes, history will be improved upon a hundredfold.

The most crucial test of freedom would arise in the relationship between the Negro Republic and the United States as a whole. It is at this point that the right of self-determination becomes the question, the pivot on which hinges the reality of freedom for the Negro. Thus, the right of self-determination for the Negroes in the Black Belt, as raised by the Communist Party, is the summation of a number of social and political steps and includes, as an integral part, the completion of the democratic revolution in the South and the creation of the Negro Republic. The realization of the right of self-determination, as has been demonstrated in the Soviet Union, does not necessarily mean separation and the creation of totally independent political states. The right of self-determination is purely a political question, a question of the relationship of political state entities, and means the right of a people to choose freely between complete independence as a separate state and federation with a state or group of states. The important, crucial point is the right to choose freely, without pressure, coercion or interference, from any other nation. This is the key political question in the relationship between nations.

One cannot say in advance under what conditions the question of the right of self-determination will present itself for solution with regard to the Negro Republic—i.e., whether at that time capitalism will still exist in the United States or a proletarian revolution will already have established a Socialist Soviet Government in the country.

In any case, the Communist supports the complete realization of the right of self-determination, no matter what the choice, because it is only on the basis of a free, democratic choice that a federation of Socialist nations can exist.

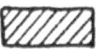 # 'ON THE RIGHT TO SELF-DETERMINATION FOR THE NEGRO PEOPLE IN THE BLACK BELT (A DISCUSSION ARTICLE)'
CLAUDIA JONES
FROM *POLITICAL AFFAIRS*
JANUARY 1946

The political attacks that are being directed against the Negro people by Big Business have once again placed serious questions before the American working class.

These attacks, reminiscent of post–World War I, are all the more serious because today the main danger of fascism to the world comes from the most colossal imperialist forces which are concentrated within the United States. The perpetrators of these attacks are the representatives of the most reactionary section of monopoly capital and of the semi-feudal economy of the Black Belt. This hookup, expressed in Congress by the reactionary Republicans and the poll taxers who draw their power from the oppression of the Negro people and the working class, makes it obvious that the two main forces for democracy are the working class allied with the Negro people.

In the short period since the war for national liberation, our nation has witnessed a revival of lynchings—three known lynchings in the

---

*   Claudia Jones, "On the Right to Self-Determination for the Negro People in the Black Belt (A Discussion Article)," *Political Affairs* 25, no. 1 (January 1946): 67–77.

space of three months. This blot of shame lies in America, while we proclaim to the world our "championship" of democracy for other nations!

The two-pronged drive of Big Business to decimate the wartime gains of the Negroes in industry and at the same time to destroy the alliance between labor and the Negro people, the fascist-inspired "race strikes" of American students, the recent attacks on Negro veterans in the South, and the closing of FEPC offices in city after city—all this necessitates the greatest political initiative and action by the trade unions and by our Party.

Coupled with this reactionary drive on the economic and political fronts, are the growing Hitler-like incitements of the Bilbos and Rankins. While popular indignation has been aroused by these events, it is obvious that labor must move more aggressively than it has so far on the vital issues affecting the Negro people.

If the alliance, crucial to progress, between the Negro people and labor is to be reinforced and extended, it is necessary to clarify the relationship between the struggle for national liberation of the Negro people and that of the working class against capitalist exploitation and oppression.

In opening this discussion, it must be made clear that the conclusions here arrived at should in no sense be regarded as a condition for the united struggle of the Negro people and the working class for Negro rights. What differences in outlook may be present as regards the thesis here presented must in no way hinder the struggle for the immediate needs of the Negro people.

The basis for this discussion article is the Political Resolution of our National Convention in July, which rejected Browder's revisionist position on the national character of the Negro question. A further basis is the preliminary exchange of opinion registered recently at an enlarged meeting of the newly established National Negro Commission of our Party. At that meeting it must be stated, the views expressed revealed varying opinions on our fundamental theoretical approach to the political essence and ultimate aim of the Negro liberation movement in the United States. Similar differences of opinion are indicated in communications, club resolutions, and articles submitted to the National Office which discuss the issue of the right of self-determination for the Negro people in the Black Belt.

'On the Right to Self-Determination for the Negro People in the Black Belt'

It is clear that a deepgoing discussion of the subject is necessary. While this article will attempt to discuss some of these views, it is to be hoped that it will be followed by further discussion. The views presented here are my own.

The National Character of the Struggle for Negro Rights

Even the worst enemies of the Communist Party cannot fail to admit that we have been in the forefront of the struggle for equality of the Negro people. It was the Communist Party which fourteen years ago made the name of Scottsboro ring the world around. It was the Communist Party which was the first, since the overthrow of the Reconstruction governments, to raise in the heart of the South the issue of full Negro freedom.

What galvanized our Party to become the initiator and vanguard of these struggles? It was our understanding of the Negro question in the United States as a *special* question, as an issue whose solution requires *special* demands, in addition to the general demands of the American working class.

It was essentially this understanding that found Communists in the forefront of the struggle to combat the imperialist ideology of "white supremacy" which is today endangering the unity of the labor-democratic coalition and of the working class itself. It was essentially this knowledge that taught white American workers to fight for Negro rights in their own self-interest, to understand that to fight against white chauvinism is to fight against imperialist ideologies and practices of America's ruling class which serves to separate Negro and white workers. It was this understanding that taught Negro workers to fight against petty-bourgeois nationalism—a result of white chauvinist ideology—and to have both Negro and white workers form strong bonds of unity with each other.

The Black Belt, an area in which the Negro people form a majority, came into existence with the growth of cotton culture and plantation economy. As the area of cotton cultivation moved over westward in the days before the Civil War, so did the area of the plantation that consisted of a white–master family with its slaves.

The Civil War, which abolished chattel slavery, failed either to break up this area of Negro majority or fully liberate the Negro people within it. Retaining their plantation lands, the ex-slaveholders soon forced the return to these lands of their former slaves as sharecroppers. A series of laws passed by Southern states—the crop lien laws, the jumping contract laws, and so on—prevented and still prevent the free migration of the Negro people. Scarcely less than before the Civil War, is the Black Belt a prison-house of the Negroes; the chains which hold them now are the invisible chains of poverty, the legal chains of debt slavery, and, when the landlords deem it necessary, the iron shackles of the chain gang.

The Civil War might have broken the bars of the Black Belt; it did not, for the Northern capitalists, who had gained a united market and field of exploitation throughout the nation as a result of the Civil War, were terrified by the simultaneous rise of Southern democracy, the Northern labor movement, and radical agrarian organizations. They betrayed the Negro people and the Southern white masses, and turned the South back to semi-slavery.

The migrations of the 1870s, of the First World War, and of the Second World War, did not appreciably diminish the proportion by which the Negroes find themselves a majority today in the Black Belt—these are virtually the same. It cannot be said that this majority is accidental, or that the Negro people continue as an oppressed people within the Black Belt by inertia or by choice. They continue so because the sheriff's posse of the twentieth century is carrying on, under new forms, the work of the slave catchers of the nineteenth. The majority remains a majority by force.

This community in which the Negro people are a majority is neither racial nor tribal; it is composed of a significant minority of whites as well. The territory stretches contiguously westward from the Eastern shore of Maryland, and lies within Maryland, Virginia, North Carolina, South Carolina, Georgia, Florida, Alabama, Mississippi, Louisiana, Tennessee, Arkansas, and Texas.

Following the Civil War, boundary lines were definitely shaped by the defeated slaveholders to prohibit the full participation of the Negroes and poor whites in political life. If it is true in the North, where certain election districts are "gerrymandered" to prohibit the full expression of the Negro vote (and of the white vote as well), it was no less true of the Black Belt, where the majority of the inhabitants were Negroes and represented its basic core.

'On the Right to Self-Determination for the Negro People in the Black Belt'

As to the other characteristics of nationhood: Have the Negro people, for example, a common language? They have a common language—English. If it be argued that this is the language of the entire country, we say that this is true. A common language is necessary to nationhood; a different language is not. When the American colonies separated from Britain; they had a common language, which was the same as that of their oppressors. Surely no one will argue that our community of language with our British oppressors should have kept us indefinitely in the status of a colonial people.

Is there an American Negro culture? The peculiar oppression of the Negro people and their striving for freedom have been expressed in songs, literature, art, the dance. This does not mean that American Negro culture is not part of American culture generally. Negro culture is part of the general stream of American culture, but it is a distinct current in that stream; it arose out of the special historical development and unique status of the Negro people; no other people in America could have developed this particular culture.

Have the Negro people a stable community of economic life? First, let us discuss what is meant by a common economic life. It is sometimes said that people have a common economic life when they make their living in the same way—they are all sharecroppers, or they are all workers. Actually, a common economic life with reference to a nation or community under capitalism means that the nation or community has within it the class or social relations that characterize society; it has capitalists, workers, farmers, and intellectuals, ranged according to their position in the production relations. In this case it means that a Negro must be able to hire a Negro, buy from a Negro, sell to a Negro, service a Negro.

Such class stratification exists among the Negro people in the Black Belt. There is a Negro bourgeoisie. It is not an industrial bourgeoisie. It is not a big bourgeoisie; the bourgeoisie of an oppressed nation never is; it is one of the results of national oppression that the bourgeoisie of the oppressed nations is retarded by the oppressors. The market of the Negro bourgeoisie is founded upon Jim-Crowism; it functions chiefly in life insurance, banking, and real estate. Its leadership among the Negro people is reflected in an ideology—petty-bourgeois nationalism, whose main purpose is to mobilize the Negro masses under its own influence.

By these distinguishing features, therefore, the Negro people in the Black Belt constitute a nation. They are an historically developed community of people, with a common language, a common territory, and a common economic life, all of which are manifest in a common culture.

As far back as 1913, Lenin emphasized that the Negro people constitute an oppressed nation. In an unfinished essay on the national and colonial question he made a *direct* reference to the Negro people as an *oppressed nation*, stating:

> In the United States 11.1 percent of the population consists of Negroes (and also mulattoes and Indians) who must be considered an oppressed nation, inasmuch as the equality, won in the Civil War of 1861–65 and guaranteed by the constitution of the Republic, has in reality been more and more restricted in many respects in the main centers of the Negro population (in the South) with the transition from the progressive, pre-monopolistic capitalism of 1860–1870 to the reactionary monopolistic capitalism (imperialism) of the latest epoch.[108]

Browder's Revision of Leninist Teachings

In discussing the right of self-determination for Negroes in the Black Belt, we surely cannot ignore the revisionist position taken by Earl Browder, as set forth in his article in *The Communist* for January 1944, which was presented as a declaration of policy for American Communists. There Browder wrote:

> ... It was in view of the gathering world crisis that we Communists at that time—in the early 30s—raised the issue of self-determination. At that time, we necessarily faced the possibility that the Negro people, disappointed in their aspirations for full integration into the American nation, might find their only alternative in separation and in the establishment of their own state in the Black Belt, in the territory in which they are a majority. We raised this as one of the rights of the Negro people, in case the

'On the Right to Self-Determination for the Negro People in the Black Belt'

Negro people found this was the only way to satisfy their aspirations.

Browder further wrote:

> The crisis of history has taken a turn of such character that Negro people in the United States have found it possible to make their decision once and for all. Their decision is for their complete integration into the American nation as a whole and not for separation.

Browder thus denied that the right of self-determination for Negroes in the Black Belt was any longer an issue, since, according to him, the Negro people had already made their historic choice!

What was the fallacy on which Browder's premise was based?

Browder's fallacy was inherently connected with a false estimate of the relationship of forces in our nation and the world. Clearly, if a rosy future was to be envisioned in which a "peaceful" capitalism would voluntarily relinquish its exploitations, solve its contradictions, etc., the Leninist program which showed that the very essence of imperialism was the distinction and conflict between oppressed and oppressing nations no longer applied to our country!

Moreover, Browder based his premise not on evaluating the right of self-determination as it applies to the Negro people in the Black Belt, but on one of its aspects, separation. That he saw fit to discuss the whole question from the standpoint of a "practical political matter," confirms this. His treatment of these two demands as being identical needs examination.

Is separation identical with self-determination? The right to separation is inherent in the right to self-determination, whether that right is eventually exercised or not. It becomes a practical political matter only when the concrete objective conditions for that choice are at hand. Therefore, to identify self-determination with separation, or to substitute one for the other, is tantamount to forcing on the Negro people a choice, which they are clearly not in an objective position to make—which, in other words, though a right, is not necessarily a function of their exercise of self-determination!

It is obvious from this that the right of self-determination is not something one can dangle, withdraw, or put forward again as a sheerly objective factor. Either the objective historic conditions of nationhood exist, in which such a right remains inviolate, or they do not. Either the objective conditions exist for the choice to be made by the oppressed nation (either for separation, autonomy, amalgamation, etc.), or they do not. Thus, and only thus, can we approach the issue as a practical political matter.

How then, does the question of integration apply? Are the Negro people demanding integration in American political life? Most certainly they are! But this is no new phenomenon insofar as the Negro people are concerned. Negro Americans have been fighting for integration for over two hundred years. Every *partial* fight—whether expressed in the demands of the Reconstruction leaders, together with the white workers and farmers in the South for land, or in the present-day demands of Negroes in Atlanta to enforce the Supreme Court ruling against the "white primary" laws; whether it be the fight against lynching and poll-tax disfranchisement, or the recent successful campaign, conducted in Negro-white unity to reelect Benjamin J. Davis Jr., to the New York City Council—is a step towards integration.

But integration cannot be considered a substitute for the right of self-determination. National liberation is not synonymous with integration, neither are the two concepts mutually exclusive.

What does integration really mean? Integration, that is, *democratic* integration, means breaking down the fetters which prohibit the full economic, political and social participation of Negroes in all phases of American life. This does not mean that a merger, or an assimilative process necessarily takes place. In a general sense, the struggle for integration waged today by the Negro people is directed toward achieving *equal rights*—economic, political and social.

But the basic difference, in fact, the touchstone of programmatic difference, between the liberals (as well as the Social Democrats) and the Communists hinges on the application of the program of equal rights to the Black Belt, and, therefore, to the *source of Negro oppression* throughout the country—a difference based on diametrically opposed concepts of the nature of the question.

In the North, the struggle for equal rights for the Negro people is chiefly that of heightening the fight to secure equal participation in every sphere of American life. The problems of the Negro people in the North are akin to those of an oppressed national minority. Particularly here, the fight for equal rights as a whole is enhanced by the presence of a large and growing Negro proletariat, in the area of the most highly developed capitalism, as well as by the participation of the advanced workers throughout the country for equal rights for Negroes. In fact, it is the existence of a strong Negro proletariat—represented today by close to one million organized trade unionists—that provides the intimate link between the American working class as a whole and the struggle for emancipation and land for oppressed Negro people and white workers in the Black Belt.

In the Black Belt the problem is chiefly that of wiping out the economic, political, and social survivals of slavery, of the *enforcement* of equal rights. Without the necessary *enforcement* of equal rights for the Negro people in the Black Belt, including social equality, it is folly to speak of integration as being equal to the achievement of national liberation. Hence, equal rights for the Negro people in the Black Belt can be achieved only through enforcement, through their exercise of the right of self-determination.

The right of self-determination does not exclude the struggle for partial demands; it presupposes an energetic struggle for concrete partial demands, linked up with the daily needs and problems of the wide masses of the Negro people and the white workers in the Black Belt. The fight for such partial demands, moreover, is a struggle for democracy. It does not divert or overshadow the working-class struggle against exploitation, it is an aid to it.

It is only by helping to interconnect the partial demands with the right of self-determination that we Communists, in concert with other progressive forces, can contribute guidance to the struggle for complete equality for the Negro people.

Certain Contentions Examined

We Communists adhere to the fundamental belief that complete and lasting equality of imperialist oppressed nations and peoples can be guaranteed only with the establishment of Socialism. The aim of Socialism is not only to abolish the present division of mankind into small states, not only to bring nations closer to each other, but ultimately to merge them. But we have never ignored the historical process necessary to the achievement of that goal. Nor can we "postpone" the question of national liberation until Socialism is established or speak solely in general nebulous phrases about national liberation. We must have a clear and precisely formulated political program to guide our work in the achievement of that goal. For we know that "mankind can achieve the inevitable merging of nations, only by passing through the transition period of complete liberation of all the oppressed nations, i.e., their freedom to secede."[109]

As Leninists, we are distinguished from the reactionary Social Democrats in that we reject, even if it is under the name of "internationalism," any denial of the right of national self-determination to the oppressed peoples. For true internationalism, that is, Marxism-Leninism, places the right of self-determination as a basic programmatic point. The "internationalism" of the reformists is nothing more or less than the nationalism of their own respective imperialist rulers, while the national program of Lenin is an essential part of internationalism. Any "internationalism" that denies the right of self-determination to the subject peoples is false, is a mere cover for imperialist chauvinism.

Our approach is based on proletarian internationalism, which recognizes that the workers of an oppressing nation best fight against national oppression—especially by their "own" bourgeoisie—once they understand that such is the road to realize their own freedom. It is based on the Marxist proposition that "no nation can be free if it oppresses other nations."

Clearly then, those who impute to the Negro people the main responsibility for "accepting" or "rejecting" the principle of self-determination ignore this tenet: they base their conclusions on the subjective factor, instead of the objective and historical conditions of oppression of the Negro people in the Black Belt.

But let us examine some of these arguments. Is it true that the Negro people do not want self-determination, that the Negro people shy away from this concept with abhorrence? Definitely not! It is, of course, quite a different matter if we speak of the Negro people as not being fully conscious of this concept in our terms. But to challenge the deepest desires of the Negro people for freedom and equality as being other than that of the fullest national self-affirmation is to fail to understand their fundamental aspirations!

'On the Right to Self-Determination for the Negro People in the Black Belt'

What do the Negro people abhor? They abhor the continuation of their *actual* status in the Black Belt—that of forcible segregation. They abhor Jim Crow from which they suffer in many forms today. They abhor the freedom with which the poll taxers and feudal landowners, by dividing Negro and white, continue their oppression of the Negro people. They abhor the ideology of "white supremacy" which flouts the basic tenets of our Constitution, as the counterpart of Hitler's "aryan supremacy." They abhor any idea which holds out the perspective, not of full freedom and equality, but of something less than these things. And the slogan of self-determination expresses precisely these aspirations in the most complete sense.

To argue that the Negro people "don't want self-determination," is unwittingly to give sanction to the poll taxers and feudal landowners in the South to continue exploiting the Negro people and poor whites on the basis that "this is what the Negroes want"; it is to argue against a conscious fight by white American workers to help achieve the objective conditions in which the Negro people can freely make their own choice. It is to blunt the struggle for national liberation, to have at best, a bourgeois-liberal approach.

Is it any wonder, then, that the most vehement voices against this principle, are *not the mass* of the Negro people, but the enemies of the white workers and the Negro people? The Social Democrats (and the reactionary mouthpieces of monopoly capital and semi-feudal economy), who advance the ridiculous charge that self-determination would "Jim Crow the Negro people," "Create a Black Ghetto," and other such arguments *ad nauseam*, are exposed in their full light when we examine their real motives. They seek to cover up their denial of the double oppression of the Negro people—as wage slaves and as Negroes. They seek to obscure the fundamental character of the status of the Negro people in the Black Belt—which is essentially *national* and rooted in economic and historic conditions of a pre-capitalist nature. Nor can all of the piety and wit of Social Democracy cancel out its real aim—which is to serve imperialism and therefore betray the Negro people and the working class.

Another view holds that the industrialization of the South and new migrations has fundamentally altered the relationship of the Negro people to the land. The proponents of this view maintain that such a development has radically changed the character of the Negro question in the Black Belt from that of oppressed nationhood, if such it was in the past, to that of a class question.

In discussing such views, we should, at the outset, distinguish between the effects of industrialization in the South as a whole and in the Black Belt. The continued existence of economic slave survivals in the Black Belt is a fundamental distinction that must be made in an examination of the characteristics of nationhood among the Negro people. Unless this is done, we shall not be able to understand the problems either of the South as a whole or of the Black Belt in particular.

There has unquestionably been some increase of industrial expansion in the South. The war requirements for victory necessitated the expansion of a number of basic Southern industries, such as steel, coal, textile, lumber, and shipbuilding. In addition, new industries, such as aircraft and munitions, were built. Capital investments, however, came primarily from the Federal government. Over $7,000,000,000 were thus expended solely as a war necessity. It is obvious that such investment for expansion of existing plants and the building of new industries no longer exists. The reverse is true—that is, the closing down of plants and a drastic curtailment of industrial production. Thus, it is clear that no trend exists at present which would permit one to speak of the industrialization of the South. The trend that was evident during the war was a temporary phenomenon.

By 1944, Mr. D. B. Lasseter of the Atlanta, Georgia, Regional Office of the War Manpower Commission was able to warn us of this trend in summarizing what war orders meant to the South. Taking note of the more than seven billion dollars in prime contracts in six Southern states alone, Lasseter wrote in *Social Forces* for October 1944:

> At first glance, these factors appear as bright prospects, but there is ample cause for anxiety lest this war-inspired prosperity prove only temporary. For while industrial activity and facilities have increased tremendously, there will be great difficulty in maintaining these gains after the war. When the shooting is over the plants responsible for the current boom will shut down entirely, or production will

be sharply curtailed. And a glance at the record shows that there is a heavy concentration of this type of industry and activity. The South is packed with Army camps, and shipbuilding, airplane and munitions plants further account for much of our industrial development. None of these offers a rosy future as a peacetime investment.

Lasseter added:

The South faces a grave readjustment. Having had its first taste of prosperity resulting from increased industrial activity, it is slated to lose the source of this prosperity.

It goes without saying that expansion and building of new industries in the Black Belt would, of course, have its influence among the Negro people. Such a process would lead to the extension of the working-class base among the Negro people. Instead of delimiting the national characteristics of the Negro people, it would help importantly to develop the national consciousness of the Negro people and thus accelerate the realization of the aim of self-determination. The extension of the working-class base in the oppressed Negro nation is fundamentally the guarantee of the successful forward movement of the national liberation cause of the entire Negro people.

Self-Determination—a Guiding Principle

It is my opinion that we again must raise the right of self-determination for the Negro people in the Black Belt, not as a slogan of immediate action, but essentially as a programmatic demand. It might perhaps be argued that, raised in this manner, the slogan is academic and should therefore not be raised at all. Such criticism fails to take into account the difference between a slogan advanced as an issue on the order of the day and a guiding principle.

We must place the question in terms of historical perspective, taking into account concretely the stage of the Negro liberation movement today and the present practical struggle for full Negro rights, in behalf of which there must be established both the broadest Negro and white alliance. Between the current struggles and the programmatic slogan here advanced there is no conflict, but a vital interconnection. The goal of national self-determination should serve as a beacon to the day-to-day struggles for Negro rights, and these struggles, in turn, should serve to hasten the realization of the right to self-determination.

'CHAPTER 6: LAND AND FREEDOM'
HARRY HAYWOOD
FROM *NEGRO LIBERATION*
1948

There is no escape from the conclusion that freedom and prosperity for the people of the South, Negro and white, can be won only through drastic overhauling of the present system of land ownership and agrarian relations of the region. The fight for such radical change must be placed in the very heart of any effective program.

The plantation system which stifles the development of the South's productive forces and warps the lives of its people must be swept away. This foul relic of the chattel slave past, subsidized from the North, can have no place in a fully democratic America. It must be relegated to the limbo of historical monstrosities.

Along with the plantation must go its odious increments of sharecropping, debt slavery, riding-boss supervision; its outmoded methods of soil usage; its one-crop system, and finally the barbarous institution of color caste, which freezes the Negroes in permanence at the bottom of the social pyramid. This democratic, agrarian revolution, which Reconstruction passed up in default, has been long overdue. It is a task which must be assumed now by the modern forces of progressive democracy as an integral part of the struggle for progress and democracy in the country as a whole.

---
*   Harry Haywood, "Chapter 6: Land and Freedom," in *Negro Liberation* (New York: International Publishers, 1948), 116–35.

The abolition of the plantation system means, first of all, land redivision, the starting point of any agrarian revolution in the South. The big plantations must be broken up and land redistributed in favor of those who work it, Negro and white. Sharecroppers, tenants, and other laborers must have ownership of the land they till. The thousands of small, mortgage-ridden, subsistence farmers who live on the fringes of the plantation belt and are excluded by planter monopoly from the best land must be given access to the good land at the expense of the big estates.

Land to Those Who Work It

At the same time, one-third of the South's eroded soil must be reclaimed and made accessible to the actual working farmers. This extension of the area of cultivable land will serve a twofold purpose: it will enhance the possibilities of developing economically sound holdings and it will relieve the frightful overcrowding endemic to the region.

Redistribution alone, however, is not enough. The new class of independent small holders must be made secure in their tenure. Here two measures are necessary: (1) The backlog of poor-farmer debt must be wiped out through a drastic scaling down of such debts or through complete cancellation. Usury must be abolished. (2) The new owners must be furnished with the essential tools of production—seeds, fertilizer, livestock, machinery—by means of cheap, long-range government credit. Land is useless without tools, and cheap government credit is essential to check the restoration of landlordism once it has been abolished.

Furthermore, the new class of independent farmers must be helped by federal funds in the cooperative purchase and operation of mechanized equipment. In a modern system there can be set up tractor pools, repair shops, groups of technical advisers, and training courses for handling the heavy machinery under government aegis. Located in each southern farm county, such technical centers and specialists would make possible the changing of the poorly equipped family farms into efficient, productive units.

In this respect, the progressive people's democracies of central and eastern Europe afford valuable lessons. The governments of these countries, representing and fighting for the interests of the workers and peasantry, have found the answer to agrarian progress on the basis of small, independent holdings to be the encouragement of cooperative enterprise, such as collective credit organizations, cooperatives for the sale and purchase of essential manufactures, and horse and tractor stations. In Poland, for example, even though agriculture continues on the basis of individual farming, modern machinery is being made available even to the smallest farms. The Polish government is supporting "Peasant Self-Help Unions" which secure implements that serve entire villages.

In short, land redivision plus cooperative farming—that is the key to the agricultural rehabilitation of the South. It would abolish the conditions which condemn the masses of soil tillers to landlessness, and at the same time assure the technical progress of agriculture by promoting the widest use of machinery and the application of science. In this way it would raise the antiquated agricultural technique of the South to modern levels, enhance the living and cultural standards of the masses of working farmers, and open the way to the ultimate development of large-scale production. In other words, this is the road towards overcoming the lag of technical development in agriculture behind that of industry which is the material basis of agricultural poverty under capitalism, and is accentuated in the South by the monopoly-nourished survivals of slavery.

Electrification and Industrialization

The modernization of southern farming methods means rural electrification together with the industrialization of the South. Cheap electric power must be made available to every farm family. This can be achieved only through a comprehensive program designed to develop the region's tremendous power resources. Rampaging rivers that have hitherto brought disaster to the South's countryside must be harnessed to useful purpose. An idea of the tremendous possibilities for rapid technological development of the South can be gleaned from the Tennessee Valley project initiated under the Roosevelt New Deal.

Despite constraints placed upon the full development of this project by the bitter opposition of reactionaries, the power trust, the railroad corporations, and their political hatchet men such as the notorious Senator McKellar, the net result of the project has been the reclamation of a large eroded and wasted area of the Southern soil. Here new industries have sprouted and tens of thousands of formerly backward people have received a higher standard of living.

Any serious program of rehabilitation of the South's agrarian economy must include the fullest extension of such projects as the Tennessee Valley Authority to every suitable site in the region, providing a basis for its all-sided industrial development. The failure to develop such a project in the much larger Missouri basin, for example, is condemning the Missouri Valley to a steady decline. Only a Missouri Valley Act (MVA) with full control over irrigation, flood prevention, power development, and the rational exploitation of natural resources could save that area. As one of the editors of the *St. Louis Star-Times* wrote, "the late President Roosevelt was an ardent supporter of the MVA idea, but his successor has given it only lip service. Even the latest floods were not enough to move him beyond that."

The chief opponents of the MVA idea, this writer explained, "are the private power interests, the railroads, cattlemen with their eyes on public lands, and such old-line pressure groups as the Mississippi Valley Association, the National Reclamation Association, and the National Rivers and Harbors Congress," whose chief "stocks in the trade are (a) the silly argument that MVA is 'communistic'—though even the *New York Daily News* favors it; (b) that methods successful in the Tennessee Valley cannot be used in that of Missouri; and (c) that there *is* no MVA plan. . . ." Despite this opposition, such projects provide the basis for effective flood control, soil reclamation, cheap rural electrification and power for local industries capable of producing cheaply the means of production and consumption for Southern agriculture, and helping to relieve the agrarian overcrowding.

Rebuilding the South's Soil

Along with the above, concrete measures must be taken to end the ruinous single-crop system and rebuild and restore to productive use the eroded, damaged, or abandoned soil wasted through the deadening influence of the plantation which prevents the application of new methods. The single-crop system which ties the South's farmers to a monopolistic market and makes the region dependent upon the outside for essential manufactured articles, must be replaced by a rational system of farming. This would include scientifically planned crop rotation and diversified farming, with emphasis on the production of food and dairy products, vegetables, fruits, and new industrial crops.

'Chapter 6: Land and Freedom'

The rebuilding of the soil would require federal outlays for such measures as the grading, ditching, and terracing of fields, and a big scale program of protective planting and reforesting of damaged hillsides, as well as an elaborate fertilizer program to supply fertilizer to all farms, especially the smallest, which need it most.

White Supremacy Must Go

The abolition of the plantation system means, finally, the complete destruction of the Jim-Crow color caste institution whereby the big planters oppress and exploit the Negro people. This institution has served both as a "moral" justification and as an effective means for maintaining and continuing plantation slavery in modern life. Without the abolition of all forms of white supremacy, it is impossible to save the land or the people who work it. Since the entire Jim-Crow system has its roots in the plantation, only the abolition of the plantation can permanently remove the soil which has produced and sustained this barbarous system. But "white supremacy" is the plantation lords' chief line of defense, the bulwark of the Bourbon exploiters' rule. Basic land reform, therefore, is unthinkable without the destruction of the entire system of Negro oppression.

Plainly, these far-reaching changes are necessary if the Negro is to be free, if the South is to rise out of the quagmire of economic and cultural blight, and if the malignant sore eating at the very heart of our country's democracy is to be cauterized and healed. They comprise the basic ingredients of the long delayed agrarian revolution in the South. If successfully prosecuted, these measures would release the imprisoned productive forces of the region, requite the gnawing land hunger of the southern tillers of the soil, Negro and white, create the conditions for the rise of a class of independent and prosperous small owners and for the further development of the class struggle for the democratic reconstruction of the South. They would strike the manacles of semi-serf bondage from the Negro people, destroy the most important material base of Jim-Crow oppression, and lay the groundwork for destroying the whole system of "color caste" which dictates inequality for America's colored citizenry throughout the country and in all walks of life.

These changes would break the backbone of Junkerism, Dixie style, whose representatives in Congress are hell-bent on essaying a role in contemporary American life similar to that of their dethroned feudalist counterparts in central and eastern Europe, as the torchbearers of native fascism. It would shake loose the putrid soil which nourishes the whole foul breed of fascist Negrophobes of the stripe of Bilbo, Ellender, Rankin, and Talmadge.

Is It Practical?

Is there any prospect for the achievement of such drastic changes within the frame of existing conditions, of a state dominated economically and politically by finance capital?

The bourgeoisie, which would not carry through this land reform during the Civil War and Reconstruction, when capitalism was comparatively youthful and waging a progressive struggle against slavery, will surely not carry it out today, when capitalism is in its decadent, imperialist era, and monopoly capital seeks to make use of the most backward feudal elements in the interests of untrammeled exploitation. The transformation of the agrarian structure of the South will not come from above. On the contrary, the real economic rulers of the South and a federal government which represents the concentrated power of big capital rather than the interests of the people can be counted on to use their maximum strength to crush any attempt at fundamental land reform in the South.

At the same time, cooperative farming, difficult at best under capitalism, is an idle dream in the South without land redivision. This was amply demonstrated by the experience of the New Deal which showed the complete futility of cooperatives for the mass of poor farmers under conditions of southern landlordism. As J. Lewis Henderson pointed out in a comparatively recent survey of the semi-feudal plantation system, the very principle of cooperation means sharing of benefits and democratic control, and this would obviously be an immediate threat to the entire white-supremacy pattern. The attempts of the Farm Security Administration to organize small farmer co-ops in the South, therefore, met with resistance and essential failure. The few existing ones are manipulated so that benefits and savings do not extend to the mass of small farmers, and Negro tenants "seldom receive the benefits of such co-ops, as any patronage dividends usually stop when they reach the landlord."

'Chapter 6: Land and Freedom'

Moreover, as long as the economy of the country as a whole is dominated by monopoly capital, there is no possibility of any far-reaching change in the technical basis of Southern agriculture. It is "normal" under capitalism for the technical development of agriculture to lag behind that of industry, and as long as capitalism prevails there can be no real prospect for all-around mechanization of agriculture in a backward area like the South, and without such comprehensive mechanization there is no way out of agricultural poverty. Indeed, under southern plantation conditions, the "normal" gap between agriculture and industry characteristic of capitalism is highly accentuated. Where mechanization does proceed in the South, tenants and farmers are tractored off the land. On non-mechanized plantations, the labor force is even more exploited as a consequence. It also means the more intensive exploitation of the hard-driven "independent" farmers who, with their "one row, one mule system," are unable to compete and survive.

The development of power projects in the South is also kept in check and obstructed, and, with the government at this time more firmly in the hands of the trusts and corporations than ever, there can be no doubt that anything done along this line will be subordinated entirely to the profit needs and military plans of big capital. With the South, the nation's so-called "economic problem number one," virtually occupying a semi-colonial position within the country, there can be no talk of any extensive development of the productive forces there, even if other conditions were favorable.

Altogether, therefore, the conclusion is inescapable that the liberation of the Negro people and the transformation of the agrarian relations in the South cannot be achieved through the further economic evolution of capitalism in that region. They can be achieved, on the one hand, only through the development and organization of the economic and political struggle of the landless masses, Negro and white, aimed against the entire "Southern system," and supported by the working class and other progressive forces of the country as a whole. On the other hand, they can be achieved only when the government is free from the influence of the monopolies, in short, is truly a people's government, firmly rooted in the public ownership of the economy, and whose first concern is the welfare of the masses and the progress of the country, and not the profits of trusts and corporations. Only under the aegis of a genuine people's government in the United States can the status quo in southern land relationships be radically altered in favor of the great bulk of the agricultural population, Negro and white. Only such a government will be capable of instituting the all-embracing social, economic, and political reforms so urgently needed by the mass of Southern common folk. But whatever one may think of the conditions necessary for the realization of the foregoing measures, there can be no question that the adoption of these measures is indispensable for progress in the South and for the democratic development of the country as a whole. There is no other way to improve the conditions of the Southern masses.

Liberal Objections

To most liberals this is tantamount to socialism and just as reprehensible. They may advocate the separate proposals advanced here, short of land redivision, or in isolated cases even admit the necessity of giving the land to the landless. But when the conditions for realizing all those proposals are clearly set forth, they see red. The fact is that every time the people have tried to improve their conditions fundamentally or have attempted to take their destinies into their own hands, or put the stamp of their needs and interests on the course of development, their action was immediately condemned as communism. But what is involved here is not communism, although the people cannot introduce fundamental measures today in their interest without removing the stranglehold of monopoly capital and consequently taking the road to a classless, socialist society. The type of measures involved is in its nature purely democratic; measures, consequently, which historically should and could have been adopted by the bourgeois revolutions. The fact that the bourgeoisie has refused to adopt them and the need for them has continued into the era when the next major stage of historical development will be socialism, and their adoption consequently becomes part of the overall historical movement and struggle for socialism, does not alter the nature of these measures. The fact that only the masses have an inexorable interest in fighting for them, and that these measures can be achieved only if the power of monopoly capital is broken, proves neither that they are socialist nor that the struggle for them can be postponed until the advent of socialism.

'Chapter 6: Land and Freedom'

In themselves, these measures represent no more than the abolition of conditions characteristic of the feudal stage of historical development. To abandon or postpone the struggle for these measures because of the conditions necessary for their realization is tantamount to abandoning the struggle for democracy and progress. As far as the masses are concerned, they cannot cease aspiring for the realization of these measures, even though this realization may be in the comparatively distant future, without entirely losing the spirit of resistance and struggle even for the smallest gains in the present. Without these bigger things, democracy is an empty shell, a fraud, and a mockery.

'Left' Objections

If the liberal, confusing the nature of these measures with the conditions for their realization, rejects radical land reform on the ground that these conditions means socialism, the ultraleft critic rejects them *in the name of* socialism. To him the whole idea of land redivision is reactionary, ostensibly because technical progress depends upon large-scale production, and land redivision would mean encouraging small, individual property as against large-scale property. As far as he is concerned the question of land and freedom for the Negro will be solved automatically with the coming of socialism, and there is consequently no need for a special struggle for these demands.

Actually, while neither the measures presented here nor the conditions of their achievement necessarily mean socialism, neither do they mean a departure from the path to socialism. On the one hand, therefore, to maintain that a people's government is an indispensable prerequisite for the realization of the foregoing measures is not equivalent to arguing that they can be achieved only under socialism. For, while it is possible that the establishment of a truly people's government in the United States might not be achieved until such a government would necessarily be a socialist government, it is also possible for a people's government to come into office which is not yet directly socialist. On the other hand, it is idle to talk of socialism in the United States without the development of the broadest struggle for the solution of precisely such democratic questions as are represented by the liberation of the Negro people and fundamental land reform in the South.

The trouble with the ultraleft argument is that it fails to understand either the conditions for the achievement of socialism or the character of the Negro liberation question. In effect it means the abandonment of the fight for both. To speak of socialism while disregarding the conditions of achieving it is to assume an end result without the process or the elements producing it. Scientifically, such an approach is intolerable; practically, it is absurd. The social character of modern production and the welfare of the people have long made socialism both necessary and possible. But it is axiomatic by now that the necessary and possible will not be transformed into living reality until the exploiters are unable and the exploited are unwilling to continue in the old way. This means that the industrial working class must not only be prepared to fight for the new way of life, but it must have as its allies in the struggle the other exploited and oppressed strata of the population suffering, directly or indirectly, from the domination of monopoly capital and that these strata, therefore, must be drawn into the struggle, which can be done only on the basis of their own demands.

In this struggle, the landless soil tillers of the South, Negro and white, are historically on the side of the industrial proletariat. But their basic aim is to be rid of landlordism and the semi-feudal conditions which keep them in bondage and poverty. While socialist agriculture could solve this problem most thoroughly, the masses of sharecroppers, as yet in the stage of aspiring to individual land holdings in the face of the feudal monopoly of the land, could hardly be mobilized to fight for a purely socialist solution. At the same time, the fight for land division is a fight for a democratic aim which cannot be waged today without hitting at one of the main bulwarks of monopoly capital and consequently at the chief barrier to the establishment of socialism. Land redivision, therefore, is progressive not only in relation to the semi-feudal plantation system, but also in relation to the task of winning fighting allies against monopoly capital among the exploited and oppressed population generally. In fact, under conditions where the government is truly a people's government, land redivision serves to advance, and not retard, technical progress in agriculture, and to prepare the necessary basis for higher forms of agricultural production.

Like the land question in the South, the question of Negro freedom is a democratic demand, the struggle for which is one of the major conditions for the ultimate achievement of socialism in the United States. At the same time, it is obvious that only under socialism will the Negro people in the United States be completely free from exploitation and oppression in any form. In this sense, therefore, socialism is the major condition for Negro freedom. But since it can actually become such only if the Negro people, supported by the white toilers, also wage an active struggle against the source of their oppression, it is absurd to talk about winning socialism first and Negro freedom will automatically follow. Actually this means telling the Negro people not to fight for land and freedom, but for socialism. This not only ignores the special feature of the Negro question, but cancels out the very element which establishes the interrelationship between it and socialism, namely, the active involvement of the Negro people in the struggle for their own freedom. It does so by presenting the question of freedom as something which will be brought to the Negro people, but also to the white working class to abandon the actual struggle for Negro freedom.

Immediate Demands

We shall discuss the special features of this question in the next chapter, especially as they bear upon the fight for basic agrarian reform in the South. Meanwhile, it should be evident that in this fight it is imperative not to neglect the immediate needs of the agricultural population. The following are some of the points towards which immediate struggle should be directed:

Reforms directed to the abolition of the sharecropping system, its economic and legal supports; lower percentage of crop yield for rentals; abolition of crop-lien laws; for the legal right of the sharecropper and share tenant to the crop, his right to sell it on the open market at his own will; for written contracts between landlord and tenant; abolition of usurious credit rates; the right of the tenant to buy where he pleases; abolition of all laws and practices supporting peonage, such as the vagrancy laws, the "jumping contract" laws and the "enticing labor" laws; allocation of adequate acreage to each tenant for the raising of essential food crops for home consumption.

Some of the most urgent needs of all tenants and small farmers can be met by: reduction of land rents, the placing of land purchasing services within the reach of small owners and of tenants; revival, extension, and liberalization of the Farm Security program, and its rehabilitation, settlement and rental cooperative programs; increased federal appropriations for the Farm Security Administration with a liberalization of loan services by reduction of collateral and interest rates so as to bring these loans within the reach of the masses of small farmers and tenants; a democratic reorganization of all local administrations, free from landlord control, with proportional representation of Negroes on all local FSA boards; the use of idle land for settlement of displaced farm families; extension of social security to include small farmers; free access to the land, and the removal of all privileges protecting the planters' land monopoly.

Farm laborers require: the removal of all semi-feudal conditions; a living cash wage and application of the Federal Wages and Hours Law; extension of Federal Unemployment Insurance to compensate for the seasonal character of the work; placing unemployment insurance once more in the hands of the federal government; abolition of all vagrancy laws and all practices enforcing peonage; the establishment of the right to organize, bargain collectively, and strike.

The needs of the Black Belt in housing, education, health, and public works can be partially met by federal and state support for adequate educational, housing, health, and public works programs; equal allocation of educational funds, equal facilities, and abolition of the Jim-Crow school system.

In the field of political democracy, demands include the abolition of the Jim-Crow caste system, abolition of the Jim-Crow laws, and establishment of full equality for Negroes in all spheres; electoral reforms, the right to vote and hold office, abolition of white primaries, the immediate passage of federal anti-poll tax legislation; the enactment of a federal anti-lynching bill, federal prosecution of lynchers, death penalty for lynching, the banning of the Ku Klux Klan, and other such extralegal terrorist organization; enforcement of the principle of the right to self-defense, the organization of mass joint defense committees, Negro and white, for active resistance to lynch terror; enforcement of freedom of speech, press, and assembly, and the right of all farming people to organize.

Lessons from Experience

The struggle for these demands has an important background of living experience to draw upon as a guide. In the deep South, from the time of chattel slavery to the present, this urge for the land has been the driving motor of the Negro's fight for human rights and justice—his

'Chapter 6: Land and Freedom'

ever-insistent and unceasing demand. The right to the soil he tills, to the ownership of a plot of earth of his own, has always constituted the hard core of his ideal of freedom.

This quest for the land was the turgid undercurrent of the hundreds of slave insurrections and conspiracies of antebellum times. It was the throbbing heartbeat of the epochal battle of Reconstruction. And today the land question, still unsolved, is the hub on which the fight of the bitterly oppressed but restive Negro people is bound to turn in the Black Belt for equality and freedom.

Aside from the migration led by Moses Singleton in 1879 and the almost legendary "Wheel and Alliance" which in the 80s organized Negro and white farmers and miners in Alabama, the first widespread movement of Negro sharecroppers in the present century seems to have been the one organized in eastern Arkansas in 1919. The United States Department of Labor explains the impetus behind this movement:

> During the period of prosperity and labor scarcity in World War I the Negro sharecroppers had shared in the profits from high cotton prices. In the postwar deflation they bore a major part of the burden. Planters attempted to shift some of their losses to tenants by manipulating accounts and in some cases practicing outright fraud.

To these reasons must be added the nationwide unrest among Negroes as a result of the broken promises of World War I. This movement was weak in that it was isolated from white sharecroppers in the region; also, it lacked the support of an organized labor movement in the urban centers. It was quickly and ruthlessly crushed. While the details of these experiences from the end of Reconstruction to the second decade of the twentieth century have yet to be pieced together by historians, the struggles of the thirties are still part of living memory and the material about them is more extensive and accessible. These struggles of the early thirties resumed the thread of the sharecroppers' movement that had been broken in 1919. They began with the organization of the Negro Farm Workers, Tenants, and Sharecroppers Union, which got off to a favorable start. It was conceived under conditions of a more matured labor movement and the presence of an active Communist Party.

As the US Department of Labor study describes it (while disparagingly referring to the historic Scottsboro case and other Southern frame-ups as mere "incidents" initiated from the "outside"):

> The most dramatic rural organization in Alabama during the thirties was the Negro farm workers' and tenants' Sharecroppers Union. This was one result of the Communist Party's organization campaign among Southern Negroes, which also gave rise to such incidents as the celebrated Scottsboro case, the Angelo Herndon trial, and the numerous mine "disorders" in the Birmingham area. Although initiated by "outside" white radical influences, these incidents were, nevertheless, symptomatic of underlying unrest and antipathy in the established relationships between the whites and Negroes. . . . The doctrines of unionism found ready response among Negro tenants, sharecroppers, and laborers, who were undergoing severe hardships during the years of depression. It is difficult to judge whether the burden of depression which fell so heavily on the cotton-growing areas of the South were especially severe in Alabama, and whether sharecroppers suffered more in this state than in others. Prof. Harold Hoffsommer in the study of 1,022 Alabama farm households receiving rent relief during 1933 estimated that in 89 percent of the years spent at sharecropping, the net economic outcome for this group was either to break even or to suffer a loss. He concluded that the so-called financial loss to the sharecropper was largely a decline of social or occupational status and an increased dependence upon landlords, since in most cases the sharecroppers had no finances to lose.

The first local of the Sharecroppers Union (SCU) was organized in Tallapoosa County, Alabama, in 1931, in the worst period of the depression, before the government had begun any measures whatever for relief. The organization was at first more successful among Negro tenants of the upper brackets—that is, cash and standing renters, and

'Chapter 6: Land and Freedom'

Negro small farm owners facing loss of their land through mortgage foreclosures.

From its inception, the union faced violent attempts at suppression on the part of the plantation owners and their local agents. The fight first broke into the open on July 16, 1931, at Camp Hill. The occasion was the breaking up, by local sheriffs and deputies, of a meeting held by sharecroppers to protest the Scottsboro frame-up. On July 17, a Negro member standing guard was alleged to have shot and wounded the local sheriff. When officers came to arrest the Negro, his house was found to be barricaded by armed unionists. In the battle that resulted, one Negro was killed and five wounded.

The local movement was not killed by suppression. During the next year, the SCU continued to grow and by the spring of 1932 it claimed a membership of 500.

The next outbreak took place in Reeltown in December, 1932. On that occasion the union came to the defense of one of its members, Cliff James. The whole affair was a frame-up by the local authorities, a plain effort to provoke the union. James had been denied the usual credit by merchants and by his landlord. The landlord served a writ of attachment on James' livestock, which James refused to give up when the writ was served. The sheriff and his deputies, attempting to seize the cattle, were confronted with armed union members who had barricaded the house. The sheriff and two deputies were wounded, one union member was killed, and several others were wounded.

Now began a manhunt accompanied by terror and violence. A mob of more than 500 tracked down Negroes in the woods. There is no account of the number of Negroes killed during those days.

Reeltown pointed up also the deep unrest among the white farmers. The officials could not get together a posse from the same county. The farmers began to see through the barrage of racist incitement, their common interests with the Negroes.

The determination of the croppers themselves was shown in the manner in which the union members packed the courtroom at Dadeville at the trial. Although the judge postponed the case and the next day the highways were blocked, the Negroes managed to get to the court, by paths which they alone knew. Sentences of several years were given to the convicted members.

However, by the following spring, the union had gained a membership of about 3,000, among which a few white sharecroppers were included. Its influence had extended to counties other than Tallapoosa.

After Reeltown, the program of the union began to make use of collective bargaining methods, attempting to enforce federal government programs for rural relief against the landlords who sought to control and, in most cases, to block that relief. In 1934, the union organized a strike of Tallapoosa County cotton workers asking 75 cents a hundredweight. In some areas, demands were won.

By 1935, the organization claimed a membership of 10,000. By this time its emphasis was more on the organization of plantation laborers and on displaced croppers and tenants driven out by mechanization and the crop restriction program.

Why did the union eventually decline? Chiefly, there was the question involved in organizing different strata of agricultural masses into one organization—small owners, tenants, sharecroppers, and wage laborers. The leaders decided that it was impractical to conduct simultaneous activities in the interests of wage workers, tenants and small owners, ostensibly because of the divergence of interest among these groups. In an attempt to solve this question, the SCU was finally dissolved, with the tenants and small owners transferred into the Farmers Union of Alabama. The wageworkers formerly in the SCU entered the Alabama Agricultural Workers Union. Later, in 1937, through an AFL charter, the Agricultural Workers Union was converted into the Farm Laborers and Cotton Cultivators Union. This union was finally absorbed in the United Cannery, Agricultural, Packing, and Allied Workers of America, CIO.

In the big plantation area of eastern Arkansas, meanwhile, a movement was developing that was to lead to one of the most dramatic and powerful organizations of the thirties. With the reduced demand for cotton came a reduced demand for labor on these plantations, most of which were absentee owned. A wholesale dispossession of tenants and sharecroppers took place, due to decreased buying power in the depression, to government crop-reduction programs, and to mechanization. Planters who dispossessed sharecroppers and replaced them with wage workers gained for themselves all the government's benefit payments.

It was in this situation that the Southern Tenant Farmers Union (STFU) had its origins. It began in Poinsett County, Arkansas, in July

'Chapter 6: Land and Freedom'

1934, interracial from the outset. Men like Claude Williams, a minister, were prominent in it. In 1937, it became affiliated with the United Cannery, Agricultural, Packing and Allied Workers.

The Southern Tenant Farmers Union conducted a series of strikes, some of which met with minor successes. The action dramatizing the plight of the South's sharecroppers and wage workers came in January 1939, when 1,300 evicted croppers camped on the main highways of Missouri. Planters had evicted a greater number of croppers than usual in order to keep all crop-reduction checks. On January 6, evicted croppers met in Sikeston, Mo. Under the leadership of a Negro preacher, Reverend Owen Whitfield, vice-president of the STFU, the croppers marched through US highways. As a result of pressure, the National Guard in Missouri was forced to supply tents and blankets to the highway campers. Declaring the camps a health menace, county and state officers broke them up. Evicted croppers were forced to scatter so that their conditions would not become a matter of public attention. Through the STFU, most of the families gained emergency relief grants from the FSA. Even the FBI was forced to agree to the claims of the demonstrators that they were protesting conditions of poverty. Unfortunately, the FBI also absolved the landlords.

What the STFU accomplished was best summarized by a union bulletin in 1940:

> The union has succeeded in exposing certain brutalizing aspects of the plantation system, and has brought to light many cases of peonage and forced labor. It was caused by governmental investigations, both State and National, to be made into conditions in the cotton industry. No lynchings have occurred in the areas where these people have organized, and constitutional guarantees of freedom of speech and assemblage have been recognized for the first time in many decades. Wages have been raised and hundreds of thousands of dollars in Government benefits and grants were secured for the sharecroppers through the union's efforts. Better contracts with planters have been effected. Members of the union had been elected to local AAA committees, and for the first time the sharecroppers have had representation on some of the policy-making agricultural bodies.

Some Conclusions

This brief resumé of modern agrarian struggles in the South emphasizes a number of points which should never be lost sight of in the struggle for Negro freedom. These points may be thus summarized:

The Negro tiller of the land is the focal point around which the democratic transformation of the South turns. In this struggle, Negro and white tillers are interdependent, having a community of interests against those of the landlords.

The history of agrarian struggle in the South emphasizes the important role of the Communist Party and indicates the necessity of support from city workers, trade unions, and liberal groups in the building of the land struggles.

This history emphasizes also the highly *political* character of the fight for southern agrarian reform, and the inseparable link between economic and political changes in that region. The fight for the most elementary demands in the sphere of agrarian reform immediately runs afoul of the political power of the landlords, entrenched in the plantation system with its anti-Negro social and legal sanctions.

In the South, as nowhere else in the country, the fight for the smallest demands to relieve the suffering of the people assumes almost at once a political character. This essentially revolutionary character of the demands of the Negro soil cultivator arises from the semi-slave economic and political setup in the region. There every demand leading in the direction of democracy becomes at once a challenge to the feudal privileges of the Bourbon ruling caste and is immediately countered by terror and the wildest racist provocation.

The observation of Lenin regarding the struggles of the Russian peasantry against feudal tsarism applies fully to the fight of their Negro American counterparts, the sharecroppers. Their partial demands, he observed, are more revolutionary than the partial demands of the city industrial workers because they represent the belated and unfinished struggle against serfdom and feudalism.

'WHAT DO WE STAND FOR?'
FROM *SOUTHERN WORKER*
AUGUST 16, 1930

This is the first number of the *Southern Worker*, which is to be published regularly every week by the Communist Party of the USA.

The *Southern Worker* is the Communist paper for the South.

It is being published because the Southern workers and farmers need it and want it. The *Southern Worker* is the voice of the Negro and white workers and farmers of the South crying in united protest against the state of starvation, suffering and persecution to which they have been subjected by the white ruling class.

This is the first really workers' paper ever published below the Mason and Dixon line. It is the first Communist publication ever issued in the South. As such it will carry the Communist program to the white and black workers and farmers, pointing out the path to struggle, offering the militant and understanding leadership of the Communist Party to the millions of Southern toilers.

The *Southern Worker* is neither a "white" paper, nor a "Negro'" paper. It is a paper of and for both the white and black workers and farmers. It recognizes only one division, the bosses against the workers and the workers against the bosses. In this class struggle the *Southern Worker* stands always, without exception, unflinchingly, for the workers. It is a workers' paper.

While fighting constantly for all the immediate demands of the workers and farmers, fighting for better conditions, we realize that the

---

* "What Do We Stand For?," *Southern Worker*, August 16, 1930, Marxists Internet Archive.

only way the workers can fully obtain their demands is through a proletarian revolution. Only by following the example of the Russian workers and farmers, who overthrew tsardom and set up their own Soviet Government, can we finally obtain our liberation. This is the final aim which will be obtained by the organized might of the toiling masses.

Never before have the workers of the South needed their own paper as much as now.

Thousands upon thousands are unemployed. And yet not a cent from either the government or the employers for the unemployed workers, although billions are spent for warships and armaments. The workers and their families are left to starve. And they do starve to death, victims of that dread disease of the South, pellagra, the disease that comes when there is nothing to eat.

The sharecroppers and tenant farmers, "poor white" and Negro, face complete ruin. Many of the tenant farmers are losing their crops to the landlords because they cannot hang on long enough to harvest them. When a crop is finally raised the farmer finds that the prices have been kept so low by the agents of the buyers that he cannot get enough money not only to pay off his debts, but to keep going at all. Potatoes and cabbage are now the only food for many of the farmers in the South.

Those who are "lucky" enough to get a job get miserably low wages, work long hours at a tremendous speed, and are never sure how soon they will be fired.

The Negro worker is the most oppressed worker in the South. His lot is worse than any. Kept Jim-Crowed at every turn, working at lower wages than the white worker, subject to lynching and persecution, he is kept a virtual slave by the Southern white bosses.

The *Southern Worker* is here to voice the rebellion against these conditions. It is here to serve as the tribunal for the demands of the Southern toilers. It is here to give them Communist leadership in their struggle.

As a Communist paper it realizes that the only way by which the Southern toilers can be victorious in their struggle is through firm and solid organization in militant unions, and, politically, in the Communist Party.

The unions we speak of are not the Jim-Crowed, weak-kneed unions of the American Federation of Labor. The Southern workers have had their experiences with the AFL. Too often have they been betrayed and sold out as at Elizabethton, Tenn., at Marion, N. C., at Anniston, Ala. We stand openly and solidly against the treacherous, boss-controlled American Federation of Labor, which is closely allied with the KKK, supports bosses' candidates in the election campaign, cries for the blood of Communist organizers.

The unions we speak of are the militant, industrial unions of the Trade Union Unity League, which, like us, recognize only one division—the one between the bosses and the workers.

The *Southern Worker* stands unalterably for full social, economic and political equality for the Negro workers and farmers. This is one of its chief planks.

The *Southern Worker* draws the workers of the South closer to the workers of the North and all countries. It builds the strong bond of workers' solidarity. It brings to the Southern workers news of the Soviet Union, the only country in the world where the workers and farmers own and run the factories and farms and have their own government. It will make the Southern workers realize that they, too, must join in the defense of the Soviet Union, must defeat the war that is being planned against it by the bosses government.

The *Southern Worker* is published from Birmingham, Ala., despite the reign of terror directed by the Tennessee Coal and Iron Company, and supported by the AFL and the KKK against the organizers and members of the Communist Party and Trade Union Unity League. That is a sign of our strength. Persecutions cannot drive us away.

We are here and we will stay. Workers of the South, here is your paper. It is for all of us to write in. It is for all of us to spread and build. The *Southern Worker* will grow and expand with the struggles of the Southern workers.

Write for, spread and build the *Southern Worker!*

 GLOSSARY

Angelo Herndon (1913-1997)

Herndon joined the Communist Party USA in 1930, while working as a rail worker in Birmingham, Alabama. Sent by the party to Atlanta to organize the Unemployment Council, Herndon was charged with insurrection under Georgia state law, and found guilty by an all-white jury in 1933. In 1937, the US Supreme Court vacated his sentence, finding Georgia's insurrection law in violation of the First Amendment.

Clara Zetkin (1857-1933):

Zetkin was a long-time member of the German Social Democratic Party and leading light of the socialist feminist movement. An outspoken critic of World War I, Zetkin joined the newly formed German Communist Party and represented it in the Reichstag (parliament) from 1920-1933. She went into exile in the USSR after the rise of the Nazi Party.

Claudia Jones (1915-1964)

Jones joined the Young Communist League in 1936, participating in the campaign to defend the Scottsboro Boys. In 1937, she joined the editorial board of the *Daily Worker,* and a year later, she became editor of *Weekly Review.* Imprisoned at Ellis Island in 1948, she was found guilty of violating the Alien Registration Act in 1951. Refused entry to Trinidad and Tobago, her birthplace, Jones left Harlem for the United Kingdom in 1955, where she would play a central role in organizing the Black British community.

Comintern/Communist International//Third International

The Third International, also known as the Comintern or Communist International, existed from 1919–1943. Emerging from the anti-war faction of European socialism after World War I, the Third International held seven World Congresses during these years, to coordinate the strategy of the world's communist parties.

Communist Party USA (CPUSA)

The CPUSA was founded in 1919 out of a split in the Socialist Party of America, over the question of support for World War I. Against waves of state repression, the CPUSA represented the US in the Third International, unifying and coordinating communist organizing within US borders.

Cyril Briggs (1888-1966)

A journalist and founder of the African Blood Brotherhood, Briggs joined the CPUSA in 1921. In 1925, Briggs became national secretary of the American Negro Labor Congress, and in 1929, he joined the Central Committee of the CPUSA.

Eugene Gordon (1891-1974)

After a decade of work as a journalist, Gordon joined the CPUSA in 1931. In 1938, he became a contributing editor for the *Daily Worker*. In 1955, he would report on the Bandung Conference.

Fair Employment Practice Committee (FEPC)

Formed in 1941 under an executive order of President Roosevelt, the FEPC banned and monitored racially discriminatory hiring practices in federal agencies, unions, and corporations involved in the World War II war effort. Amidst opposition from segregationist Southern Democrats, a wave of hate strikes, and racist violence in industrializing cities across the US, alongside organized popular support for the committee, its jurisdiction was widened in 1943, to include all federal agencies.

George Padmore (1903-1959)

Padmore joined the CPUSA in 1927, actively participating in the work of the American Negro Labor Congress. In 1929, he headed the Negro Bureau of the Red International of Labor Unions (Profintern).

In 1930, Padmore edited The *Negro Worker* from Austria, until its offices were ransacked by fascists. Expelled from the communist movement in 1934, and refused reentry into the US on the basis of his earlier membership in the Communist Party, Padmore moved to France, the United Kingdom, and eventually Ghana, remaining deeply involved in Pan-African struggles.

Harry Haywood (1898–1985)

Haywood joined the CPUSA in 1925, after becoming radicalized by the racist pogroms across US cities in 1919, remembered as "Red Summer." From 1925–1930, Haywood lived in the USSR, contributing to the research that led to the Black Belt thesis. He would later spearhead the campaign to defend the Scottsboro Boys. By the late 1950s, as the CPUSA changed its position on Black self-determination, Haywood was expelled from the Party, remaining active in organizational and political work until his death. Haywood's legacies are felt in the Black Belt Thesis itself, alongside his books *Negro Liberation* (1948) and *Black Bolshevik* (1978).

International Labor Defense (ILD)

Established by the Third International from 1925-1947, ILD provided legal advocacy for political prisoners, civil rights organizations, and the campaign against lynching. The ILD played a major role coordinating the international campaign in defense of the Scottsboro Boys.

James Allen (1906–1986)

Born Sol Auerbach, Allen joined the CPUSA in 1928, and became editor of *Labor Defender*, the official publication of International Labor Defense. In 1930, he was appointed editor of the *Southern Worker*, the CPUSA's Southern newspaper, which was produced as an underground newspaper. In this role, he publicized the case of the Scottsboro Boys, which would become a major international movement. In later decades, Allen would go on to head International Publishers.

Jim Crow

The legal, political, and social system of white supremacy governing the United States, from the late nineteenth century reaction against Reconstruction, to the late 1960s.

Ku Klux Klan (KKK)

A white supremacist, fascist terror organization in the US that has seen three waves, from 1865–1872, 1915–1944, 1946 to the present. The Klan is one of the premier white nationalist organizations to have emerged out of US society.

Louise Thompson [Patterson] (1901–1999)

Thompson became associated with the CPUSA by 1931, joined in 1933, and was active in the National Negro Congress and the Civil Rights Congress. With Langston Hughes, she founded the Harlem chapter of Friends of the Soviet Union in 1932, and played an active role in the campaign to defend the Scottsboro Boys. In 1951, she helped form Sojourners for Truth and Justice.

Red International of Labor Unions (RILU)

Also known as Profintern, the RILU was founded in 1921, to coordinate communist work within trade unions, and it dissolved in 1937, upon the Third International's adoption of the Popular Front strategy.

Scottsboro Boys

In 1931, nine Black teenagers hopping a freight train in Alabama were charged with raping two white women. In the ensuing rushed trials, all but one of them were found guilty, and sentenced to death. The CPUSA supported the defendants as they appealed their sentences, leading to a major international campaign against the Jim Crow system.

Sharecroppers

A system of agricultural labor, where land is cultivated by families who do not own it, paying rent and meeting living expenses by selling their harvest to the landowner. Sharecropping was a common agricultural system in situations of uneven transition from feudal to capitalist agriculture, particularly in the colonies during the late nineteenth and early twentieth centuries. Sharecropping was the most common agricultural system in the US South, from the late 1870s through the mid-twentieth century.

Sharecroppers Union

Founded with the support of the CPUSA, the Sharecroppers Union, or SCU, organized Black sharecroppers and tenant farmers in Alabama, in the teeth of police and vigilante violence, from 1931–1936.

Trade Union Unity League (TUUL)

An umbrella organization for industrial trade unions, organized under the CPUSA from 1929–1935. Channeling radical work in and against the more conservative AFL, the TUUL prioritized efforts to support Black workers within the union movement.

V. I. Lenin (1870–1924)

Lenin was a leader of the Russian revolutionary movement, and a founder of the Bolshevik Party. His theories of organization, imperialism, and the state shaped the development of the communist movement.

W. E. B. Du Bois (1868–1963)

Du Bois, a founder of the Pan-Africanist movement and the NAACP, long-time editor of *The Crisis,* and a prolific author and campaigner, he is widely considered to be the greatest intellectual in US history. Held on trial in 1951 for his peace activism, Du Bois moved to newly independent Ghana in 1960, joining the CPUSA in 1961.

ACKNOWLEDGMENTS

About the Black Belt Study Group

The Black Belt Study Group was a group of nine organizers, majority of whom are from the US South, who came together in 2020 to study the Black Belt Thesis, its contemporaries and impact, and its legacy. Over the course of their research, they compiled the writing you see here.

About Eugene Puryear

Eugene Puryear is a journalist, activist, politician, and host on Breakthrough News. He is a founding member of the Party for Socialism and Liberation, and is the author of *Shackled and Chained: Mass Incarceration in Capitalist America.*

Many thanks to all who had a hand in making this book possible. First, to the participants of the Black Belt Study Group: Kenia Alcocer, David Chung, Dan Jones, Lindsey Jordan, Manu Karuka, Eugene Puryear, Kym Smith, Leonardo Vilchis, and Ben Wilkins. To the publishers and editors at 1804 Books (Layan Fuleihan, Kate Gonzales, and Manu). To the Tricontinental Institute for Social Research; University of Minnesota Press for the Haywood excerpts, originally published in *Black Bolshevik: Autobiography of an Afro-American Communist,* copyright 1978 by Harry Haywood; and the comrades of the International Peoples' Assembly for their support and solidarity. To Andrew Nance for a gorgeous cover design that highlights the workers who were at the center of the thesis, and the region it impacted.

ENDNOTES

Editor's Note: Where necessary, we have kept notes as is in the original text, with added citations in brackets whenever possible.

Introduction

1. William H. Frey, "A 'New Great Migration' Is Bringing Black Americans Back to the South," *Brookings Institution* (blog), September 12, 2022, https://www.brookings.edu/research/a-new-great-migration-is-bringing-black-americans-back-to-the-south/.
2. Mohamad Moslimani et al., "Facts About the U.S. Black Population," *Pew Research Center's Social & Demographic Trends Project* (blog), n.d., https://www.pewresearch.org/social-trends/fact-sheet/facts-about-the-us-black-population/.
3. Moslimani et al.
4. Moslimani et al.
5. Tracy Hadden Loh, Christopher Coes, and Becca Buthe, "The Great Real Estate Reset, Separate and Unequal: Persistent Residential Segregation Is Sustaining Racial and Economic Injustice in the U.S," *Brookings* (blog), December 16, 2020, https://www.brookings.edu/essay/trend-1-separate-and-unequal-neighborhoods-are-sustaining-racial-and-economic-injustice-in-the-us/.
6. Moslimani et al., "Facts About the U.S. Black Population."
7. Jon Whiten, "Several States Make New Moves to Tax Wealth," *Institute on Taxation and Economic Policy (ITEP)* (blog), https://itep.org/several-states-make-new-moves-to-tax-wealth/.
8. Stephen Miller, "Black Workers Still Earn Less than Their White Counterparts," Society for Human Resource Management (SHRM), June 11, 2020, https://www.shrm.org/resourcesandtools/hr-topics/compensation/pages/racial-wage-gaps-persistence-poses-challenge.aspx.
9. Moslimani et al., "Facts About the U.S. Black Population."
10. J. V. Stalin, *Marxism and the National Question*, https://www.marxists.org/reference/archive/stalin/works/1913/03a.htm#s1.
11. A Phillip Randolph and Chandler Owen, "The Bolsheviki," *The Messenger*, January 1918, Marxists Internet Archive.
12. A Phillip Randolph and Chandler Owen, "Bolshevism and World Democracy," *The Messenger*, July 1918, Marxists Internet Archive.

13 Tony Pecinovsky, ed., *Faith in the Masses: Essays Celebrating 100 Years of the Communist Party USA* (International Publishers, 2020), 75; interestingly enough the very first issue of *The Messenger* had a historical fiction essay by Lovett Fort-Whiteman, one of the very first Black American communists.
14 Cyril Briggs, "Letter to Theodore Draper in New York from Cyril Briggs in Los Angeles, March 17, 1958 [Long Extract]," March 17, 1958, Early American Marxism, http://www.marxisthistory.org/history/usa/groups/abb/1958/0317-briggs-todraper.pdf. Interestingly enough Briggs notes he was "more interested in the national revolution than the social revolution." This seems somewhat belied by the clear "class struggle" rhetoric of earlier *Crusader* issues.
15 Briggs.
16 Lowell B. Denny III, "The Bolshevik Revolution: Unacknowledged Inspiration of Liberation Movements Everywhere," *People's World* (blog), November 3, 2017, https://www.peoplesworld.org/article/the-bolshevik-revolution-unacknowledged-inspiration-of-liberation-movements-everywhere/.
17 V. I. Lenin, *Lenin Collected Works*, vol 18 (Moscow: Progress Publishers, 1975), 543–544.
18 Joe Pateman, "V. I. Lenin on the 'Black Question'" *Critique: Journal of Socialist Theory* 48, no.1 (January 2, 2020): 77–93, https://doi.org/10.1080/03017605.2019.1706786.
19 Joe Pateman, "V. I. Lenin on the 'Black Question.'" John Riddell, "Black Liberation and the Communist International," *John Riddell* (blog), September 11, 2011, https://johnriddell.com/2011/09/11/black-liberation-and-the-communist-international/.
20 V. I. Lenin, *Draft Theses on National and Colonial Questions for the Second Congress of the Communist International*, 1920, https://www.marxists.org/archive/lenin/works/1920/jun/05.htm.
21 Harry Haywood, *Black Bolshevik: Autobiography of an Afro-American Communist* (Chicago: Liberator Press, 1975), 219.
22 Haywood, 228; In his speech to the Sixth Comintern Congress, Black communist leader James Ford would reveal that the Comintern had sent no less than 50 messages to their American comrades imploring them to conduct more work in the Black Liberation Movement.
23 Haywood, 221.
24 Haywood, 222.
25 Barbara A. Reynolds, *Jesse Jackson: America's David* (Washington DC: JFJ Associates, 1985), 115.
26 Haywood, *Black Bolshevik: Autobiography of an Afro-American Communist*, 248.
27 Mary G. Rolinson, *Grassroots Garveyism: The Universal Negro Improvement Association in the Rural South, 1920–1927* (Chapel Hill, N.C.: University of North Carolina Press, 2007).
28 Haywood, *Black Bolshevik: Autobiography of an Afro-American Communist*, 230.
29 Haywood, 231–32.
30 Haywood, 232.
31 Haywood, 234.
32 Tony Pecinovsky, "Anne Burlak: The Red Flame," *Communist Party USA* (blog), March 27, 2020, https://www.cpusa.org/article/anne-burlak-the-red-flame/.
33 Communist Party USA, "Mass Work: Work Among Negro Masses (Examples of How Not

to Work)," *Party Organizer*, March 1931, 19–20; This appears to be a reference to the case of a J. Peters, framed for rape in Linden New Jersey. "Frame Linden, N.J. Negro Worker: 'Attack Charge Raised Against J. Peters,'" *The Daily Worker*, June 22, 1931, 1.
34 "Carry On the Struggle," *The Daily Worker*, May 2, 1932, Library of Congress: Chronicling America, 1.
35 "Carry On the Struggle."
36 Mary Helen Washington, *The Other Blacklist: The African American Literary and Cultural Left of the 1950s* (New York: Columbia University Press, 2014), 36.
37 Larry Neal, "The Black Arts Movement," *Drama Review* 12, no. 4 (Summer 1968): 29–39.
38 Claude Andrew Clegg, *An Original Man: The Life and Times of Elijah Muhammad* (St. Martin's Press, 1997), 150.
39 "Black Power!" was coined by Ture during the "March Against Fear" in 1966, conducted after racist vigilantes attempted to assassinate civil rights leader James Meredith. Ture and his colleagues in the Student Non-Violent Coordinating Committee (SNCC) had tested the slogan along the route, and unveiled at a spirited rally in Greenwood, Mississippi in June. Kwame Ture, *Ready for Revolution: The Life and Struggles of Stokely Carmichael* (New York: Scribner, 2005), 504–11.
40 Charles V. Hamilton and Kwame Ture, *Black Power: Politics of Liberation in America* (New York: Random House, 1967), 5.
41 Hamilton and Ture, 6.
42 Hamilton and Ture, 16.
43 Hamilton and Ture.
44 Harold Cruse, "Revolutionary Nationalism and the Afro-American," *Studies on the Left* 2, no. 3 (1962): 12–25.
45 For instance: Harry Haywood, "The Crisis of Negro Reformism and the Growth of Nationalism," *Soulbook: The Quarterly Journal of Revolutionary Afroamerica* 1, no. 3 (Fall 1965): 203–7.
46 Eldridge Cleaver, *On the Ideology of the Black Panther Party: Part I* (San Francisco: Ministry of Information: Black Panther Party, 1969), 6, http://www.freedomarchives. org/Documents/Finder/Black%20Liberation%20Disk/Black%20Power%21/SugahData/ Books/Cleaver.S.pdf.

The 1928 Comintern Resolution

Endnotes for the two Comintern Resolutions are taken from http://www.marx2mao.com.
47 *The American Negro Labor Congress* was founded in Chicago in October, 1925. The Workers (Communist) Party of America, the dominant force within the Congress, intended the Congress to be a vehicle for uniting all of the organizations of Black workers and farmers then existing. The stated two-fold task of the Congress was to agitate for the admission of Black workers into heretofore White unions and to struggle against the Garvey-inspired Black ambivalence toward the American trade union movement. The Congress, however, with very few exceptions, was unsuccessful in establishing proposed local branches and in reality amounted to little more than a paper organization. It remained in existence until 1930, when what was left of it served as the foundation for the *League of Struggle for Negro Rights*, a no longer existing mass organization of similar char-

acter, through which the Communist Party U.S.A. unsuccessfully attempted to extend its influence among Black people generally and in particular among Black workers.

48   *The Trade Union Educational League* (TUEL) was founded in Chicago in November, 1920 by William Z. Foster for the purpose of organizing the "militant minority" in the trade unions. At its founding, the TUEL was an independent united front organization and nominally remained such throughout its nine-year existence. In reality, however, from the time Foster joined the Workers (Communist) Party of America in 1921, the TUEL functioned as the Party's principal vehicle for work within the trade union movement.

49   *The Negro Champion* was the organ of the American Negro Labor Congress. The journal ceased to exist upon the Congress's demise in 1930.

50   *The International Labor Defense* (ILD), an affiliate of the Comintern's legal defense mechanism (the Red International of Class War Prisoners Aid), was founded in 1925. Its purpose was to provide legal defense for radical and Communist activists and non-political victims of the American judicial system. The ILD often employed mass campaigns as a means of bringing about the acquittal and release of those on whose behalf it was acting. A good deal of the ILD's activity was devoted to defending the legal rights of Black people, with its most prominent undertaking being the defense (and rescue from the electric chair) of the nine Scottsboro Boys, the last of whom was finally released from prison in 1950. The ILD was dissolved in 1941.

The 1928 Comintern Resolution

51   [*Transcriber's Note:* There is no item "1." preceding this. Presumably, it was in the previous section, but mistakenly omitted. –DJR]

52   *The Trade Union Unity League* (TUUL), the successor to the TUEL, was founded in Cleveland on September 1, 1929. The organization was disbanded in July, 1935, in order to clear the path for affiliation by the various unions comprising the TUUL with the A. F. of L.

Capitalism and Agriculture in the United States of America

53   (op. cit., Vol. V, pp. 102, 104) [*Census Reports.* Twelfth Census 1900. Vol. V. Agriculture, Wash. 1902.]

54   See present edition, Vol. 3, pp. 585–90. — Ed. [Vladimir Ilyich Lenin, *Development of Capitalism in Russia: The Process of the Formation of a Home Market for Large-Scale Industry*, Second, vol. 3 (Moscow: Progress Publishers, 1908), https://www.marxists.org/archive/lenin/works/1899/devel/.

'Further notes on Negro Question in Southern Textile Strikes'

55   The change to which Comrade Briggs refers as well as the wrong page captions were both due to typographical and technical reasons; but of course Comrade Briggs' remarks are fully justified. —The Editor.

Excerpt from *Let Me Live*

Chapter Fifteen

56   I am disguising his true identity for obvious reasons.

Endnotes

Chapter Sixteen

57 Unemployed workers were being arrested by the hundreds and sent back to the farms. There were special police assigned to arrest everyone who did not have any "visible means of support."

'Sharecroppers with Guns: Organizing the Black Belt'

58 *The New York Times*, April 12, 1933, as quoted in Carter, *Scottsboro*, 247 [Dan T. Carter, *Scottsboro: A Tragedy of the American South* (New York & London: Oxford University Press, 1969), 247.]

59 In 1932, my close friend, William L. Patterson, had been elected national secretary of the ILD at its Cleveland convention. Earl Browder and I attended as delegates from the Party's Central Committee. We pushed for Patterson's election, but Pat, a brilliant dynamic man, needed no pushing! He was quite popular, having played a leading role in publicizing the Scottsboro case.

Louis Engdahl, former national secretary of the ILD, was on tour for Europe and the Soviet Union with Scottsboro mother, Ada Wright, at the time of the convention. He was elected chairman of the ILD at that time, but died while on tour in Europe.

60 See Carter, 248. [Carter, *Scottsboro: A Tragedy of the American South*, 248.]

61 At this time, the LSNR and the ILD were involved in a number of local struggles against police brutality and lynching, which raised similar slogans. Most notably, we helped to build a broad united front on Maryland's eastern Shore. A reign of terror had struck the area after the legal lynching of Euel Lee and the lynching of George Armwood. Both men were Black and both were innocent.

At the initiation of the LSNR, we built the Baltimore Anti-Lynch Conference (November 18–19, 1922). Some 773 delegates, Black and white, attended including Monroe Trotter who along with DuBois was a co-founder of the Niagara movement, Dr. Harry F. Ward of the Union Theological Seminary in New York and Mary Van Cleek of the Russell Sage Foundation. Even some of the local NAACP types were forced to attend.

I believe that the widely publicized movement around the conference was successful in bringing a temporary halt to the open terror on the Eastern Shore. Masses of people became aware that the deaths of Armwood and Lee were not isolated incidents. The anti-lynching movement won many new friends and supports as a result of the conference.

62 Ruby Bates was one of the two women supposedly raped by the nine youths. She recanted her testimony at the Decatur, Alabama, trial of Haywood Patterson and became an active member of the defense movement.

63 "The Scottsboro Struggle and the Next Steps: Resolution of the Political Bureau," *The Communist*, June 1933, 575–76, 578–79.

64 Hosea Hudson, *Black Worker in the Deep South* (New York: International Publishers 1972), 57.

65 The following account of the sharecroppers' struggles is based on what I learned at the time from personal observations and reports of comrades. Much of it is confirmed by Stuart Jamieson, *Labor Unionism in American Agriculture*, Bureau of Labor Statistics Bulletin No. 836 (1945), 290–98; and Dale Rosen, *The Alabama Sharecroppers Union*, Radcliffe Honors Thesis (1969), 19–20, 30–41, 48, 56, 130–35. [Stuart Jamieson, "Labor Unionism in American Agriculture," Bulletin (United States Department of Labor,

1945), 290–98; Dale Rosen, "The Alabama Sharecroppers Union" (Radcliffe Honors Thesis, Cambridge, Harvard University, 1969), 19–20, 30–41, 48, 56, 130–35.]
66. *The Daily Worker*, December 28, 1932. ["Cliff James Dead of Infected Wounds; Denied Medical Aid," *The Daily Worker*, December 28, 1932.]
67. Ibid., December 21–22, 1932, and April 17, 1933. ["News Flash from Alabama: White Croppers Shield Hunted Negroes," *The Daily Worker*, December 21, 1932; "White Croppers Shield and Defend Negroes Hunted by Alabama Landlord-Police Lynch Gangs," *The Daily Worker*, December 22, 1932; "Tallapoosa Sheriff Threatens to Have Defense Lawyer Flogged," *The Daily Worker*, April 17, 1933.]
68. Ibid., January 7 and 9, 1932.]
69. Ibid., April 27, 1933. ["Ex-Senator Heflin Leads Prosecution in Trial of Tallapoosa Sharecropper," *The Daily Worker*, April 27, 1933.]
70. Benjamin J. Davis, *Communist Councilman from Harlem* (New York: International Publishers, 1969), 44. See also pp. 27, 34, 40, 43, 46–48, 51.
71. Kenneth E. Barnhart, "A Study of Homicide in the United States," Birmingham-Southern College Bulletin (May 1932), 9. Figures for 1930. [Kenneth E. Barnhart, *A Study of Homicide in the United States* (Birmingham-Southern College, 1932).

Selections from *The Reds in Dixie*

72. Soviet means "Council." In Russia these Soviets are the governing bodies which rule the country (as the Congress and President rule this country). The members of the Soviets are elected by the workers and farmers, whom they represent.

Selections from *The Negro Question in the United States*
From Chapter 1, 'The Black Belt: Area of Negro Majority'

73. These figures have been collected by Evarts B. Greene and Virginia D. Harrington, *American Population Before the Federal Census of 1790*, 1932.
74. Ulrich B. Phillips, *American Negro Slavery, A Survey of the Supply Employment and Control of Negro Labor as Determined by the Plantation Regime*, 1929, p. 87. [Ulrich Bonnell Phillips, *American Negro Slavery: A Survey of the Supply, Employment and Control of Negro Labor as Determined by the Plantation Regime* (New York & London: D. Appleton and Company, 1929).]
75. Ibid., p. 75.
76. Cited by Phillips, Ibid., p. 83.
77. The counties and the proportion of Negroes in their total populations in 1930 are: Amelia, 51%; Hanover, 37%; Lancaster, 45%; Middlesex, 46%; New Kent, 59%; Richmond, 39%; Surry, 60%; and Warwick, 37%.
78. Ibid., 1929, 95–96.
79. Ibid., 159–160.
80. Ibid., pp. 166–167

From Chapter 2, 'The Black Belt: Area of Negro Majority'

81. Sen. Ex. Doc., 38th Congress, 2nd Session, No. 28, p. 2
82. Ho. Ex. Doc., 39th Congress, 1st Session, Vol. 7, No. 11; p. 23.
83. Ibid., Vol. 7, No. 11, p. 23.

Endnotes

84 Walter L. Fleming, Freedmen's Saving Bank, pp. 7–13. [Walter L. Fleming, *The Freedmen's Savings Bank; a Chapter in the Economic History of the Negro Race*. (Chapel Hill: University of North Carolina Press, 1927), 7–13.]
85 *Weekly Advertiser*, Mobile, Sept. 16, 1865.
86 Quoted by Moulton, Ala., *Advertiser*, Dec. 4, 1868.
87 Walter L. Fleming, *Documentary History of Reconstruction*, pp. 355–356; also Fleming, "Forty Acres and a Mule," North American Review, May, 1906. [Walter Lynwood Fleming, *Documentary History of Reconstruction: Political, Military, Social, Religious, Educational & Industrial, 1865 to the Present Time* (Cleveland: A.H. Clark Company, 1906), 355–56; Walter L. Fleming, "Forty Acres and a Mule," *The North American Review* 182, no. 594 (1906): 721–37.]
88 A. A. Taylor, Reconstruction in Virginia, p. 35. [A. A. Taylor, *The Negro in the Reconstruction of Virginia*, First Edition (Washington DC: The Association for the Study of Negro Life and History, 1926), 35.]
89 Fleming, *Documentary History*, pp. 353–354, 357–358; Whitelaw Reid, *After the War, A Southern Tour from May, 1865, to May, 1866*; Jesse T. Wallace, *History of the Negroes in Mississippi*, p. 23; John R. Ficklen, *History of Reconstruction in Louisiana*, pp. 226–227; and others. [Fleming, *Documentary History of Reconstruction*, 353–54; Whitelaw Reid, *After the War: A Southern Tour. May 1, 1865 to May 1, 1866, 1866*; Jesse Thomas Wallace, *A History of the Negroes of Mississippi from 1865 to 1890* (Columbia University, 1927), 23; John Rose Ficklen, *History of Reconstruction in Louisiana (through 1868)* (Baltimore: The Johns Hopkins Press, 1910), 226–27.]
90 Cox *v.* Jones, 40 Ala. 297.
91 James W. Garner, *Reconstruction in Mississippi*, pp. 4–6. [James Wilford Garner, *Reconstruction in Mississippi* (Macmillan, 1901), 4–6.]
92 Robert P. Brooks, *The Agrarian Revolution in Georgia*, 1865–1912, p. 27. [Robert Preston Brooks, *The Agrarian Revolution in Georgia*, 1865–1912, vol. 3, no. 3, Bulletin of the University of Wisconsin; History Series 639, 1914, 27.]
93 *Clarke County* (Ala.) *Journal*, Sept. 9, 1865.
94 *Mobile Weekly Advertiser*, Sept. 9. 1865.
95 *Clarke County Journal*, Nov. 8, 1865.
96 *Mobile Weekly Advertiser*, Sept. 16, 1865.
97 Ibid., Jan. 20, 1866.
98 Tuskaloosa, Ala., *Independent Monitor*, Dec. 11, 1867.

From Chapter 5, 'Financing the Plantation'

99 Vance, *Human Geography*, p. 155. [Rupert Bayless Vance, *Human Geography of the South; a Study in Regional Resources and Human Adequacy* (Chapel Hill, N.C.: The University of North Carolina press, 1932), 155.]
100 W. Eustace Hubbard, *Cotton and the Cotton Market*, 1928, pp. 139–141. [William Hustace Hubbard, *Cotton and the Cotton Market* (D. Appleton, 1927), 139–41.]
101 In 1933, the United States government owned 64.2% of the total capital stock of the Federal land banks, and national farm loan associations, operating under the supervision of and with funds made available by the Farm Credit Administration, owned 35.2%.
102 The Farm Debt Problem, Letter from the Secretary of Agriculture, Washington, 1933, p. 11.

From Chapter 7, 'Northern Industry and Black Belt'

103 See Appendix II. Table 5. [reproduced below]

Year	U.S.	Black Belt	%	Border Territory	%	South Other Territory	%	Non-South	%
1930	11,891,143	4,790,049	40.3	2,358,302	19.8	1,627,493	13.8	3,115,299	26.1
1920	10,463,131	4,806,565	45.7	2,192,457	21.0	1,411,183	13.5	2,052,926	19.6
1910	9,827,763	4,842,766	49.3	2,032,773	20.7	1,379,266	14.0	1,572,958	16.0
1900	8,833,994	4,488,991	50.8	1,608,411	18.2	1,410,978	16.0	1,328,614	15.0
1890	7,488,676	3,866,742	51.6	1,373,471	18.3	1,169,608	15.6	1,078,855	14.4
1880	6,580,793	3,466,924	52.7	1,120,844	17.0	1,042,356	15.8	950,669	14.4
1870	4,880,009	2,560,263	52.5	802,617	16.4	749,837	16.3	722,292	14.8
1860	4,441,830	2,461,099	55.4	705,095	15.8	673,223	15.1	602,413	13.6

104 Greene and Woodson, op. cit., Chaps. XIII and XIV. [Lorenzo Johnston Greene and Carter Godwin Woodson, *The Negro Wage Earner* (Association for the study of Negro life and history, Incorporated, 1930).]

105 Ibid., Chap. XVI.

From Chapter 9, 'The Right of Self Determination'

106 *Proceedings of the Colored People's Convention of the State of South Carolina, Charleston, 1865.* [*Proceedings of the Colored People's Convention of the State of South Carolina* (Charleston: South Carolina Leader Office, 1865).]

107 V. I. Lenin, "Lecture on the 1905 Revolution," Jan 22, 1917, *Little Lenin Library*, Vol. 6, p. 40. [V. I. Lenin, "Lecture on the 1905 Revolution," in *Little Lenin Library*, vol. 6, 1931, 40.]

'On the Right to Self-Determination for the Negro People in the Black Belt'

108 V.I. Lenin, *Miscellany*, Collected Works, Vol. XXX, Russian Edition.

109 Lenin, *Selected Works*, Vol. V. International Publishers, p. 271.

www.ingramcontent.com/pod-product-compliance
Lightning Source LLC
Chambersburg PA
CBHW060550080526
44585CB00013B/508